SEX ROLE STEREOTYPING IN THE MASS MEDIA

GARLAND REFERENCE LIBRARY
OF SOCIAL SCIENCE
(VOL. 47)

SEX ROLE STEREOTYPING IN THE MASS MEDIA
An Annotated Bibliography

Leslie J. Friedman

GARLAND PUBLISHING, INC. • NEW YORK & LONDON
1977

Library of Congress Cataloging in Publication Data
Friedman, Leslie, 1948-
  Sex role stereotyping in the mass media.

  (Garland reference library of social science; v. 47)
  Includes indexes.
  1. Sex roles in mass media—Bibliography. I. Title.
Z7164.S42F74   [P96.S5]   016.30141   76-52685
ISBN 0-8240-9865-X

PRINTED IN THE UNITED STATES OF AMERICA

CONTENTS

v

INTRODUCTION:
Media Socialization and Sex Roles

The communications media touch every one of us every day of our lives. We may avoid family, church and school for days at a time, but we rarely go through a twenty-four-hour period without seeing a newspaper, television program, billboard, magazine, movie or book, or hearing a radio program or record. Because the media are so powerful in reaching their audience, media treatment of the sexes is extremely important—the media project the image people acquire for themselves and are therefore primary agents of socialization.

Studies within this bibliography indicate that people, especially children, pay close attention to media portrayals of characters of their own sex. In order to recognize personal talents, we need inspiring role models. Boys have models in every occupation from railroad conductor to astronaut to President. Husbanddom and fatherhood are asides to other professional responsibilities and fulfillment. Meanwhile, girls are groomed for domesticity when they are given their first doll; they see apron-clad television and textbook women surrounded by children or limited to professions that provide services, such as teacher, waitress, librarian, nurse. Rarely is a child exposed to female role models who function as pilot, surgeon, accountant, carpenter or construction worker, although women successful in these fields have been cited by Betty Medsgar (see 0106), Suzanne Seed (see 0110) and the PBS program "Woman Alive." Several of my childhood friends loved animals and occasionally daydreamed about becoming veterinarians, but none seriously aspired to a profession so inappropriate for women. How many female role models were in the field? Girls on television didn't even own animals, much less administer to them. Even Lassie was owned by boys. We learned then that we could be close to animals only by following the fictional lead set by Jan Clayton, Cloris Leachman and June Lockhart, farmers' wives and mothers of Jeff and Timmy, Lassie's male owners. A girl could live on a farm, but Lassie would never be her very own dog.

Without role models in a variety of fields, female high school students prepare for the future by learning to type, but rarely by learning to run a camera. The media provide young women with few female images to emulate and provide few positive images of womanhood for people of either sex to respect. Female invisibility not only deprives the female audience of inspiring role models but also produces what George Gerbner has called "symbolic annihilation" (see 0340). Women are often considered unworthy sources to quote in news stories, are ignored in rock concert performer chatter (see 0616), and comprise a low percentage of advertising's authoritative voiceover announcers (see 0156).

The audience naturally identifies with like-sexed characters. After continually viewing portrayals of women as only sexy and/or stupid, the audience is ultimately led to believe these distortions. Female confidence is undermined by the constant depiction of women as socially inferior. As many entries in this bibliography indicate, women's aspirations are limited by the subtle picture of themselves as incompetent. Without adventurous girls in textbooks, all children learn that girls are dull (see 0847). With few career-bound role models supplied by the media, the percentage of actual career women remains low (see 0025). The like-sexed identification that will result from future positive portrayals of women as talented, vibrant, self-sufficient people making decisions and controlling their own lives and destinies will produce more confident, competent women with increased potential. An improved media image of women should socialize men, also, to regard female intelligence more respectfully. The present emphasis on woman as sex object inhibits the audience's ability to see past the female body to the powerful female brain. Women should be treated with the same deference given Robert Redford, whose physical beauty is considered almost irrelevant. Not only is his sex appeal not exploited, but his interests in ecology and the Old West are given full expression in television documentaries and magazine articles.

Within this bibliography, several authors discuss the brainwashing of society as many people come to accept the notion of inherent female inferiority. When advertising, television programming and comic books constantly strip women of dignity and stress supposed female inferiority, people are socialized to believe the false image. Even though women are acquiring confidence, advanced degrees and technical skills, and although affirmative action laws are being enacted, the mass media tend to neutralize their effects. The constantly trivialized and objectified image of women not only undermines newly formed female confidence, but also subtly affects all aspects of life—economic, political, social and personal. Male employers distrust women's ability to handle important decisions or jobs, and women distrust themselves and each other: women rarely run for political office and don't vote for women who do. Elimination of this suggestion of feminine inferiority within the communications media, the most pervasive collective phenomenon of our society, will facilitate recognition of female competence and dignity, and women will less frequently be degraded and humiliated in the name of feminine helplessness.

The very specific 1974 complaints by Stewardesses for Women's Rights—which concerned airline advertising (see 0217–0223) that stripped them of female dignity and professional integrity by implying that the flight attendants were sex toys rather than highly trained savers of lives—are less blatantly true of media treatment of women in general. But though more subtle, unrealistic media treatment is no less insidious. According to automobile advertising, woman's place is in the passenger seat or as a decorative ornament sitting on the hood. Women are rarely portrayed driving automobiles, reading newspapers, voting or going to work or school. On television's adventure programming, women are usually rescued by men. The female police officers on "Starsky and Hutch" are ignorant of self-defense techniques and must depend on male heroes to save them from crises. Although the female protagonists on "Charlie's Angels" rescue one another, their autonomy is limited by an off-screen male boss and an on-screen male chaperone. Female fictional characters rarely control their situations by physically overcoming men or by mentally outwitting them. Most television adventure programs ignore women while relating exploits of intellectually and physically active men who solve crimes as well as commit them. Women often appear on screen only to be victimized by male criminals.

Symbolic annihilation, so common in television programming and pre-1977 film, is not a problem in advertising. Though women are visible in almost every advertisement, however, the female image is predominantly negative. Advertising shows us women who cannot make a decent cup of coffee or buy the right dog food, women who cannot learn from experience and require laundry instructions from a man who probably does not wash his own clothes, and women who spend the major part of the day cleaning the toilet bowl or admiring their reflections in the dinner dishes and leave the home only to run to the supermarket, where they become Mr. Whipple groupies. While a bookmobile librarian distributes laxatives and a business executive promotes sleeping pills, advertising shows few women whose daily activities take them outside the kitchen or bathroom, and even fewer female authority figures whose voices project the conclusive voiceover sales pitch. According to a Screen Actor's Guild study (see 0189), voiceover product representatives earn more per ad than other actors. The position is apparently open only to men (see 0156, a 1975 study showing token 7% female voiceovers). Not only is this discrimination illegal, but in light of other research (0096, 0119, 0270), it is poor business practice. Product recall is higher when a female announcer's voice is used, and the general public has no conscious preference regarding sex of authoritative voice. Now that Barbara Walters is coanchoring network news and ratings have neither decreased nor increased, opening disc jockey slots, television game show emcee positions and advertising voiceovers to female talent should not prove detrimental. Since the female voice provides higher product recall, women may actually increase sales.

A frequently heard argument compares the image of half-wit women in the media to that of half-wit men. However, the Mr.

Whipples, Archie Bunkers, Fred Flintstones and Dagwood Bumsteads are rare compared to the positive images of male authority in advertising, the Kojaks, Columbos and McGarretts on television adventure programming and the Dick Tracys in comic strips, not to mention all the male heroes in the "buddy" films. Although masculine figures are overly aggressive, especially in television programming and movies, and although there should be less attention focused on violence and more frequent recognition of the often peaceful, compassionate male nature, nevertheless these masculine figures' penetrating minds, wit and overall control of situations are common positive male qualities rarely ascribed to female characters. Also, a more positive overall human image of men is becoming apparent. The news camera has recently captured not only the tears of joy or disappointment of male politicians, but also those of ordinary male citizens faced with personal tragedy. In light of this humanized portrayal of men, some feminists hope that the media will soon take advantage of themes explored by feminist collectives and humanize the image of women throughout the commercial media. At present, one of the few commercial works to readily come to mind in which a woman truly celebrates herself is Shirley MacLaine's record album *Live at the Palace*. As the artist rejoices in her energy and talent, the listener becomes energized and confident by extension. However, Shirley MacLaine's self-celebration is an exception: the commercial media more often specialize in female inferiority and self-effacement. For confidence and strength, women usually avoid the male-based mass media and turn to productions of woman-centered media.

While mass communications have been misleading the public by promoting false insecurity among women with the image of the dull, flighty, superficial, helpless, hopeless, scatterbrained "normal" woman, feminist collectives have been discarding these exaggerated stereotypes. The *Media Report to Women Index/ Directory* (see 0105) lists forty pages of feminist collectives who meet the specific needs of women by publishing, producing and organizing periodicals, presses, news services, recording companies, and radio, television, film and music programs. Although the women operating woman-based collectives possess the philosophy required to offset the influence of the commercial media, distribution is still a problem, but one which, according to Dr. Donna Allen, director of Women's Institute for Freedom of the Press and editor of *Media Report to Women,* will eventually be solved. The large growth of collectives continues; women are reaching each other. "We don't know how outreach will take effect, but we know that it will. We're still at the exploring stage," Dr. Allen explained in a telephone conversation.

The experience and philosophy engendered by the collectives will have an ultimate influence on the commercial media, as will other changes effected by FCC litigation, legislative measures, and, most important, by the promotion of women to management-level, decision-making positions within each medium. The nagging wife and the brainless blonde and other exaggerations will disappear. Mass-produced records and films will provide images of female dignity and celebrations of womanhood, commercial television will offer inspiring fictional role models and perhaps biographical series documenting notable female accomplishments, the news media will often quote female sources of authority and accurately report both the advances and defeats of the women's movement, comic books and cartoons will offer independent, adventurous women, and mammory fetishism in jokes and news photography will end. The more enlightened but still entertaining image of women will show women of every race, economic background and lifestyle as intelligent, ambitious, level-headed, talented, interesting, and active. People will become socialized by the communications media to regard women as equal and societally vital. Most important, the media will show women *as women* and not as the caricatured pseudomen on Norman Lear's latest production, "All That Glitters." As evidenced by Amy Gross's "What are they doing to women now?" (0484) and Jane Wilson's "Hollywood flirts with the new woman" (*The New York Times*, May 29, 1977, p. D-1+), the film industry is beginning to portray women realistically as exciting and strong individuals; independent filmmakers and feminist film collectives have paved the way for the commercial film industry's emancipated image of women. Meanwhile, Joan Ganz Cooney, president of the Children's Television Workshop, has announced that "Sesame Street" will show 50% women "on the Street" in 1978. It shouldn't be long before the other commercial media follow these leads.

This bibliography brings together the many studies, content analyses and published opinions concerning sex stereotypes in the media in order to put past research into historical perspective and to offer direction for future research. Although many of the articles are scholarly, the annotations are written in language easily understood by the undergraduate. Since it is college students who have most often solicited my help in researching the issue of sexism and the media, they are the primary target audience. However, serious scholars and media professionals researching ways to limit sex stereotypes will also appreciate technical features of the book: all references to U.S. government documents include standard Superintendent of Documents call numbers, and series notations and sources for reprinted material are included whenever available. Although the annotations usually reveal the most significant message of each article, occasionally an annotation will deal only with an interesting perception not mentioned elsewhere.

The significance of this bibliography lies in the style of articles included. Because the communications media reach literally everyone, the articles indexed are written by people with many different backgrounds and points of reference. Writing styles run the gamut from pure academic scholarship to feminism's early, but justifiable, tones of outrage. Works include entertaining speeches, statistical evidence gathered by women's and church groups, consciousness raising slide programs and films, and works tracing the imagery of womanhood throughout the history of film, rock music and women's magazines. To maintain objectivity, I included every article I found defending sexism. There were twelve. Such a low percentage (0.01%) indicates either that media moguls know that sexism is indefensible or that they fail to recognize it as an issue. If the latter is the case, this book should destroy the myth. The dissatisfaction with sex role stereotypes in the media is expressed not by a lunatic fringe, but by people of many racial groups, lifestyles and educational backgrounds. Demonstrating the great demand for positive media images of women and more compassionate portrayals of men was one of my purposes in compiling this bibliography, along with the wish to raise consciousness among producers, publishers, station managers, board members and upper-level management in general. Of course, when meeting the public, these powerful men all claim to be sensitive to the sex role issue and committed to change. Reading *Madison Avenue*'s special December, 1976, issue (see 0254), I couldn't help thinking of advertising's women for whom spotted glasses spell doom or the quasi-obscene advertising in which cameras follow the motion of female derrieres. With such "sensitive" men at the top, just who is responsible for this female trivialization? It is possible that only the employment of women in management-level positions will facilitate a positive image of women in the commercial media. Perhaps under those circumstances the media will meet their social responsibility to reflect reality creatively but honestly. Equal opportunity laws alone will not produce equality until socialization of female inferiority ends. Only when the media, a major perpetrator of second-class status for women, discontinue the portrayal of women as semiretarded sex objects can true social equality between the sexes begin. As media approaches reflect female capabilities, mass attitudes will change.

For their help in searching references, I'd like to give special thanks to Terry Camp and Susan Morris of the University of Georgia's Inter-Library Loan Department, without whom this bibliography would be much less complete. Special thanks also go to Donna Allen, Dan Baisden, Maija Blaubergs, Mary Ellen Brook, Laura Bulkeley, Joan Dominick, Joe Dominick, Margaret Holt, Molly Howard, Jeanne Lansman, Nellie Moffit, Karen Persons, Richard Press, Leslye Seltzer, Vernon Stone, John Via, Kathy Waller and Irene Zahava for sharing material, expertise and encouragement, to all the researchers who sent reprints and other information along with notes of support, and thanks also to my parents and brothers, Margaret Williams, the typist, and Rita Smalling, my editor, for all their wonderful support and encouragement.

LJF

MASS MEDIA

Media in General

0001

Amundsen, Kirsten. "The American woman, myth
and reality," *The Silenced Majority, Women and
American Democracy*, by K. Amundsen. Englewood
Cliffs, NJ: Prentice-Hall, 1971. pp. 1-18.

The image of American womanhood projected in advertising and TV is that of a young, pretty, slender creature
whose major life concerns are changing her hair color and
softening her skin in order to please her American man.
In return he loves, protects and indulges her with plush
carpeting and a gleaming kitchen. Her companion image,
found in men's jokes, is that of the scheming, grasping,
coy woman who selfishly manipulates her man for his money.

The media malign manhood by projecting him as naive,
clumsy and dependent on female approval. He'll buy bigger
cars and masculine accoutrements in order to attract
women.

0002

Bardwick, Judith M. and Elizabeth Douvan. "Am-
bivalence: the socialization of women," *Women
in Sexist Society; Studies in Power and Powerlessness*, ed. by Vivian Gornick and Barbara K.
Moran. NY: Basic Books, 1971. pp. 147-159;
also in *Readings in the Psychology of Women*, ed.
by J. M. Bardwick. NY: Harper and Row, 1972.
pp. 52-58.

Sex role stereotypes exist in their purest form in
the media. The simplistic, unidimensional, romantic role
model is no longer valid, especially for women who compare the romanticism of the media image to the reality
of a repetitive world of child care and housekeeping.

0003

Barrett, Karen. "Daughters," *Houston Breakthrough, Where Women are News.* January 1977, 2(1):4-5.

In an interview with six girls, aged three to thirteen, several comment on women's role in the media. One child complains that books and TV only show widowed women working while married women are portrayed as housewives. She'd like to see commercials where men do the dishes and women are portrayed in a variety of fields.

0004

Bass, Lois and Meta Sylvester. "You women are all alike," *Up from Under.* Winter, 1971-1972, 1(4):21-22.

A collage of platitudes and cliches about women from advertising, motion pictures, nursery rhymes, pop music, television, literature and the bible.

0005

Beasley, Maurine and Sheila Silver. *Women in Media: a Documentary Sourcebook.* Washington, DC: Women's Institute for Freedom of the Press, 1977.

A compilation of "documents representing the struggle of women who needed to communicate about changes in society and culture, from the early journalists, Jane G. Swisshelm and Margaret Fuller, to the founders of the National Women's Press Club and the present advocates of non-sexist images in journalism."

0006

Bem, Sandra L. and Daryl J. Bem. "Case study of a non-conscious ideology: training the woman to know her place," *Beliefs, Attitudes, and Human Affairs,* ed. by D. J. Bem. (Basic Concepts on Psychology series), Belmont, Ca: Brooks/Cole, 1970. pp. 89-99; also in *Women: a Journal of Liberation,* 1969, 1(1): 8-14; also in *Roles Women Play: Readings Toward Women's Liberation,* ed. by Michele Hoffnung Garskoff. Belmont, Ca: Brooks/Cole, 1971, pp. 84-96; also in *Sexism and Youth,* ed. by Diane Gersoni-Stavn. NY: Bowker, 1974. pp. 10-22; also in *Female Psychology: the Emerging Self,* ed. by Sue Cox. Chicago: Science Research Associates, 1976. pp. 180-190.

The mass media is one of five cultural references who define "natural" sex roles. Through this definition, or non-conscious ideology, male and female children are taught different aspirations and motivations. Men are socialized against displays of tenderness and sensitivity, and are "especially discouraged" from participating in the "glamour" of housework, while women as well as men are taught prejudices against women.

0007
Bem, Sandra L. and Daryl J. Bem. "We're all non-conscious sexists," *Psychology Today*, November, 1970, 4:22+.

Adapted from article, "Case study of a non-conscious ideology: training the woman to know her place." See 0006.

0008
Bernstein, Paula. "Women rap media's messages," *New York Daily News*, December 10, 1974, p. 55.

Although the media coverage of the Betty Ford and Happy Rockefeller breast operations was helpful in exposing women to the need for self-examinations, the media was negligent in avoiding the controversy of radical mastectomy vs. less extensive surgery.

0009
Blakey, William A. "Everybody makes the revolution, some thoughts on racism and sexism," *Civil Rights Digest*, Spring, 1974, 6(3):11-19.

Sex and race stereotypes in movies, books and the news and entertainment media limit the self-image, goals and accomplishments of women and minority group members by steering them toward traditional occupations. By failing to include women and minorities in a variety of roles, the media present a distorted picture of the real world.

0010
Boersma, Dee. "A report on the United Nations Commission on the Status of Women and Mass Media." *The Journal of the University Film Association*, 1974, 26:3-4.

The United Nations Commission on the Status of Women suggests that the mass media depict women contributing effectively to society. In contrast to reality, advertising shows women predominantly in the home when 35-55% of the world's labor force is female. Such a stereotyped image of women may limit female participation in society.

3

The implications are especially serious when considering that underdeveloped nations learn ideas and values from the TV and film models of developed countries. The goal of human equality will be evident in the media when women are employed and promoted to positions of authority in media industries. Developing nations will then acquire positive feelings of sexual equality and therefore not waste valuable womanpower.

0011

Brandon, Liane. *Anything You Want To Be*. 16mm. 8 min. b/w., rental, $15, purchase $100. New Day Films, Box 315, Franklin Lakes, NJ 07117.

When a high school women acts on the promise indicated by the title, she finds herself blocked at every turn by the television-style voiceover who leads her through the acceptable feminine role stereotypes.

See 0740. M. Brenton, "The Dagwood Bumstead syndrome."

0012

Brownmiller, Susan. "Victims: the setting," *Against Our Will, Men, Woman and Rape*, by S. Brownmiller. NY: Simon and Schuster, 1975. pp. 309-346.

The setting of rape is in fairy tales where Red Riding Hood is attacked by the wolf, in the news tabloid where the victim's physical attractiveness is mentioned before (or instead of) reporting her place in society, and in the confession magazine where the theme of women inviting rape is common. It is through exposure to these settings that women learn to accept brutal rape and death as punishments for deviating from the stereotypes.

0013

Busby, Linda Jean. "Mass media research needs: a media target for feminists," Michigan. University. *Women's Studies Papers*, 1974, 1:9-29.

When researching the image of women in the media most scholars and feminists have concentrated on content analysis. Dr. Busby suggests that future studies include cultural, control, audience, media and effects analyses as well, in order to facilitate significant media change. Women should be writing, directing, and producing programs. Television should no longer aim at a common denominator audience, but should reach the changing culture.

0014
    Busby, Linda J. "Sex-role media research and
sources," *New Research on Women and Sex Roles
at the University of Michigan,* ed. by Dorothy
Gies McGuigan. Ann Arbor: University of Michigan Center for Continuing Education of Women,
1976.

    The mass media are "projective-reflective mirrors"
of society. They project traditional societal roles and
do not reflect the social impact of the women's movement
on 1970's lifestyles. A select bibliography is included.

0015
    Busby, Linda J. "Sex-role research in the mass
media," *Journal of Communication,* Autumn, 1975,
25(4):107-131.

    An assimilation of important content analyses and
effects studies measuring sex role stereotypes in television, print advertising, newspaper coverage, and children's media. The studies indicate that the audience
acquires personal sex role behavior from media images.

0016
    Busby, Linda J. "Women and society: the mass
media," *SISCOM '75, Women's (and Men's) Communication;* Proceedings of the Speech Communication Association's Summer Conference XI, 1975,
ed. by Barbara Eakins, R. Gene Eakins, and
Barbara Lieb-Brilhart. pp. 100-113; also in
ERIC (ED 127 643), pp. 106-119, and full text
of ERIC (ED 112 449).

    The mass media, especially television, reinforce
certain social values. By projecting women in low status
positions politically, socially and in employment, the
media have reinforced low female career aspirations and
low self-esteem. While the media consistently portray
the female sex in low status positions, men and boys are
seen with wider varieties of roles and goals. The effect
of this differential treatment is that children grow up
believing the stereotyped images which are further reinforced by the media sex role stereotyping they encounter
as adults. An extensive bibliography is included.

0017
    Butler, Matilda and William Paisley. *The Flawed
Mirror, Sourcebook on Women and the Media.* Washington, DC: Communications Press, 1977.

5

As the media "mirrors" society it sometimes presents a distorted reflection. It is from this distorted reality that audiences draw their self-images and aspirations. Sexism in the media, its effect on the audiences, its perpetuation by the media industry, and recommendations for media change are explored.

0018
   Chafetz, Janet Saltzman. "The media and sex role stereotypes," *Masculine/Feminine or Human?, An Overview of the Sociology of Sex Roles*, by J. S. Chafetz. Itasca, Il: Peacock, 1974. pp. 41-53.

Widely accepted sex role stereotypes in the media include the typical newspaper accounts of "ladies'" sports, but never "gentlemen's" sports, while the content of women's magazines are written for women but are about men. A comparison of the cartoons in *Good Housekeeping* with those in *Playboy* reveals fewer sex role stereotypes in *Playboy*. Also discussed are sex role stereotypes in pop music, underground newspapers and comic strips.

0019
   Collins, Bud. "Billie Jean King evens the score," *Ms.*, July, 1973: 39-43+.

Billie Jean King reveals that she is not disenchanted with the press for creating a false picture of her as radical, notorious and tough, because any good or bad treatment helps women's tennis. However she resents the double standard treatment given her by reporters who ask about her domestic lifestyle when male athletes are not questioned about their marriages or vasectomies.

0020
   "Cynthia F. Epstein: Women's exclusion from news media - a product of social control," *Media Report to Women*, June 1, 1975, 3(6):16.

Although a few script writers have dealt sensitively with women's problems, and a few actresses have created characters who shine through the banality of their parts, most media tend to undermine female achievements and project a negative image of womanhood.

0021
   Daniels, Arlene Kaplan. "The mass media and social change," *A Survey of Research Concerns on Women's Issues*, by A. K. Daniels. Washington,

DC: Association of American Colleges, 1975.
pp. 4-5.

In order to end media perpetuation of sex stereotypes women should be employed in high level positions.
If necessary, legal charges should be filed against the
media for underemployment of women.

0022
Daniels, Arlene Kaplan. "The mass media as 'edu-
cational supplements'," *A Survey of Research
Concerns on Women's Issues*, by A. K. Daniels.
Washington, DC: Association of American Col-
leges, 1975. pp. 14-15.

Now that the existence of sex role stereotypes in the
mass media has been thoroughly documented, the author suggests approaches for future research: How do media
stereotypes affect the self-image and behavior patterns of
various age groups? How do children react to women's
image? How do media stereotypes affect one's motivations,
occupational goals, achievements? Are stereotypes re-
versible?

0023
Davis, Elizabeth Gould. "The prejudice lingers
on: woman's image," *The First Sex*, by E. G.
Davis. NY: Penguin, 1972. pp. 322-326.

During news interviews Senator Margaret Chase Smith
is called "Mrs." Smith while her male colleagues are ad-
dressed as "Senator." Women in television commercials
are shown in either the image of sex object, or as sex-
worshiper of a condescending male. Television drama
depicts women as subservient - never as a serious partner
or breadwinner. Magazines dehumanize women as sex kittens
or bunnies. The media's overt contempt for women indoctrinates women and men alike to regard female as the
inferior sex.

0024
DeCrow, Karen. "The seventh wave," *Young Woman's
Guide to Liberation: Alternatives to a Half-
Life While the Choice is Still Yours*, by K.
DeCrow. Indianapolis: Bobbs-Merrill, 1971.
pp. xl-xxvl.

While the mass media encourages intellectual curiosity in boys, the only aspiration they seem to encourage
in girls is to grow up to become human Barbie dolls.
Women's magazines, edited by men, condition women to be

helpless beauties. Movies show female executives who
sacrifice careers for love and a full-time position as
domestic servant. Television advertising further demeans
women as people whose most important challenge is to have
the whitest wash on the block. Ambitious women are beginning to reject the media's misogynistic messages.

0025

> Epstein, Cynthis Fuchs. "Models and images,"
> *Woman's Place, Options and Limits in Profes-*
> *sional Careers,* by C. F. Epstein. Berkeley:
> University of California Press, 1970. pp.
> 28-32.

The young female audience is rarely exposed to female
professionals in books, films, television and magazines.
The few they do see are usually embittered and forsaken:
the homewrecker of the cinema, television's divorced
career women, and Lois Lane of comic book fame who is
most effective professionally when Superman is by her
side. The low percentage of career women in society is
at least partially caused by the paucity of role models
in the media.

See 0742. W. Farrell, "Image and aggression."

0026

> Faust, Jean. "Testimony before the New York City
> Commission on Human Rights," *Women's Role in*
> *Contemporary Society.* NY: Avon Books, 1972.
> pp. 682-700.

The movie and television industries have consistently
denigrated women's image. Women have few lead parts, are
televised participating in only the "suitable" sports
that don't induce sweating, and are either omitted, re-
jected or killed off in television western, spy/adventure
and science/space dramatic programs. Television commercials' god-like voiceovers patronizingly rescue helpless
women from domestic crisis and teach them their ultimate
feminine value and fulfillment as consumers. On television's variety programming, popular song lyrics teach
women to be untroublesome, and berate the women who reject submissiveness by two-timing their lovers. Male
comedians who specialize in "wife jokes" mercilessly mock
their wives' dumb, helpless, flighty characters. These
prejudiced images deny little girls the inspiring female
role models they should emulate and deny adult women respectable images with which to identify.

See 1004. H. Franzwa, "Working women in fact and fiction."

0027
Gerbner, George. Teacher image in mass culture; symbolic functions of the 'hidden curriculum'," *Communications Technology and Social Policy, Understanding the New "Cultural Revolution"*, ed. by George Gerbner, Larry P. Gross, and William H. Melody. NY: John Wiley, 1973. pp. 265-286; also in *Media and Symbols: The Forms of Expression, Communication, and Education*. (National Society for the Study of Education. Yearbook. v. 73, pt. 1) Chicago: N.S.S.E., 1974. pp. 470-497.

The negative media image of the teacher shows spinster schoolmarms teaching children, while absent-minded professors teach college students. The media teachers are usually unloved and sexless people who have either failed in romance, or in the case of women, have been forced to choose between career and marriage.

0028
Goldfield, Evelyn, Sue Munaker, and Naomi Weisstein. "A woman is a sometime thing, or cornering capitalism by removing 51% of its commodities," *The New Left: a Collection of Essays*, ed. by Priscilla Long. Boston: Extending Horizons Books, 1969. pp. 236-271.

Media men, in their advertising, broadcasting and magazine industries, define women as sexual objects and brainless people whose consumption of unnecessary products is motivated by the sole obsession to catch or keep a man. Women's image fares no better in underground newspapers where left wing male editors stereotype women as "revolutionary cheesecake."

0029
Hansen, L. Sunny. "We are furious (female) but we can shape our own development," *Personnel and Guidance Journal*, 1972, 51:87-93.

The sex role stereotypes and myths found in advertising, textbooks, television and motion pictures socialize girls and women to regard themselves as incapable of significant contribution to society. The myths about women as the weaker sex become self-fulfilling prophecies. School guidance counselors are offered suggestions to counteract media socialization.

9

0030
Harbeson, Gladys E. "Challenge of the seventies:
the new self-image," *Choice and Challenge of the
American Woman*, by G. E. Harbeson. Cambridge,
Mass: Schenkman, 1971. pp. 1-13.

Ancient mythical images of woman are still being
perpetuated by the mass media, with the profit motive suggested as the primary cause of the media's indifference
toward the debilitating effects of this outdated image.
The image of a non-aggressive, non-intellectual woman who
gains her identity solely through husband and children
neither reflects the reality of who women are, nor presents the intelligent womanly qualities valued by most
people.

0031
Harris, Janet. "A role without a script," *The
Prime of Ms. America, The American Woman at
Forty*, by J. Harris. NY: Putnam, 1975. pp.
11-24.

While the middle-aged man is portrayed in popular
magazines as a tanned, virile business tycoon or rugged
outdoors-type, the image of the middle-aged woman is less
dignified. She is portrayed as a sad joke: the silly
club woman, perennial shopper, castrating female or carp-
ping mother-in-law.

She is absent from ads - too old to sell perfume,
floor wax or even wrinkle cream, but she does appear in
dishwashing soap ads to demonstrate her youthful hands.
The older woman's movie image is even worse as aging
villainess, invalid sister or ax-murderer.

0032
Harrison, Barbara Grizzuti. "June, 1971: a
new beginning," *Unlearning the Lie: Sexism in
School*, by B. G. Harrison. NY: Liveright,
1973. pp. 131-160.

Extracts from a video tape reveal sex role stereotypes in a Norman Rockwell illustration, *Sesame Street*,
advertising, fashion magazines and children's picture
books. Most effective is the montage of television commercials whose message implicitly states that girls'
futures lie in "the womb, the kitchen, and the toilet
bowl."

0033
Henley, Nancy. "The American way of beauty -

of parlors, beauty and/or funeral," *The Paper*,
November-December, 1970. Available from KNOW,
Inc., PO Box 86031, Pittsburgh, PA 15221. #141.

A comparison of beauty parlors and funeral parlors
based on media applications. Both parlors advertise the
"natural" look in cosmetics. Daytime television programming projects beautiful women as "the living dead" and
fosters a pill culture of drugged zombies.

0034
Hole, Judith and Ellen Levine. "Feminist social
critique," *Rebirth of Feminism*, by J. Hole and
E. Levine. NY: Quadrangle Bks, 1971. pp. 194-
225.

In movie ads women are described by their adjunct relationships to men. Children's toys and books teach sex
role stereotypes in which boys are chemists and girls are
"little homemakers." When they become adults men balk at
sharing the drudgery of housework while women are brainwashed to find total fulfillment in waxed floors, spark-
ling ovens and ringless collars.

0035
Hole, Judith, and Ellen Levine. "Media," *Re-
birth of Feminism*, by J. Hole and E. Levine. NY:
Quadrangle Books, 1971. pp. 247-277.

An examination of coverage of the women's movement,
women's image and employment status of women in the mass
media and in the feminist media. Highlights of the article include descriptions of the 1970 feminist takeovers
of the *Ladies' Home Journal* and *Rat* underground newspaper
offices.

0036
Holter, Harriet. "Role models in mass media and
literature," *Sex Roles and Social Structure*.
Oslo: Universitetsforlaget, 1970. pp. 204-206.

The conclusions of several American studies show that
magazine fiction projects an acceptable image of woman as
parasite. Her passion, ambition and goal is the pursuit
of a man. Women's magazines in Poland, as long ago as the
early 1950's, described economic and familial equality between the sexes. Swedish children's books show girls as
competent, independent and emancipated only in those
books which include no male characters. Girls are passive when playing with boys. Biographies of Florence
Nightingale portray her as a gentle, saintly woman although

11

historical records report a more aggressive personality.

0037
    Holter, Harriet. "Sex roles and social change,"
    Acta Sociologica 1971, 12:2-12; also in *Toward
    a Sociology of Women*, ed. by Constantina
    Safilios-Rothschild. Lexington, Mass: Xerox,
    1972. pp. 331-343; also reprinted as *Sex Roles
    and Social Change*, by Harriet Holter. Andover,
    Mass: Warner Modular Publications, 1973; also
    in *Women and Motivational Analysis*, ed. by
    Martha T. S. Mednick, Susan S. Tangri, and Lois
    W. Hoffman. Washington, DC: Hemisphere Publ,
    1975. pp. 6-19.

Since housewives are fairly isolated, "their conceptions of themselves and each other are mediated to them
through a 'third party' - the mass media. Such stereotyped self-images of women are less conducive to feelings
of solidarity among women than direct contact and cooperation."

0038
    "How do you feel about being a woman? - the
    results of a *Redbook* questionnaire," *Redbook*,
    January, 1973, 140(3):67-69+.

A reader survey revealed that 75% of the 120,000 respondents agreed that "the media degrades women by portraying them as mindless dolls."

0039
    Israel, Joachim. "Consumption society, sex roles
    and sexual behavior," *Acta Sociologica*, 1971,
    14:68-82.

Because advertisements and commercial propaganda use
women as a means to sell commodities, American society
views women as sexually passive *objects* while men are considered active *subjects*. The role of women as objects is
further strengthened by mass media television, cinema and
weekly magazines which have strong indoctrinating effects.

See 0608. "Joan Nicholson: on using employee publications for affirmative action.

0040
    Komisar, Lucy. "The ideology of feminism," *The
    New Feminism*, by L. Komisar. NY: Franklin Watts,

1971. pp. 152-169.

Inequities facing women in media treatment include advertising which typically portrays men instructing women on proper performance in their "place", the kitchen. Female bodies are used to sell everything from cigarettes to airline tickets to movie plots. In the movies women alternately play sex objects and "man-eaters." Television news is dominated by men and newspapers offer women a "woman's section" while men are given the rest of the paper.

0041
Komisar, Lucy. "The new feminism," *Saturday Review*, February 21, 1970, 53(8):27-30.

The early goals and strategems of the "new feminism" include purging women of the self-hatred that drives them to laugh at jokes about women drivers, mothers-in-law and dumb blondes, and purging advertising of the image of women as decorative sex objects.

0042
Lerner, Gerda. "The feminists: a second look," *Columbia Forum*, 1970, 13(3):24-30.

Women occupy an oppressed caste in society because the mass media, literature and Freudian psychology have all reinforced a stereotyped femininity. Women who feel dissatisfied with the role are called neurotic or deviant.

0043
Martin, Joanna Foley. "Confessions of a non-bra-burner," *Chicago Journalism Review*. July, 1971, 4(7):11+.

Of all the stereotypes perpetuated by the media concerning advocates of women's equality, the ubiquitous burning bra is still with us. This article reveals the truth about the bra-burning myth, where it originated and how the media distorted a symbolic, non-flammable act.

0044
"Mass communication media," *Declaration of Mexico Plans of Action*, by World Conference of the International Women's Year. United Nations, 1975. pp. 45-47; also in *Journal of Reprints of Documents Affecting Women*, 1976, 1:602-604. also as "The media," *Decade for Women: World Plan of Action*, by Women's Equity Action League, National

Press Bldg, Washington, DC 20045, 1975; also
in ERIC (ED 123 173).

The World Plan of Action concerning the media adopted
by the United Nations Conference of the International
Women's Year suggests that the mass communications media
direct their great potential for social change toward influencing the removal of prejudices and stereotypes by
accelerating the acceptance of women's expanding roles.
The media should depict women's present and historical
achievements, should seek to develop women's self-confi-
dence, and project an image of female value as human
beings. The greater numbers of women working in the media
should be promoted to decision-making levels.

0045
"Mass media: friend or foe?" "...to Form a
More Perfect Union ...", Justice for American
Women, report of the National Commission of the
Observance of International Women's Year, 1976.
pp 18-21. (Y3.W84 1/976).

Commercial and public broadcasting and the print
media are examined for cases of employment discrimination
and for the effect of media content in shaping and reinforcing stereotyped sex role behavior patterns.

0046
"'The media are educable ...' - consensus of
panel at TX Conference," Media Report to Women,
January 1, 1976, 4(1):6.

Incisive quotes from a panel discussion of prominent
media women.

0047
Media in Montana: Its Effects on Minorities and
Women: A Report of the Advisory Committee to
the U.S. Commission on Civil Rights, 1976. (CRI.2/
M76); also ERIC (ED 129 514), 1976.

"The broadcast and print media have become major
transmitters of cultural standards, myths, values, roles
and images, reaching people of every socioeconomic status."
False imagery conveyed by the powerful media can prove
detrimental in promoting misconceptions about minorities
and women. Montana has few female reporters to provide
positive role models in the media, and further derogates
women with biased reporting. Photographs of women athletes
show them with eyes crossed or biting tongues, while no
such unattractive shots of Jack Nicklaus are printed in

14

the sports pages. A survey revealed that respondents
would like to see authoritative women appearing on television as professional career women, promoting national
products, hosting talk shows and anchoring the news. The
images of women and minorities are neither truthful nor
believable.

See 0105. *Media Report to Women*.

See 0748. K. T. Mehlinger, "Image of the black man and
the media."

0048
> Murphey, Mary. "Superstar women and their mar-
> riages," *New York*, August 9, 1976, 9(32):24-33.

The old Hollywood fantasy-stereotype of ambitious
women gladly dropping successful careers for the promise
of marriage is demythologized. Interviews with Helen
Reddy, Carol Burnett, Ann-Margret and Mary Tyler Moore and
their husband/managers show that the husbands bask in the
glow of their superstar-wives' talent, hard work and ambition. The article mentions Mary Tyler Moore's revolu-
tionizing of the image of women: she is sexually active,
demands equal pay, refuses to marry any available man and
brings dignity to the image of the unmarried career woman.

0049
> "Nancy Seifer on the source of stereotypes," *Media
> Report to Women*, October 1, 1976, 4(10):5.

The mass media, particularly newspapers and television tend to exaggerate stereotypes of women and minority
groups, and therefore mislead the audience who believes
the stereotypes to be true reflections of reality.

0050
> National Organization for Women. New York Chap-
> ter, Image of Women Committee. "Images of women
> in the mass media." Available from author, 47 E.
> 19th St., NY, 10003.

A short pamphlet with brief descriptions of the type
of sexism inherent in each medium. Suggestions offered
for combatting sexism in the media include controlling
"badvertising by writing protest letters to the presidents
of national corporations responsible for sexist ads. A
similar approach may be taken with broadcasting, magazines
and newspapers, films and popular music.

0051
    Nelson, Gayle. "The double standard in adolescent novels," *English Journal*, February, 1975, 4(2):53-55.

The media provide young women with few inspiring female role models. Women in ads are worried about rings around husband's collars, those in television programs and movies function as secretary to the male lead, and women in adolescent fiction, as evidenced in the five novels examined, function as personified wombs more often than not.

0052
    Nunes, Maxine and Deanna White. *The Lace Ghetto*. (New Woman Series, 3). Toronto: New Press, 1972.

A visual cluster of ads, comic strip illustrations, photos and quotes which demean and/or reinforce the traditional image of woman as coy, cute, scatterbrained being.

0053
    Peck, Ellen. "The Media Trap," *The Baby Trap*. NY: Bernard Geis Assoc, 1971. pp. 39-59.

Advertising's image of "mother" shows a fulfilled and glamorous woman. Magazine articles further the glamour of motherhood by enshrining the state in a religious dimension, complete with cults and subcults. Media men realize that motherhood is neither chic, fun, nor glamorous but project it as such for the sake of consumerism. Peck labels the most common media models of motherhood as Professional Mother, Glamour-Doll, Out-of-Wedlock Mother, and the Hippie Mother. She denounces women's magazines and Hollywood pulps for irresponsible journalism in promoting pregnancy in this age of population problems.

0054
    Pogrebin, Letty Cottin. "Down with sexist upbringing," *Ms*, Spring, 1972, pp. 18+.

The female (and male) child's spirit is being ruined by portrayals of lazy, frightened and eccentric women in nursery rhymes, sex role stereotypes in math books, the manly burden defined by the Hardy boys, the image of women as slaves or scatterbrains on television situation comedies, the role of women as cook and cleaner on *Sesame Street* and the conditioning of television commercials that teach girls an obsession with beauty. Sugar, spice, snails and puppydog tails are no longer relevant metaphors. Human dignity, the birthright of every child, should be reflected in the mass media.

0055
"Portrayal of women by the mass media," *American Women, the Report of the President's Commission on the Status of Women*, by US President's Commission on the Status of Women. NY: Scribner's, 1964. pp. 214-219.

The image of women in the mass media contains myths, misconceptions, and distortions of reality. Women are projected as subservient, non-political, non-working, and non-creative. Advertising shows women as shallow and grotesque, demoting them through a female quest for glamour. Worse still is the Negro girls' equation of being glamorous with being white. Daytime television includes no educational programming for women and women's magazines are delinquent in offering Negro women in fiction and non-fiction, even though heroic women exist in real life. All communications media project an onus about the career woman. By portraying her as aggressive, brash and pushy, career women are given an additional psychological barrier. The commission identified the necessity for showing pluralistic images of women: full-time working women (both single and married), the woman who supports her family, the professional intellectual, and the Negro woman.

0056
"Really socking it to women," *Time*, February 7, 1977, 109(6):58-59.

Misogyny in magazine and record album illustrations take a new turn in the form of physical violence against women. Attempts to counteract the trend include mass manufacturer boycotts organized by Women Against Violence Against Women.

0057
Reich, Michael and Margery Davis. "On the relationship between sexism and capitalism," *The Capitalist System*, ed. by Richard C. Edwards, Michael Reich and Thomas E. Weisskopf. Englewood Cliffs, NJ: Prentice-Hall, 1972. pp. 348-359.

The media preserve male power within the nuclear family by promoting the image of the successful woman as one who is fulfilled by pleasing her husband and caring for *his* children. The media fail to demonstrate female fulfillment as derived from significant activity in the labor market.

0058

Reichert, Julia and James Klein. *Growing Up Female*, 16mm., 60 min. b/w., rental, $60, purchase, $375. New Day Films. Box 315, Franklin Lakes, NJ 07117.

Demonstrates the impact of advertising, television and pop music on the socialization of American women. (See also 0063.)

0059

Rooms with no View; A Woman's Guide to the Man's World of the Media, compiled by the Media Women's Association, edited by Ethel Strainchamps. NY: Harper and Row, 1974.

Personal testimonies of employment discrimination at four commercial and educational television networks, 17 magazine and 24 book publishing houses, nine newspaper and wire services and in the editorial arena in general. The appendix includes guidelines for filing sex discrimination complaints.

0060

Saperstein, David. "Your time, your station: changing woman's thinking and lifestyle through the great communication revolution," *Woman in the Year 2000*, ed. by Maggie Tripp, NY: Arbor House, 1974. pp. 309-320.

In the 1970's people are questioning the values that once dictated a woman's place to be in the home. Creative women no longer subvert their desires and talents but now create the advertising copy rather than functioning strictly as the cleaning and cooking machines seen within ads. By the year 2000, the author foresees women taking even more active roles as the writers, producers, directors and technicians in the media explosion to come.

0061

Stannard, Una. "The mask of beauty," *Woman in Sexist Society: Studies in Power and Powerlessness*, ed. by Vivian Gornick and Barbara K. Moran, NY: Basic Books, 1971. pp. 118-130.

All men are created equal and all women are created beautiful (or potentially beautiful through cosmetics). Little girls grow up seeing models of female beauty in ads for soap powder, on television, movies and magazine covers. Every girl watches dozens of beauty contests per year and is trained to regard the mask of beauty as the feminine ideal.

0062

"Statement of Lucy Komisar, writer and a National Vice President of the National Organization for Women, New York Chapter," *Discrimination Against Women, Congressional Hearings on Equal Education and Employment,* ed. by Dr. Catharine R. Stimpson. (Bowker/CIS Congressional Document Series). NY: Bowker, 1973. pp. 105-118.

Discrimination against women in media employment and the negative image of women in television, newspapers, magazines and advertising are two sides of the same coin. While media image of women harms the female self-image and aspirations, it also contributes to the image of women that makes job discrimination respectable.

0063

Sternburg, Janet. "Revealing herself," *Film Library Quarterly,* Winter, 1971-1972, 5(1):7-12+.

The causes of woman's common self-image of worthlessness are explored in four novels and one film, all written by women. One cause, the stereotyped image of women in advertising, is especially potent in the film, *Growing up Female* (see 0058) when a hip advertising executive matter-of-factly describes advertising's manipulation of women as consumers. When a woman is constantly surrounded by a "Barbie Doll" image of what she should be, it's difficult to maintain a "self-determined identity" in order to avoid feelings of worthlessness.

0064

"Sugar and spice ...," *School Library Journal,* January, 1971, 17(5):5.

Television, magazines and book publishers seem to be cashing in on their latest fad: laughing at the women's movement as they continue to stereotype the sex roles. Even "our hallowed Newbery-Caldecott winners aid in the insidious process of socialization." By cutting through this socialization process perhaps the new dictum will read "Psychology (not Biology) is destiny."

0065

Teltsch, Kathleen. "U.N. reports on sexist attitudes around the world," *The New York Times,* January 31, 1974, p. 24.

A United Nations report quotes worldwide complaints concerning woman as sex symbol in advertising, as seductress or nagging wife in television, and jokes about mothers-in-law and dumb blondes throughout broadcast media.

See 0200. "This ad insults women."

0066
Tobias, Sheila and Ella Kusnetz. "For college students: a study of women, their roles and stereotypes," *Journal of Home Economics,* April, 1972, 64(4):17-21.

The images of women in fairy tales, children's books, women's magazines and television programming all reinforce the stereotype of woman as physically beautiful but incompetent.

0067
Walstedt, Joyce Jennings. "Women as marginals," *Psychological Reports,* 1974, 34:639-646.

A marginal group is one who lives on the margin of two cultures but is not easily assimilated into the dominant culture. Our communications media affirm the value of the dominant male business/professional/government leadership culture, which effectively excludes women. The other culture which women do not fit into is the lifestyle of super-wife and super-mom as idealized by the media.

Female children learn of their marginal status from negative indoctrination received from picture books, television programming and sex-typed toys. Walstedt further notes that "despite the need for zero population growth [girls are encouraged] to feed, dress, and caress dolls in much the same way they might nurture real babies when they grow up."

0068
Ward, Jean. "Attacking the king's English: implications for journalism in the feminist critique," *Journalism Quarterly,* 1975, 52:699-705.

The *AP-UPI Stylebook* offers no guidelines for eliminating sexist language in journalistic practice. Feminist groups have picketed the *New York Times* for its ban on the title "Ms.," and have written letters to editors and broadcasters deploring the use of words "girl" to

describe woman, "housewife" to describe legislator, and
"man" to describe all humanity. The practice is especially
discriminatory when male subjects are not called "boy",
male legislators are not called "husbands," and the word
"woman," which does include "man", is not considered a
generic noun. The author offers smoothly flowing sentence
construction as evidence that the word "person" and third
person plural pronouns do not obscure understanding.

0069
"Woman-as-object," *Up Against the Wall, Mother...*,
ed. by Elsie Adams and Mary Louise Briscoe. Beverly Hills: Glencoe, 1971. p. 33.

Big business has thrived at woman's expense by promoting the ornamental function of the American woman in
advertising, playgirl of the month foldouts and the Miss
America ideal.

0070
"Your daughter's education," *Ladies' Home Journal*,
August, 1970, 87(8):65-66.

From childhood girls are taught certain role behavior.
Popular songs teach her to "make him your reason for living," school books teach her math with images of housewives in the grocery store (and men in the bank) and
television advertising offers her the choice of becoming
castrator or sex object when she grows up.

News Media

0071
Akamatsu, Muriel. "Liberating the media: news,"
Freedom of Information Center Report, 289. Co-
lumbia: University of Missouri, School of
Journalism, 1972.

An overview of the common stereotypes found in newspapers, magazines, television programming and media employment. Sexist reporting occurred which did not quote
the female cement truck driver featured nor reveal any
struggle she may have experienced being hired. Activity
within the feminist movement is having some impact on
raising consciousness and overthrowing some stereotypes
in the media.

21

0072

American Association of University Women, Sacramento, California Branch. *The Image of Women in Television, A Survey and Guide*. Sacramento: AAUW, 1974.

Monitoring of 470 news programs for word usage, omission of women and sex stereotyping indicated that television news projects two images of women: helpless victim or opinionless, supportive wife and mother. More prevalent than these images was the common omission of women from news stories. Women appeared in the news less than 10% of the 221.5 hours monitored. Recommendations for improving the image of women on news programming included an affirmative action program to recruit more female reporters, more interviews with prominent female newsmakers, rejection of commercials in which women appear stupid, subservient or helpless, and programs featuring women's role in law, employment, politics and medicine.

0073

"Analysis of news programming aired by WRC-TV during the composite week," *Women in the Wasteland Fight Back*, by National Organization for Women, National Capitol Area Chapter. Washington, DC: NOW, 1972. pp. 105-117.

WRC-TV news programming was monitored for story type, newsmaker, sex, race and name of each reporter, as well as length of time allocated each story. Of 505 minutes of news programming less than 3½ minutes were given to stories about women's rights, women's rights leaders, the women's movement, women's changing role. The longest story (1 minute, 45 seconds) was a humorous anecdote about "non-women's libbers," while no coverage was given to the first woman admiral and first woman rabbi who were featured in newspapers that day. Women were 10% of the newsmakers featured and 12% of the reporters. Women reported 1.9% hard news, 5.6% mini-documentaries, 11.8% features.

0074

"Australian media women examine their media's rape reportage," *Media Report to Women*, April 1, 1977, 5(4):6.

By reporting rape attacks and trials in terms of mock horror, complete with suggestive euphemisms, Australian news media perpetuate the myth that rape is the fault of the victim. The news media fail to report the true atrocities of rape - anal rape, use of broken bottles, defecation, gang rape, photographs, and rape's aftermath of disease, familial rejection and nightmares. The authors call on the media to lay aside the mock horror and begin honestly reporting violence against women.

0075
"Barbara Walters - star of the morning," *Newsweek*, May 6, 1974, pp. 55-61.

The sex role double standard operates to hurt Ms. Walters' reputation among some viewers. Her detractors consider her "aggressive and pushy" when these are the very qualities that they admire in successful male interviewers.

0076
Barnett, Julie. *A Content Analysis of the National Organization for Women (N.O.W.) in News Magazines*. M.A. thesis, University of Georgia, 1976.

News coverage of NOW activities by *Newsweek*, *Time* and *U.S. News & World Report* revealed that most coverage was neutral although *Newsweek* had a greater tendency for negative reporting while *U.S. News & World Report* was most likely to be positive.

0077
Bowman, William Winslow. *Distaff Journalists: Women as a Minority Group in the News Media*. Ph.D. dissertation, University of Illinois-- Chicago Circle, 1974.

Women do not advance in their media careers with the same ease as men, and are limited to "minor league" areas of journalism. One reason given for this limiting of female potential has been that it is compatible with the traditional sex roles in American society.

0078
Chacon, Estelle. "Women journalists on television should be positive role models for other women," *Media Report to Women*, January 1, 1977, 5(1):8.

In an open letter to female broadcasters, the President of San Diego County NOW asks them to treat female viewers with dignity. She reminds the broadcasters that it was NOW's challenges of FCC license renewals that opened jobs for women in broadcast news.

See 0023. E. G. Davis, "The prejudice lingers on:

Woman's image."

0079

Delsman, Mary A. "Media organizations," *Every-*
thing you Need to Know about the ERA, by M. A.
Delsman. Riverside, CA: Meranza Pr, 1975.
pp. 105-107.

The author claims that news reporters created an
artificial 50-50 situation when the ERA faced little
national opposition in 1970. The media further treats ERA
advocates prejudicially by using "tough" language to describe their appearance and attitudes while using softer
adjectives to describe ERA opponents. The male dominated
media is also responsible for the insistence in covering
Mr. Blackwell's list of worst dressed women while failing
to carry stories about the need for day-care centers, adequate facilities for delinquent girls, and inhumane treatment of poor women.

0080

Diliberto, Gioia E. *Profiles of Three Newswomen.*
M.A. thesis, University of Maryland, 1975.

Pauline Frederick, Meg Greenfield and Helen Thomas
are interviewed about pressures, obstacles, treatment and
effects on personal lives common to female journalists.

0081

"Ellen Cohn on media's picture of women," *Media*
Report to Women, June 1, 1974, 2(6):12.

Female lobbyists are influencing legislation and flexing political muscles, yet the media still undervalue,
overlook and trivialize women and their accomplishments.
The media are guilty of patting women of all ages on the
head and calling them "girl" (though they would never refer
to other groups as "kike" or "nigger"), proudly refer to
themselves as male chauvinist pigs and refuse to acknowledge Billie Jean King as "Ms.", even though they do comply
with Lew Alcindor's request to be called Kareem Abdul-
Jabbar.

0082

Good, Mashinka. "Hotline set: erase sexism from
media," *Editor and Publisher*, June 8, 1974,
107(23):24.

A conference of female journalists plans to set guidelines to erase sexism in the news media by covering issues

24

relevant to women, ending language abuse, determining a standard age whereby girls become women, advising on affirmative action cases, and redefining the news so that it applies to the female as well as male perspective.

0083
    Hennessee, Judith, "Some news is good news," *Ms.*, July, 1974, 3(1):25-29.

The stereotyped attitudes television newswomen must face include the desirability of masculine voices for reading the news, the fact that a newswoman's attractive appearance often destroys her credibility, and the "ghetto mentality" at the assignment desk where women are expected to cover White House weddings rather than hard political stories, while child care, abortion and rape are left uncovered altogether.

0084
    "How would a woman shoot a story differently than a man?," *Media Report to Women*, April 1, 1975, 3(4):5.

Testimony of job discrimination faced by a news camerawoman includes evidence of her news footage being edited to remove the image of an "unattractive" woman digging and lifting trees. Sex role stereotypes prevail and women of average appearance engaged in realistic non-"feminine" activity are not reflected in news coverage.

0085
    "Jill Volner: How news media make the issues - and the stereotypes of women," *Media Report to Women*, March 1, 1977, 5(3):7.

Jill Volner's role as prosecuting attorney in the Watergate trials was consistently reported in stereotypical terms. Cheesecake photos of her body from the toes up appeared in newspapers while her male colleages were photographed from the shoulders up. Her hair color and skirt lengths were treated as hard news though physical descriptions of male prosecutors did not appear in the news. The sexist tilt to news coverage was also evident in the reporting of Judge Sirica's remark that Volner not squabble with the witness when the same remark, warning male prosecutors to discontinue squabbling, was not reported in the press. Such incomplete coverage perpetuates a stereotype that women are less professional than men.

0086
>   Kirkpatrick, Curry. "Getting into the picture
>   with sports broadcasters and journalists," *Sports
>   Illustrated*, April 21, 1975, 42:84-96.

Initial discrimination faced by female sportscasters
eventually leads to acceptance.

0087
>   Kohler, Pam Sebastian. "Objectivity ends at the
>   hemline," *The Quill*, October, 1972, 60(10):25-
>   27.

News reporters who now refer to Mexican-Americans as
Chicano and who no longer call black men "boy" do not
maintain the same journalistic objectivity when reporting
women's activities. Photographs of semi-clad women are
never matched by those of men in brief attire. Women's
achievements are neglected as the story reports female appearance and 60 year old women are called "girl."

0088
>   McNeely, Patricia G. *Woman's News: A Changing
>   Image*. M.A. thesis, University of South Carolina,
>   1975.

A content analysis of women's news sections from
metropolitan newspapers in every US region, for 1960 and
1975, documents the trend from society news toward general
and women's features.

0089
>   Mannes, Marya. "Should women only be seen and
>   not heard?," *TV Guide*, November 23, 1968; also
>   in *Television*, by Barry G. Cole. NY: Free
>   Press, 1970. pp. 276-284.

Calls for female voices of authority as news com-
mentators, rather than limitation of women as reporters.

0090
>   "Marlene Sanders: the other woman in network
>   news," *Broadcasting*, November 8, 1976, 91:105.

As the first female newscaster in 1962 Marlene
Sanders helped change the image of women in broadcasting
by writing and producing a weekly documentary program,
and covering such hard news stories as the 1963 civil
rights march on Washington, and Vietnam.

0091
  "Marlene Sanders: 'We have found a new
  comraderie. We must continue to work together',"
  Media Report to Women, March 1, 1975, 3(3):11.

  Marlene Sanders describes programs she has produced
concerning sex role stereotypes and the women's movement.
As one of the early women in broadcast news she has been
a positive role model for viewers by covering Vietnam and
occasionally anchoring the news.

0092
  "Media misogyny," *Off Our Backs*, February, 1977,
  7(1):6.

  After reporting a rape story on local New York City
news, the reporter told a joke about rape. Two weeks
after the reporter had been suspended, the news anchor
told another joke alluding to the original one. Picketing
feminists demanded the reporter's dismissal as well as
sensitivity training for the news staff and positive programming on the issue of rape.

0093
  National Organization for Women. San Francisco
  Chapter, Media Task Force. *The Image of Women
  in the Media*. C. Neuman, 2001 California St.,
  no. 503, San Francisco, CA 94109. $2.00.

  NOW monitoring of 228 news programs on four San
Francisco television stations documented sexual discrimination. Results showed 15% appearances by female reporters and 20% on-camera interviews of women. Stories
about men outnumbered those about women 3:1. Conclusions
include: the four stations cover women's news inadequately, female reporters most often deliver soft news
and features, women's roles are inadequately reflected,
women are interviewed less frequently than men, female
employees are concentrated in clerical positions while
male employees are most often in the top four job categories. Monitoring instructions and forms are included.

0094
  "New 'guidelines for eliminating sexism in the
  media' proposed," *Media Report to Women*, June 1,
  1975, 3(6):12.

  The newspaper guidelines, reprinted here in their
entirety, offer alternatives to sexist phraseology, the
ghettoization of women's news, suggestions for less
derogatory treatment of the women's movement in the news.

0095

Pogrebin, Letty Cottin. "Ten cogent reasons why
TV news fails women," *TV Guide*, October 4, 1975;
also in *Media Report to Women*, December 1, 1975,
3(12):12.

All three commercial networks are guilty of ignoring
hard news concerning women. Employment, education, insurance discrimination, and issues concerning rape, childcare and health are not covered adequately by the news
media. Women's issues are systematically ignored, but
sports events are covered as hard news.

0096

Stone, Vernon A. "Attitudes toward television
newswomen,"*Journal of Broadcasting*, 1974, 18:
49-62.

Although NBC President Reuven Frank had publicly announced his opinion that 1971 audiences were less prepared
to accept news from a woman's voice than from a man's, by
1972 60% of RTNDA stations had female newscasters. A
survey of university professors, fourth and fifth grade
children, their parents and news directors revealed that
only the news directors overwhelmingly favored male
anchors. Sixty-six percent of the audience admitted no
preference to sex of reporter.

See 0446. V. Stone and A. J. Nash, "A survey of women
in broadcast news."

See 0447. V. Stone, "Surveys show younger women becoming
news directors."

0097

"Survey of WRC-TV public affairs and news programming since February, 1972," *Women in the
Wasteland Fight Back*, by the National Organization for Women, National Capitol Area Chapter.
Washington, DC: NOW, 1972.

Public affairs programming and talk shows were most
often hosted by men (91%), had male guests (77%), and mentioned male occupations more often than female (81%:62%).

The local news primarily covered foreign policy,
sports, crime and weather. Women's issues covered included the first female traffic police officer, female
circus clown; women's issues neglected by the news included abortion legislation, Congressional ERA debates,

hearings on discrimination against women and credit, though these issues were covered in *The Washington Post* during the same time period.

See 0604. L. Van Gelder, "Women's pages: you can't make news out of a silk purse."

See 0068. J. Ward, "Attacking the king's English: implications for journalism in the feminist critique."

0098
  "'We must do a better job of covering news about women,' says V-P of U.P.I.," *Media Report to Women*, July 1, 1976, 4(7):7.

H. L. Stevenson, editor in chief of UPI, was influenced in this decision by data from IWY proceedings and discussion of women's coverage with Jill Ruckelshaus and Liz Carpenter.

0099
  Whitlow, S. Scott. *The Perception of Women as News Principals: An Analysis of the Cognitive Set of Gatekeepers and of Situational Correlates.* Ph.D. dissertation, Southern Illinois University, 1975.

Relationship between employment roles of women in news media and the image of women within the news.

0100
  Whittaker, Susan McDargh, "Male vs. female newscasters - a study of the relative effectiveness, believability and acceptance," paper presented at the annual meeting of the Association for Education in Journalism, 1975. ERIC (ED 120 770).

An experiment to measure audience believability and acceptance of female as well as male newscasters was conducted with two female and two male newscasters, each reading two factual and two fictitious news stories. Results indicate no significant difference in audience acceptance of either sex as newscaster, and no differences in effectiveness of female and male newscasters.

0101
> Adato, Perry Miller. "Imagery in communication media," *Arts in Society*, 1974, 11:41-46.

A forum at which members discuss successful techniques used by various women's groups to improve the image of women in the media.

See 0072. American Association of University Women. *The Image of Women in Television, A Survey and Guide.*

See 0953. L. Artel and W. Wengraf, "Positive images: a guide to non-sexist films for young people."

0102
> *Booklegger Magazine*, 555 29th St., San Francisco, CA 94131. Quarterly, $8/yr, ISSN 0092-7686.

Regular columns "Mediamaze," "Kids" and "Grapevine" review the latest non-sexist publications in both print and non-print formats.

0103
> Kennedy, Florynce. "Kicking Ass," *Color Me Flo: My Hard Life and Good Times*. Englewood Cliffs, NJ: Prentice-Hall, 1976. pp. 52-81.

In 1966 Flo Kennedy organized Media Workshop whose purpose was to oppose racism and sexism in advertising. Their picketing an ad agency facilitated a meeting with agency vice-presidents. Stories of a NOW picket of a radio station, and the Atlantic City beauty contest protest are relayed in connection with limiting sexism in the media.

See 0544. S. Lowell, "Women in film."

See 0930. L. Z. McArthur and S. V. Eisen, "Achievements of male and female storybook characters as determinants of achievement behavior by boys and girls.

0104
> "Media guidelines proposed by the National Commission of the Observance of International Women's

Year." Available from Office of Public Information, IWY Commission, Room 1004, Department of State Building, Washington, DC 20520. Specify Leaflet L-1-July, 1976. free; also reprinted by the title, "Guidelines for the treatment of women in the media and checklist for the entertainment program and advertising industries," "...*To Form a More Perfect Union*..." *Justice for American Women; Report of the National Commission of the Observance of International Women's Year*, 1976, pp. 250-253. (Y3.W84 1/976).

Because media stereotypes limit women's aspirations, the IWY Commission proposed ten guidelines concerning employment of women in the media, news coverage of women's activities, the image of women, gender free language, and respectful treatment of women's organizations. Also included is a 16-point checklist for a positive portrayal of women in entertainment programming and advertising.

0105
    Media Report to Women, A Monthly Report on What Women are Doing and Thinking About the Communications Media and Related Media Information. 3306 Ross Place, N.W., Washington, DC 20008.

Reports news of women's publications, conferences, surveys, and quotes from unpublished speeches, legal testimony and proposed guidelines. The annual *Index/Directory* lists accomplishments of individual media women and women's media groups as well as 40 pages of women's periodicals, presses, speakers bureaus, distributors and other feminist collectives and groups.

0106
    Medsgar, Betty. *Women at Work, A Photographic Documentary.* NY: Sheed & Ward, 1975.

In order to convey real images of working women rather than the stereotypes of "women's work" regularly fed the American public by the mass media, Betty Medsgar traveled the country documenting female occupations as heavy equipment operator, bus driver, air traffic controller, industrial designer, stewardess, mother, and potter. Women of all ages, colors, and ethnic backgrounds, who are not often seen in the media reflection of reality, are pictured and quoted here.

0107
    "New media reform task force," *Media Report to Women*, July 1, 1974, 2(7):8.

Major concerns of the National Organization for
Women's new Media Reform task force include working with
industry and government agencies in writing codes and
policies regarding fair treatment of women in all communications media. The negative image of women in the media
is one of the biggest roadblocks to women's equality because it encourages male power by promoting female
inadequacy and powerlessness.

0108
　　　Pogrebin, Letty Cottin. "Women on the tube:
　　　four insiders report," *Ladies' Home Journal*,
　　　April, 1975, 92:18+.

Four female broadcast correspondents discuss legal
measures countering sex segregated want ads and sexist
language in newspapers, and their personal participation
with television documentaries.

0109
　　　Rennie, Susan and Kirsten Grimstad. "Communica-
　　　tions," *New Woman's Survival Sourcebook*, ed. by
　　　S. Rennie and K. Grimstad. NY: Knopf, 1975.
　　　pp. 139-159.

Feminist communications listed include women's
periodicals, directories, broadcasting studies, bookstores,
speaker's bureaus, feminist presses, feminist publications.

0110
　　　Seed, Suzanne. *Saturday's Child: 36 Women Talk
　　　about Their Jobs*. NY: Bantam Books, 1974.

To counter the influence of gender related occupational stereotypes her daughter met in elementary school
readers and on television, Suzanne Seed wrote this book
which contains interviews of 36 women in traditionally
male dominated professions - sportswriter, oceanographer,
letter carrier, lawyer.

0111
　　　Ten-point plan developed to advance women in
　　　media, *Editor and Publisher*, September 27,
　　　1975, 108:11.

Education, publicity, legal recourse and a talent
bank are a few points suggested to advance women professionally in the media.

0112
　　United Nations Economic and Social Council. Com-
　　mission on the Status of Women. *Influence of the
　　Mass Communication Media on Attitudes Towards the
　　Role of Women and Men in Present-Day Society.*
　　1976. (E/CN.6/601).

A 19 page report of the Secretary-General of the UN
includes proposals for creating a more positive image of
women in the mass media. Instead of perpetuating sex role
stereotypes, broadcasting, print media, films, songs and
puppet shows should more positively influence the formation of dynamic attitudes toward women's roles in today's
society. Suggested measures include those to be taken by
the media, by governments and by the UN.

0113
　　"Women and media," *Women's Agenda,* February,
　　1977, 2(2): entire issue.

The special issue on media reports accomplishments
of five activist groups: United Methodist Women, National Organization for Women, American Association of
University Women, National Gay Task Force and Population
Institute concerning feminist activist pressure on the
media.

0114
　　"Women in the media," *National Business Woman,*
　　March, 1976, 57(2):23-24.

The absence of women in policy making positions in
the broadcast and print media accounts in part for the unrealistic portrayal of women in the media. To counter
this employment discrimination Business and Professional
Women suggests three projects: 1) a personnel file of
local television stations and newspaper offices which
tallies the number of women at the highest and lowest employment levels, 2) awareness of changes in FCC regulations which would affect the status of female employees,
3) club sponsorship of a musical concert featuring the
music of female composers.

0115
　　"Women's proxy pressure," *The New York Times,*
　　August 31, 1975. p. F-11.

Feminist activist shareholders submitted proposals
to Procter and Gamble, Columbia Pictures and Gulf and
Western in order to influence the development of positive
images of women in advertising and film roles. Both media

were criticized for not reflecting women's changing status in today's world.

ADVERTISING

Stereotypes in General

0116
    Aaron, Dorothy. "About face: towards a posi-
    tive image of women in advertising," 1975. On-
    tario Status of Women Council, 801 Bay St., 3rd
    Floor, Toronto, Ontario. $1.00.

    An advertising survey conducted by the Ontario Status
of Women Council yielded 1,017 mail responses. Most common
objections were directed to ads implying that a woman's
worth is determined by how well she does her housework,
that her main interest is catching a man, that she lacks
confidence and therefore requires male advice and approval,
and ads implying that she's a sex object. Many women further expressed embarrassment from personal women's products
advertised on prime time television and on public bill-
boards. They felt that ads for these products should be
more appropriately confined to women's magazines. A table
lists the products, half of which are manufactured in the
US, whose ads were most frequently cited as objectionable.
Other tables list Canadian and US magazines and television
programs whose ads are considered objectionable. Also
listed are the stations, magazines and television programs
with the *lowest* frequency of objectionable ads. Suggestions are offered for steps to be taken by consumers and
advertisers in order to eliminate offensive advertising.

See 0069. E. Adams and M. L. Briscoe, "Woman-as-object."

0117
    "Advertising," *Women and Corporations: Issues
    and Actions*, by Interfaith Center on Corporate
    Responsibility, Task Force on Women and Cor-
    porations. NY: ICCR, 1975. p. 15. Available
    from ICCR, 475 Riverside Dr, Room 566, NY 10027.
    $.35.

    In 1974 women were shown in 12% of the ads showing

35

people working. Their typical occupations were clerk, stewardess, entertainer and teacher.

See 0072. American Association of University Women. *The Image of Women in Television, a Survey and Guide.*

See 0751. American Association of University Women. "Jack and Jill; This is the world that Jack built and Jill came tumbling after."

0118.
 Andreas, Carol. "Keeping people in their places: St. Paul, Freud and Madison Ave: the marketplace," *Sex and Caste in America,* by C. Andreas, Englewood Cliffs, NJ: Prentice-Hall, 1971. pp. 87-91.

 Sex role stereotypes in advertising proclaim man "the provider" and woman "the consumer." Children learn their roles from the GI Joe *action figure* and the Barbie *doll* to the images of father waxing his car while mother waxes her floor.

See 0373. M. J. Arlen, "Three views of women."

0119
 Atkin, Charles K. "Effects of television advertising on children. Report #2: second year experimental evidence. Final report." East Lansing: Michigan State University College of Communication Arts, 1975. ERIC (ED 116 784).

 A study exposing 400 elementary school students to television advertising yields the following results: Ss who viewed ads showing women in traditionally masculine occupations were more likely to label those occupations as appropriate for women. Those who viewed ads with girls playing with racing cars were more likely to exhibit attitudes of acceptance toward girls playing with these toys than were the control group who did not see these ads. Recall of product was higher when female announcer's voice was heard, than when male voice was heard.

0120
 Bardwick, Judith M. and Suzanne I. Schumann. "Portrait of American men and women in TV commercials," *Psychology,* 1967, 4(4):18-23.

 A catalogue of advertising's preoccupation with

certain desires, fears and themes including beautiful body, orifice sterilization, youth, dirt and sex. Sex role stereotypes include differential treatment of men as bumblers when they are with family members and as elegant or exciting when not shown with a family.

0121
Belkaoui, Ahmed and Janice M. Belkaoui. "A comparative analysis of the roles portrayed by women in print advertisements: 1958, 1970, 1972," *Journal of Market Research*, 1976, 13:168-172.

This statistical study follows up the research of the Courtney and Lockeretz 1970 study (see 0132) and the Wagner and Banos 1972 study (see 0209) to determine that the portrayal of women in advertising has improved marginally from 1958 to 1972, but does not yet reflect the average woman's lifestyle.

0122
Bell, Inge Powell. "The double standard," *Transaction*, November/December, 1970, 8:75-80.

Advertising reinforces societal loathing of the older and/or aging woman while glamorizing the aging man. Aside from the sweet grandmother image, women 50 and older are conspicuously absent from advertising, while men of the same age are seen in ads for many types of products. The author also examines want-ads for employable age ranges of each sex.

0123
Berger, John. *Ways of Seeing*. London: British Broadcasting Corporation and Baltimore: Penguin Books, 1972.

Essay two is a textless photographic montage of nude, semi-nude and dressed female sex objects taken from art, advertising and news media. Especially effective is the photographic juxtaposition of female breasts and derrieres beside a tray of sliced meat.

The development of female nudity for the sake of the male spectator, begun in traditional European painting, has been adapted by twentieth century advertising. This Western tradition in which passionless female nudity exists only to feed the male spectator's appetite does not exist in traditional Eastern art. There female nakedness combines with male nakedness; female sexuality is as active as male sexuality. In most traditional and contemporary Western examples of female nudity, the passive

woman ignores the male lover in the painting or ad while
looking outside the picture to a spectator-lover. However a few examples by Rembrandt and Rubens defy this
tradition by picturing autonomous and dynamic female nudes.

0124

>Bernstein, Henry R. "Ads ignore real women, use
>stereotypes: Levine," *Advertising Age*, June 16,
>1975, 46(26):86.

Speaking before the California Commission on the
Status of Women, Joan Levine blamed the perpetuation of
sex role stereotypes in advertising on the absence of
women from decision making levels in the industry. Consequently ads have seriously derogated the intelligence of
women in order to sell coffee and floor wax. The standard
argument that advertising reflects rather than shapes society is a cop-out. When corporations like Procter and
Gamble have ad budgets of $245 million, the by-product of
their ad message is the shaping of a supplementary image
along with the advertising.

See 0910. J. Betancourt, *Women in Focus*.

See 0015. L. J. Busby. "Sex role research in the mass
media."

See 0314. M. Butler. "The image of women in advertisements: a preliminary study of avenues for change."

0125

>Callahan, Michael A. *Do Blondes Have More Fun?*
>16mm., 1:30 mins., color, rental, $30. Women's
>Film Cooperative, Valley Women's Center, 200 Main
>St., Northhampton, Mass. 01060.

Glamorous blonde models from print advertising, juxtaposed with a final shot of a black child, remind the
viewer of the difference between advertising's image of
women and reality.

0126

>Cantarow, Ellen, Elizabeth Diggs, Katherine
>Ellis, Janet Marx, Lillian Robinson, and Muriel
>Schien. "I am furious (female)," *Roles Women
>Play: Readings Toward Women's Liberation*, ed.
>by Michele Hoffnung Garskof. Belmont, CA:
>Brooks/Cole, 1971.

Advertising may define woman as "the angel in the house," but actually portrays her less ethereally as the custodian of consumer goods for whom fulfillment is streak-free windows, odorless armpits and cavity-less offspring. It is time for women to put down the nail polish and re-discover real needs.

0127
Cantor, Muriel. "Comparison of tasks and roles of males and females in commercials aired by WRC-TV during the Composite Week," *Women in the Waste-land Fight Back: A Study of the Treatment of Females and Males in WRC-TV Programming Aired During a Composite Week*, by National Organiza-tion for Women, National Capital Area Chapter. Washington, DC: NOW, 1972. pp. 12-51.

During a composite week 2,750 ads were monitored. Overall statistics indicate that product representatives were 93% male, 7% female. On weekday ads voiceovers were 46% male, 54% female before 4:30 p.m., and 67% male, 33% female after 4:30 p.m. On weekends product reps were 80% male, 20% female, while on Saturday morning children's programming they were 86% male, 14% female. Other prod-uct representative demographics show those over age 40 to be 44% male, 18% female, and those of ethnic minorities to be 5% male, 2% female. Domestic roles were 34% male, 77% female. Male product reps were most often assigned professional occupations while female professional status was virtually ignored. Concludes with tables and Duncan SEI scores for every occupation and activity.

0128
Cappo, Joe. "Advertising - its own worst enemy?," *Chicago Daily News*, July 7, 1975; also in *Mass Media: The Invisible Environment Revisited*, by Robert J. Glessing and William P. White. Chicago: Science Research Associates, 1976. p. 132.

A survey conducted by ad agency Foote, Cone and Beld-ing indicates that 58% of the women and 39% of the men questioned admit to being insulted by some advertising. The most insulting were ads for sanitary protection aids and "dumb housewife" ads.

See 0914. J. S. Chafetz. "The bringing up of Dick and Jane: media."

0129
Cheles-Miller, Pamela. "An investigation of

39

whether the stereotypes of husband and wife presented in television commercials influence a
child's perception of the role of husband and
wife," paper presented at the annual meeting of
International Communication Association, 1974.
ERIC (ED 094 439).

Preliminary research on which "Reactions to marital
roles in commercials" is based. See 0130.

0130
Cheles-Miller, Pamela. "Reactions to marital
roles in commercials," *Journal of Advertising
Research*, August, 1975, 15(4):45-49.

A stereotype acceptance test was given to 276 fourth
and fifth grade students who accepted as typical the rigid
sex role stereotypes found in television commercials, and
would incorporate into their personalities more honest
portrayal of marital roles if exposed to them.

0131
"The commercial woman," *Boston: Published by
Greater Boston Chamber of Commerce*, September,
1970, 62:54-57.

Two opposing viewpoints concerning the image of
women in advertising. See 0172 and 0211.

0132
Courtney, Alice E. and Sarah Wernick Lockeretz.
"Woman's place: an analysis of the roles por-
trayed by women in magazine advertisements,"
Journal of Marketing Research, February, 1971,
8:92-95.

A content analysis of 729 print ads revealed that 45%
of the ads picturing men and 9% of the ads picturing women
featured the subjects in working roles. None of the 9%
working women were portrayed as business executives or
professionals. Men were pictured alone in 40% of the ads
surveyed, pictured with other men (25%) in working situations, and with women (34%) in recreational situations.
Women were pictured alone 26% of the time, with men 34%
and with other women only 11%, therefore women were most
often seen in the recreational company of men. In ads
women rarely smoked, drank, traveled, drove cars or used
banks unless in the company of men. Women without men
were usually decorations, sitting on cars.

0133
　　Courtney, Alice E. and Thomas W. Whipple. Women
　　in TV commercials," *Journal of Communication*,
　　1974, 24(2):110-118.

The findings of four studies are compared in terms
of sex of voiceovers, sex of product representative, occupations portrayed by sex, and average age per sex. The
results indicate that women are not portrayed as autonomous, independent human beings. Advertising's portrayal
of women is lagging far behind the realistic change in
women's roles.

0134
　　Culley, James D. and Rex Bennett. "Selling women,
　　selling blacks," *Journal of Communication*, Autumn,
　　1976, 26(4):160-174.

A 1974 updating of the 1971 research by Dominick and
Rauch involving television ads (see 0140) and the 1970
Courtney and Lockeretz research involving print advertising (see 0132) reveals little significant change. Advertising's portrayal of women still deals with personal
appearance and household matters while men are still shown
concerned with durable goods purchases and complex decisions. Women in ads are conspicuously absent from the
professions: women are not shown as lawyers, doctors,
engineers or judges, but remain concentrated in kitchens
and bathrooms.

0135
　　Culley, James D. and Rex Bennett. "The status of
　　women in mass media advertising: an empirical
　　study." Newark, Delaware: College of Business
　　and Economics, University of Delaware, 1975.
　　$1.00; abstracted in *Southern Marketing Associa-
　　tion. Proceedings*, 1974. pp. 19-20.

The full research on which "Selling women, selling
blacks" is based. See 0134.

0136
　　Danzig, Fred. "Sales execs panel tells feminists
　　ad obstacles," *Advertising Age*, June 16, 1975,
　　46(24):27.

A panel discussion entitled "100,000,000 American
Women: How Do You Sell Them?" discussed the problems of
showing a female doctor using laundry detergent in a 30
second commercial.

0137
     Densmore, Dana. "On the temptation to be a
     beautiful object," *No More Fun and Games: A
     Journal of Female Liberation*, February, 1969,
     n2:43-48; also in *Toward a Sociology of Women*,
     ed. by Constantina Safilios-Rothschild. Lexing-
     ton, Mass: Xerox, 1972, pp. 96-99.

The shimmering, magical beauty promised by hypnotiz-
ing cosmetics ads does little more than imprison women by
their appearance. Women who become manikin-like objects
of beauty are rarely taken seriously because they are "too
pretty to be smart."

0138
     Diamond, Barbara Reingold, "Ad-lib," *The New York
     Times*, December 19, 1971, p. K-14.

Advertising insults men and children as well as
women by implying that whiskey and floor wax bring prestige.

0139
     Dispenza, Joseph E. *Advertising the American
     Woman*. Dayton: Pflaum, 1975.

An examination of the cultural conditioning of
woman's role by "one of the most accessible image-rein-
forcers we have, advertising in the popular press."
Dispenza analyzes the image of women in 285 ads appearing
in popular magazines from 1900-1975. The book is divided
by advertising theme: facial beauty, the domestic role,
courtship and marriage, women's figure and undergarments,
products dealing with isolated functional areas of the
body (eyes, teeth, perspiration), health care, and woman
as sex object. Each ad is pictured and subtleties discussed.

0140
     Dominick, Joseph R. and Gail E. Rauch. "The
     image of women in network TV commercials,"
     Journal of Broadcasting, 1972, 16:259-265.

That women are still stereotyped despite the continuing activism of the women's liberation movement is
clearly demonstrated in the study of a sample of early
1971 network television ads. Focusing on the advertising
viewed in millions of homes during prime time, the authors
conclude that women are most often seen as decorative
(sex objects) or useful (housewives or mothers) but hardly

ever as professionals or working wives.

Document Abstract

0141

Doolittle, John and Robert Pepper. "Childrens's TV ad content: 1974," *Journal of Broadcasting*, 1975, 19:131-141.

There is no evidence that television advertising is making efforts to reflect a society in which the sexes are equal. Sex role stereotypes have increased from a 1971 report of 72% male authority in children's commercial announcements to this 1974 evidence of 85% male authority.

0142

Embree, Alice. "Media images I: Madison Avenue brainwashing - the facts," *Sisterhood is Powerful, an Anthology of Writings from the Women's Liberation Movement*, ed. by Robin Morgan. NY: Vintage Books, 1970. pp. 175-191.

Advertising is examined in terms of its war motif: a certain detergent is the weapon which "wins the war against dirt and stains." One of the consequences of advertising's "psychological warfare" is the socialization of woman to accept herself as such an extremely passive and unquestioning being, that corporations easily mold her into a consumer.

0143

"European women hit mass media image of being robots, sex objects," *Advertising Age*, August 9, 1971, 42:26.

An organized protest against the image of women in European ads was waged by 120 European women meeting in Geneva. The two biggest complaints were against the practice of using scantily clad women to sell everything from liquor to cars, and against the portrayal of housewives as robots.

See 0562. "Everything you ever wanted to know about advertising and were not afraid to ask."

0144

Ewen, Stuart. "Advertising as a way of life," *Liberation*, 1976, 19:16-34.

Condensed version of *Captains of Consciousness*. See 0145 and 0741.

0145
　　Ewen, Stuart. "Comsumption and the new woman,"
　　Captains of Consciousness: Advertising and the
　　Social Roots of the Consumer Culture, by S.
　　Ewan. NY: McGraw Hill, 1976. pp. 159-176.

Advertising of the 1920's capitalized on suffrage
rhetoric: "The toaster that *Freed 465,000 Homes* ... from
ever watching, turning or burning toast." Another ad campaign, designed to open the cigarette market to women,
hired a feminist and her cigarette puffing friends to
march down 5th Avenue in the 1929 Easter Parade.

See 0741. S. Ewen. "Father - the patriarch as wage
slave."

See 0743. W. Farrell. "Masculine images in advertising."

See 0026. J. Faust. "Testimony before the NY City Commission on Human Rights."

0146
　　Ferris, Abbott, Lamayne. *Indicators of Trends in*
　　the Status of American Women. NY: Russell Sage
　　Foundation, 1971.

By way of introduction to this book of statistical
trends in the educational, marital, employment and health
status of women, the author briefly discusses the impact
of mass communications. One factor possibly responsible
for the feminist movement is the American woman's dis-
enchantment with the impossible standards of pulchritude
and male adoration set by advertising.

0147
　　Fine, Gary Alan. "The psychology of cigarette
　　advertising: professional puffery," *Journal of*
　　Popular Culture, 1975, 8:513-522.

The author defends the macho image of some cigarette
advertising because "implicit in American popular culture
is the belief that women long for men like these ..." He
does not mention where he uprooted this information on
women's longings. He also discusses the association of
female smoking with female independence.

0148
　　Firestone, Shulamith. "The culture of romance,"

The Dialectic of Sex. NY: Morrow, 1970. pp. 165-175.

The advertising medium is guilty of overkill. Female eroticism as portrayed by advertising has lost its quality of natural excitement with the stereotyping of woman as a tummy-controlled, false-eyelashed, bleached blonde being.

0149
Foster, Anne Tolstoi. "Is that really me," *TV Guide*, June 19, 1971. pp. 18-20.

A proposal for "Ad Lib" could close the reality gap between advertiser and consumer. With almost half the female population over 16 working in the job market, television advertising still features working women only in roles of entertainer, secretary or waitress, while the 21 million working wives are not reflected realistically. This reality gap extends to the ad image of incompetent woman driver, when studies prove that women are better drivers than men. The consumer can facilitate closing the reality gap by sending complaint letters to ad agencies and television networks.

0150
Friedan, Betty. "The sexual sell," *The Feminine Mystique*, by B. Friedan. NY: Norton, 1963. pp. 206-232.

Motivational techniques advertisers use to sell household items to women include: the guilt of being an inadequate wife or mother, desire to be creative in the kitchen, and the appeal to teenagers with the "happiness through things" motivation.

See 0337. B. Friedan. "TV and the feminine mystique."

0151
Friedman, Leslie J. *Sexism in Advertising, A Humorous Portrayal of the Image of Women*. 35mm slides. Available from the author, 1704 Stony-brook Drive., Cincinnati, Ohio 45237. Rental, $25.

A slide program dealing with the stereotypes of woman in all her media incarnations: man-chaser, servant, sex object, mother. She serves coffee but never drinks it, cooks food but never eats it. She seeks eternal youth and beauty, and allows her naked body to decorate the most unusual commodities. The author calls for a more realistic professional and social presentation of women in advertising, in order to give young women inspiring female role models, to restore the self-esteem of adult women, and to give men images of women to respect. One way to achieve this realistic presentation in advertising is to send protest letters to the presidents of manufacturing corporations responsible for the demeaning ads. The program includes 90 slides and a supplementary booklet detailing how to write the letter and where to find the president's name and corporate address. See 0316.

0152
Gadlin, Howard. "Private lives and public order: a critical view of the history of international relations in the US," *Massachusetts Review*, 1976, 17:304-330.

The image of woman as homemaker hit commercial proportions in the 1920's with the advent of canned goods and electrical appliances. These industries as well as women's magazines and advertising all depended on keeping women in the home, fulfilling their female role as consumer.

0153
Gelber, Alexis. "Toughness is all," *Art Direction*, November, 1976, 28(8):55-58.

Where once vacuous manniquins smiled at the camera, today's fashion model glares at it. No longer the submissive ornament, she shows her new image as tough, brainy and sexually secure. The new sophistication and confidence reflected in advertising is credited to the women's movement which encourages women to take themselves seriously.

See 0028. E. Goldfield. "A woman is a sometime thing."

0154
Gorney, Sondra and Claire Cox. "Beware of the youth-cult sickness," *After Forty*, by S. Gorney and C. Cox. NY: Dial Press, 1973. pp. 12-14.

Objections are made to advertising's "Lolita Syndrome" in which youth is glorified and age is regarded with contempt. Wearing false teeth does not bring forth imbecility, as advertising implies.

0155
    Greyser, Stephen A. "The social impacts of adver-
    tising," *Advertising Quarterly*, Spring, 1972, 9:
    17-22.

    Regarding advertising's impact on values and life-
styles the author deals with the issue of whether advertising creates or reflects values. In terms of the
portrayal of women he asks, Should ads show society as it
is or as someone (the advertiser) thinks it should be?"
Research should identify the impact of ads on the learning
process.

See 0031. J. Harris, "A role without a script."

See 0032. B. G. Harrison, "June, 1971: a new beginning."

0156
    Harvey, Mary. "Images of women in advertising,"
    CIC Brief, July, 1975. Interfaith Center for
    Corporate Responsibility, Room 566, 475 Riverside
    Dr., NY, 10027. 60¢.

    The image of women in advertising tends to strengthen
sex role stereotypes while not adequately reflecting contemporary attitudes toward women, men, manners and morals.
Advertising defines women by service-oriented or sexually
liberated roles, and very rarely shows women in occupational roles. Female voices are featured as product
representatives in 7% of the off camera announcements.

0157
    Hennessee, Judith Adler and Joan Nicholson. "NOW
    says: TV commercials insult women," *The New York
    Times Magazine*, May 28, 1972, pp. 12-13+; also in
    Women: Their Changing Roles. (The Great Con-
    temporary Issues). NY: Arno Press, 1973. pp.
    446-450.

    In 1972 NY NOW filed a petition with the FCC for vio-
lation of the Fairness Doctrine by WABC-TV, NY. Grounds
for violation were based primarily on news coverage which
ignored or ridiculed female achievement. The challenge
also covered a NY NOW study of 1,241 commercials, which
determined that 42.6% of advertising's women were involved
in household tasks, 37.5% were domestic adjuncts to men
and 16.7 were sex objects, while 0.3% were portrayed as
autonomous people leading independent lives. Women were
rarely given advertising credibility - 89% of authoritative voiceovers were male. Women sought male approval

in 33.9% of television ads, were submissive in 24.3%.
Meanwhile 43% of the female population - working women -
were virtually ignored in television commercials. Women
should be portrayed in a more dignified light. When shown
as poor drivers women not only lack dignity, but the image
is false. Insurance tables prove that women have fewer
auto accidents than men.

See 0034. J. Hole and E. Levine, "Feminist social
critique."

0158
 "How appearance divides women," *Ladies' Home
Journal*, August, 1970, 87(8):69-70.

Advertising's peddling of young women in the arms of
men 30 and older implies that women over 25 are no longer
attractive or interesting.

See 0039. J. Israel, "Consumption society, sex roles and
sexual behavior."

0159
 Kaplan, Milton. "Women in advertising," *The
Quarterly Journal of the Library of Congress*,
October, 1975, 32:366-369.

Examples of historic ads from the Library of Congress
Prints and Photographs Division ranging from 1869-1898,
show women serving a decorative function in whiskey and
cigar ads, as neoclassical goddess serving coffee, in more
mundane surroundings washing clothes, and in a before/
after pose advertising a hair care product.

See 0745. H. E. Kaye, "Male survival; masculinity without
myth."

0160
 Keck, Donna. "The art of maiming women," *Women,
A Journal of Liberation*, 1969, 1(1):40-42.

Television advertising's dichotomy of woman as either
household drudge or alluring sexmate is finally brought
together in the persona of a 1969 well dressed woman who
cleans her toilet. Sexism is also apparent in ads where
teenage women are encouraged to learn to paint their
faces and to cook greaseless chicken in order to catch and
keep a man, while the teenage men, by way of public

service announcements, are taught the value of education
and career.

0161
    Klemesrud, Judy. "On Madison Avenue, women take
    stand in middle of the road," *The New York Times*,
    July 3, 1973. p. 28.

    Interviews with seven heads of ad agencies reveal at-
titudes toward sexist advertising. Most agree with
feminist principles but feel little responsibility to
change the image of women in advertising. More than the
others, Franchellie Cadwell and Jane Trahey acknowledge
inequities in the female ad image. Cadwell polled 600
women to determine the ten most hated commercials, and is
personnally offended by images of women who argue with
doves and chat with little men in toilet bowls. Trahey
has developed a slide program with ads showing women as
sex objects, in stereotyped household roles, and ads that
use liberation jargon without offering a liberated message.

0162
    Komarovsky, Mirra. "Cultural contradictions and
    sex roles: the masculine case," *American Journal
    of Sociology*, 1973, 78:873-884; also in *Changing
    Woman in a Changing Society*, ed. by Joan Huber.
    Chicago: University of Chicago Press, 1973. pp.
    111-122; also in *Sex:Male/Gender:Masculine; Read-
    ings in Male Sexuality*, ed. by John W. Petras.
    Port Washington, NY: Alfred Publishing, 1975.

    Sixty-two college men were interviewed and given
psychological tests to determine attitudes concerning
women's roles. A slow change in attitude is evident. One
man reported preference for a career wife rather than a
housewife as he has little respect for the women he sees
in advertising.

See 0040. L. Komisar, "The ideology of feminism."

0163
    Komisar, Lucy. "Image of women in advertising,"
    *Woman in Sexist Society; Studies in Power and
    Powerlessness*, ed. by Vivian Gornick and Barbara
    K. Moran. NY: Basic Books, 1971.

    Advertising projects the image of woman as a sex ob-
ject who buys sleek, shining pens in order to feel prettier, and as housewife who takes laundry instructions from
male voiceover authority figures who presumably have

never washed their own clothes. Suggestions are made for an improved image of women in ads.

0164
    Kotzin, Miriam. "Women, like blacks and orientals, are all different," *Media and Methods*, March, 1972, 8(7):18-26.

    Although advertisers did not create the feminine mystique, they are its most powerful perpetrator. They have sent women home and kept them there by glamorizing the role of housewife.

    Suggestions for classroom consciousness-raising activities include discussion of soap opera themes, sex role images in comic strips and the image of women in film.

0165
    Krassner, Paul. "Naked emperor," *Crawdaddy*, December, 1973, p. 10.

    Discussion of 11 sexist commercials aired during the television special, "A Woman's Place," whose purpose was to expose "the evils of role conditioning." The ads showed men as doctors and professional chefs while housewives made coffee and did laundry.

0166
    "Libs have had little effect on ads to women," *Advertising Age*, March 19, 1973, 44(12):44.

    In spite of feminist pressure advertising continues to show dunce-like women delighted by clean floors and ringless collars. Poor timing may be one reason why the feminist movement has revolutionized other areas of the culture but has failed to effect significant advertising change. The liberation movement peaked at the same time as the economic recession, thereby causing apprehension among advertisers who otherwise may have changed their approach.

0167
    Lipman-Blumen, Jean, "How ideology shapes women's lives," *Scientific American*, January, 1972, 226:34-42.

    The behavior of women is implicitly shaped by certain ideology. A study of 1,012 college women of both traditional and contemporary ideologies revealed that contrary to television advertisements, not all women delight

in cleaning house and doing laundry. However women of
both ideologies do enjoy opportunities for creative self-
expression in the home: cooking, entertaining, interior
decorating.

See 0746. B. Lohof, "The higher meaning of Marlboro
cigarettes."

0168
    McArthur, Leslie Zebrowitz and Beth Gabrielle
    Resko. "The portrayal of men and women in Ameri-
    can TV commercials," *Journal of Social Psychology*,
    1975, 97:209-220.

Television advertising influences sex role stereotypes by exposing people to stereotyped behavior more
often than to individualized behavior. Female viewers
are constantly reminded to stay home when ads show women
in the home setting even while selling non-home-oriented
products. Men are the authority figure or voiceover for
home products in 86% of the ads, but are shown using the
home products in only 16% of the ads.

0169
    McGhee, Alexandra. "Sex and the salesman,"
    Women in Today's World, by A. McGhee. Portland,
    Maine: J. Weston Walch, 1974. pp. 30-31.

Television commercials place little emphasis on
brains. Men react not to reason but to slinky, sultry,
sexy objects. The objects are women who hide their brains,
emphasize their bodies and encourage other women to attract men by flashing teeth that glimmer like neon. Although men are sometimes treated as objects in order to
sell hair tonic or deodorant, it is women who are most
encouraged to worry about appearance.

0170
    McKnight, Diane. "Sexism in advertising: what's
    a nice girl like you ...," *Technology Review*, May,
    1974, 76:20-21.

An examination of the ads in 130 engineering and
trade magazines published in November, 1973 revealed that
35% of the magazines had at least one sexist ad, 9% had
two, 6% had three, and 4% had more than four ads which
denigrated women as passive, silly or incompetent, or used
their semi-clad or naked bodies to attract attention to
equipment. The author calls for the elimination of
blatantly sexist trade ads, inclusion of female engineers

in ads, and eradication of the male slant in textbooks.

0171

McLuhan, H. Marshall. *The Mechanical Bride,
Folklore of Industrial Man.* NY: Vanguard Press,
1951.

In sections "Coke and cheesecake," "How not to offend," "The mechanical bride" and others, McLuhan relates
1951's advertising image of the "good girl": she is
scrubbed, deloused, germ-free and depilatorized. Inhibi-
tions, misgivings and marital grief dissolve when she
relies on Lysol for feminine hygiene and extends this cult
of hygiene to her gleaming bathroom. She is sweet, non-
sexual and innocent when sipping a coke, she grows up to
become "woman in a mirror" who poses as the cool sophisticated dream walker, or to become the wide-awake, peppy,
semi-clad "good-time girl". Another image, the "Love-
goddess assembly line" is the mechanical bride incarnate.
Her female legs and other spare parts are interchangeable
from pedestal to pedestal as the image of woman becomes
that of a synthetic robot lacking a soul. McLuhan pro-
phetically asks if the mechanical bride will "feel a dim
resentment at being deprived of full human status?"

0172

Mannes, Marya. "Female of the Specious," *Boston;
Published by the Greater Boston Chamber of Commerce,* September, 1970, 62:54-56.

Mannes describes the stereotypes used by advertising
to brainwash women and to glorify single men and demean
married men.

0173

Mannes, Marya. "Television: the splitting image,"
Saturday Review, November 14, 1970, 53:66-68.

While television advertising concentrates on the
swinging sex object and the constipated granny it misses
all the intelligent, sensitive, talented women in between.
If women in ads "change overnight from plaything to floor-
waxer" after marriage, men also switch from swinging
bachelor to paunchy slob. The article ends with Mannes'
reflections on the social and moral obligations of mass
media advertisers.

0174

Meehan, Eileen Rose. *Sex-Typing in Dramatiza-
tions of Advertising Presented During Television*

Commercials, M.A. thesis, University of Pennsylvania, 1975.

Commercial dramatization constituted 20% of the messages aired during 42 hours each of afternoon and prime time viewing. Performers were primarily white adults with advisor/advisee roles "utilizing traditional sex-types."

0175
Miller, Judith and Leah Margulies. "The media: new images of women in contemporary society," *The American Woman: Who Will She Be?*, ed. by Mary Louise McBee and Kathryn A. Blake. Beverly Hills, CA: Glencoe Press, 1974.

Advertising exploits and distorts the term "liberation" by selling cosmetics, clothes, style and image of independent, emancipated women. The authors protest that women do not want to become surrogate "he-men ... We don't want male nude centerfolds."

0176
Millum, Trevor. *Images of Woman: Advertising in Women's Magazines*, Totowa, NJ: Rowman and Littlefield, 1975.

Although the stereotypes of women in advertising range from "Wanda the abuser to Justine the abused," the four most common images of woman are Mannequin, Narcissist, Hostess, and Wife/Mother. The four stereotypes are discussed in terms of props, ad locations and types of products used for each image. For example the Mannequin is usually aloof, set in exotic locations, and rarely directs her attention to things or to people. She is dramatic and beautiful. Her props are not functional but rather add to her sophistication. Clothing ads often feature several of the mannequin type who never look at one another nor interact in any way. They are untouchable. The Mannequin differs from the Narcissist who directs her attention toward herself, her body, and her own beauty. The Narcissist's nudity in women's magazine ads is contrasted with the nude woman as alienated object found in men's magazines.

Men are restricted to rigid stereotypes as well. Sophisticated men are heroes or mannequins; plain men are husbands and brothers. In women's magazines men play a supportive role and often function as a prop for the sophisticated female mannequin. As a husband the male role is often that of buffoon.

These distorted stereotypes fail to encourage women to

be self sufficient, inward looking, independent spirits
who function as equals to men.

See 0050. National Organization for Women. New York
Chapter, Image of Women Committee, "Images of women in the
mass media.

0177
    Nelson, Gunvor and Dorothy Wiley. *Schmeerguntz*.
    16mm, 15 mins., b/w, rental, $15, purchase $210.
    Serious Business Company, 1609 Jaynes St.,
    Berkeley, Ca 94703.

    Satirizes the sex roles portrayed in advertising and
beauty contests.

See 0694. J. Nicholson, "The packaging of rape: a
feminist indictment."

See 0625. "No comment."

See 0052. M. Nunes and D. White, *The Lace Ghetto*.

0178
    O'Kelly, Charlotte G. and Linda Edwards Bloomquist.
    "Women and blacks on TV," *Journal of Communica-*
    tion, 1976, 26(4):179-184.

    Of 2,309 characters coded on 28 hour-long segments of
morning television, 4.9% were non-white characters and 37%
were female. Women appeared as 46% of the commercial
characters. Although women were nearly equal in distribution with men during commercials, they are almost always
shown in traditional roles, as housewives or in six traditionally female occupations. Men were shown in husband/
father roles in 6% of the ads, and were shown in 16 other
occupations as well. While blacks were represented in
2.8% of the television commercials, female blacks appeared
in only 1/3 of that 2.8%.

0179
    "The packaging of women: how women are portrayed
    in advertisements," by Women in Media, available
    from author, 37 Brondesbury Rd, London, N.W. 6. L 1.00.
    1976.

    A 1976 Women in Media seminar held in London included

formal presentations, workshops and a debate between representatives of the advertising industry and feminist consumers. Salient points include an ad woman's perception that sex role stereotypes in advertising show "women wearing one of three things - an apron, a G string or a confused look" and men who are "physically incapable of giving themselves cough medicine," and a professor's remark that consumer education is vital. When disappointed with a product women should complain. A survey indicated that consumer complaints measure 4% even when product dissatisfaction is 50%.

0180
    Passovoy, Janice Sue. *A Study of Advertising Appeals from Selected Advertisements in the Ladies' Home Journal from 1920-1973.* M.A. thesis, University of Oregon. 1975.

The most frequently used psychological appeals found in 2,160 ads directed specifically to the female audience include: "good taste," "sex appeal/romance," and "love."

See 0053. E. Peck, "The media trap."

0181 Pingree, Suzanne. *A Developmental Study of the Attitudinal Effects of Nonsexist Television Commercials Under Varied Conditions of Perceived Reality.* Ph.D. dissertation, Stanford University, 1975.

A study of third and eighth grade children exposed to television commercials showing women engaged in traditional or non-traditional occupations revealed that television promulgates sex-typed behavior and attitudes. Television commercials can manipulate children's perceptions of reality and therefore socialize them to accept traditional sex role stereotypes.

0182
    Poe, Alison. "Active women in ads," *Journal of Communication,* 1976, 26(4):185-192.

Because female participation in sports has increased recently and advertising has the power to reinforce sports acceptability for women, the author examined the advertising in women's and general interest magazines for years 1928, 1956, 1972 for the image of women in sports activities. The results indicate that while female participation in sports has increased, advertising's representation of women in sports has decreased. When

55

women are shown participating in sports they are usually coed activities rather than same sex competitive sports. Advertising is not reflecting this change in women's activities.

See 0054. L. C. Pogrebin, "Down with sexist upbringing."

0183
    Porter, Sylvia. "Women and the ads," *New York Post*, March 24, 1975, p. 28.

In her report of the NARB's "Advertising and women" (see 0278), Porter notes the distinction between the portrayal of woman as sexy and portrayal as sex object, comments on sex role nouns like "her kitchen" and "his car", and reminds the reader of advertising's underrepresentation of over 50% of American women between ages 18-64 who are gainfully employed outside the home.

0184
    "Prehistory to playboy, a woman's place is in the body," *Life*, August 13, 1971, 71(7):44-45.

The image of woman's body in advertising and art.

0185
    "Procter and Gamble ads assailed for their depiction of women," *The New York Times*, October 15, 1975, p. 59.

A coalition of church groups owning stock in Procter and Gamble proposed a resolution eliminating the degrading sex role stereotypes in Procter and Gamble ads: the female obsession for soft hands and Mr. Whipple's fetish for unsqueezed Charmin. The major disagreement was with Procter and Gamble's concentration of housewives. Vast numbers of women are neither mothers nor housewives, and most of those who are do not define themselves solely by those roles.

0186
    Rea, James Michael. *A Content Analysis of the Portrayal of Men and Women in Prime Time Television Commercials*. M.S. thesis, Kansas State University, 1975.

Examination of 759 prime time commercials revealed that men dominate commercial voiceovers while on camera selling is evenly split between both sexes. Women were

most likely portrayed in the 21-35 age group, while more
men were in the 36-50 group. Most of the occupational and
sex roles were uncodable.

0187
   A Redstocking Sister. "Consumerism and women."
   Notes from the Second Year: Women's Liberation.
   NY, 1970. pp. 72-75; also in *Woman in Sexist
   Society: Studies in Power and Powerlessness,* ed.
   by Vivian Gornick and Barbara K. Moran. NY:
   Basic Books, 1971. pp. 480-484.

   Advertisers insist on presenting stereotyped pictures
of women as domestic slaves or sex objects, not to sell
goods, but to reinforce the ideology of male supremacy.
Ads for male grooming products appeal to a man's desire
for autonomy and freedom while ads for female grooming
products appeal to her need to please a male oppressor.
Male supremacy and female subordination are exploited in
advertising. Advertising further supports the sexist
status quo by aiming ads for "feminine hygiene" at men
more than at women.

0188
   Rivers, Caryl. "How to be spotless, sexy and
   loved," *The New York Times,* April 28, 1974,
   p. D-15.

   In selling their products to women, advertising
messages support two common themes. "Approval/Disapproval"
(and with it the manufacture of guilt) operates in ads for
products that remove dirt rings from collars, water spots
from drinking glasses and imperceptible household odors
from living rooms. The theme of competition and envy
traditionally runs in detergent ads for the whitest,
brightest, most spotless clothes on the block. With these
themes of guilt and jealousy, television commercials have
molded womanly attitudes and behavior, according to
John Kenneth Galbraith.

0189
   Screen Actors Guild. New York Branch Women's
   Conference Committee. "The relative roles of
   men and women in television commercials," 1974.
   Available from SAG, 551 Fifth Ave., NY, 10017.
   $1.00.

   A statistical analysis compared the roles of men and
women in 656 television commercials submitted to the Clio
competition. The sample commercials were distributed
among 28 product categories, with results indicating that

the principal characters are male in almost every category including supermarket products. On camera speaking principals were 74.1% male, while off camera speaking principals were 100% male. Women were principal characters in 3 of the 28 categories: apparel, cosmetics and household products.

See 0940. A. A. Sheikh, "Children's TV commercials: a review of research."

0190
    Silverstein, Arthur and Rebecca Silverstein. The portrayal of women in television advertising," *Federal Communications Bar Journal*, 1974, 27:71-98.

The distorted image of women in advertising content is measured by sex of voice-over, sex within home environment, those unnecessarily confined to home environment, those requiring/providing help, variety of occupations by sex, type of physical and psychological appearance, and role of dominance, neutrality or subservience.

0191
    Simmons, Marcia Kay. *The Portrayal of Adult Sex Roles: A Content Analysis of Advertising Pictures in Six Women's Magazines.* M.S. thesis, Kansas State University, 1974.

Examination of 519 ads from the first three 1974 issues of *Family Circle, Good Housekeeping, Ladies' Home Journal, McCall's, Ms.,* and *Redbook* revealed that parents of both sexes were pictured with children though men were rarely pictured alone with children in ads. Other statistics showed the glamour role 48.4% female, 10.9% male; leisure recreation 14.9% female, 42.4% male; working role 10.2% female, 25% male. Women populated ads for everyday household purchases while men dominated ads for expensive household appliances. Women were most often seen in ads for beauty and cleaning products while men were most often in ads for cigarettes and food.

0192
    Sissman, L. E. "Best worst TV commercials of 1975," *Atlantic*, May, 1975, 235-20+.

Expounds on current Geritol ("My wife...I think I'll keep her") and Wisk ("Ring around the collar") television commercials. The Wisk ad has a soap opera format with humiliation as the theme.

0193
     Slatton, Yvonne LaBelle. *The Role of Women
     in Sport as Depicted Through Advertising in
     Selected Magazines, 1900-1968*. Ph.D. dis-
     sertation, University of Iowa, 1970.

     Advertisements in two women's magazines and three
general interest magazines were examined for attitudes
toward women's participation in sports. The conclusions
were: 1) societal attitudes toward women's participation
in sports reflect changing attitudes toward women's role
in general, 2) advertising's portrayal of women in individual and dual sports as suitable for women, and 3)
ads generally depict women in recreational sports rather
than competitive sports.

0194
     Sontag, Susan. "The double standard of aging,"
     Saturday Review of the Society, September 23,
     1972, 55(39):29-38.

     The standards of beauty which dictate that youth is
acceptable but natural age among women is ugly is compared
to advertising's promotion of the extremely thin female
body as ideal, when it is this kind of body that looks
more desirable clothed than naked.

0195
     "The sponsor," *Woman; A Multimedia Resource for
     Human Liberation*. Catalog #9335. Record avail-
     able from Teleketics, Franciscan Communication
     Center, 1229 S. Santee St., Los Angeles, CA
     90015. $2.95.

     "A sound collage that contains a half serious spoof
on the dictates of Madison Avenue."

0196
     Stemple, Diane and Jane E. Tyler. "Sexism in
     advertising," *American Journal of Psychoanalysis*,
     1974, 34:271-273.

     Predominate advertising themes by decade since 1910
include: mother/cook (1910), fashion plate (1920), cook/
housecleaner (1930), beauty (1940), appliance (1950), food,
clothing, beauty (1960) and sexual liberation (1970).

See 0063. J. Sternburg, "Revealing herself."

0197

Teitz, Joyce. *What's a Nice Girl Like You Doing
in a Place Like This?* NY: Coward, McCann,
Geoghegan, 1972.

Active women in powerful or exciting careers are
rarely visible in the media. Instead advertising offers
a disproportionate number of ecstatic housewives who
"find fulfillment in the sparkle of dishes and the dazzle
of linens." Teitz offers alternatives to this advertising image of "pathological femininity" as well as to the
myth of the career hag, by interviewing 11 active women
involved in traditionally masculine careers and either
egalitarian marriages or otherwise independent lifestyles.

0198

Terry, Robert. "The white male club, biology and
power," *Civil Rights Digest*, Spring, 1974, 6(3):
66-77.

A 1974 ad for US Savings Bonds, headlined "Welcome
to the club" pictures ten white male executives buying
savings bonds. The exclusion of all women and all non-
white men constituted more than half of the US population
who were not invited to buy Savings Bonds. The article
continues with a discussion of other "clubs" open only to
white men.

0199

Sexton, Donald and Phyllis Haberman. "Women
in magazine advertisements," *Journal of Advertising Research*, August, 1976, 14:41-46.

A statistical study measuring the treatment of women
in cigarette, automobile, office equipment and airline
advertisements indicates, for example, that women have
cigarettes in their mouths only in those ads where men are
helping them light it.

0200

"This ad insults women," *The Silenced Majority,
A Women's Liberation Multimedia Kit*. Media Plus,
Inc., 60 Riverside Dr., Suite 7E, NY 10024. Com-
plete 13 piece kit, $89.

The filmstrip and tape document the following media
protests: Miss America Pageant - 1968, *Ladies' Home
Journal* - 1970, *Playboy* - 1970. Examples of ads raise
consciousness as they show women being judged by appearance and whiteness of wash, while men are judged by
brains. Language further insults women when they're
called "chick," "tomato" and other endearments of fruit,

vegetable and animal. Typical dialogue in commercial
films implies that women are brainless, while literature
portrays the female sex as "fallen." In order to overcome
second class female status history must be researched and
rewritten to include the many women's contributions here-
tofore ignored.

0201
Truby, J. David. "Women's lib vs. Madison
Avenue," *Sexual Behavior*, October, 1972, 2:44-48.

Looking at sexism in advertising, a journalism professor quotes objectively from both the complaints of the
feminists and the justifications of the ad writers.
Feminists claim that advertising reinforces female subservience, and advertisers charge that feminists lack
humor. The article is illustrated with examples of heavy
female masochism and sexual innuendo, in advertising, including an ad in which a young woman is bound in leather.

0202
Tweedie, Jill. "How liberated are Soviet Women?,"
New Statesman, September 21, 1973, 86:376+.

Because of the complete absence of advertising in the
Soviet Union, there is no "profit motivated standard of
beauty." Soviet women do not compare themselves to glamorous models, but rather each respects herself regardless of
weight or facial features.

0203
"UN Status of Women reports advertising 'hurting' women's image," *Montreal Star*, January 24,
1974, p. B-2.

The United Nations Commission on the Status of Women
reports that advertising promotes the following demeaning
images of womanhood: the media portrayal of women as
children or sex symbols reinforces stereotypes about women
held by employers who do not hire women for executive
level positions; ads for commodities enhancing social
status are aimed at men while household gadgets are advertised to women; stereotyped images of mothers-in-law,
nagging wives and dumb blondes are compared to the now
defunct image of the kindly, illiterate, "Uncle Tom"
black; newspaper articles should not reveal the height and
weight of female dentists if they do not commonly give the
same irrelevant information in articles about male dentists.

0204
    Unitarian Universalist Association. Unitarian
    Church of Westport, Women's Alliance. "Images
    of women in television advertising, report on
    the Westport Alliance project," 1976. Avail-
    able from ICCR, 475 Riverside Dr., Rm 566, NY
    10027.

    Monitoring of the image of women in television com-
mercials revealed that women are most often seen in the
kitchen. When compared to men, women are less likely to
be portrayed as self-assured, and more often seen nagging,
complaining or exhibiting foolish behavior. Voiceover
messages were 508 times male and 78 times female. No
percentages given.

0205
    Venkatesan, M. and Jean P. Losco. "Women in
    magazine ads: 1959-1971. Journal of Advertis-
    ing Research, October 1975, 15(5):49-58.

    A content analysis of the portrayal of women in ads
appearing in 12 general interest, women's and men's magazines for the years 1959-1971 revealed that the themes
"woman as sex object" and "happy housewife" have decreased
in women's magazines since 1961, although women were still
portrayed as dependent on men. The image of women in the
advertising of general interest and men's magazines had
not changed significantly from years 1959-1971.

0206
    Ventura, Charlene. "Impact of women's liberation
    movement on advertising trends," 1974. Available
    from author, 7225 North Bend Rd., Cincinnati,
    Ohio 45224. $1.00; also as "Ad liberation: the
    feminist impact," *Sybil-Child*, 1975, 1(1):37-
    54.

    Advertising and magazines manipulate consumers, par-
ticularly women, by creating needs where none had existed
before (e.g., feminine deodorant spray, fake fur eye-
lashes). Furthermore fear of age, germ phobia, masochism
and sexual insecurity are so exaggerated by advertising
that they are no longer considered examples of human insecurity, but have become regarded as typically female
neuroses.

    Protests of the image of women in television and
print advertising were held at the offices of *Ladies'
Home Journal*, *Playboy*, CBS and National Airlines. Because
of these protests and others, some advertising has shown
a more respectable image of women, while other advertising

co-opts feminist rhetoric to sell products of dubious "liberating" value. Another perversion of feminist values is the male centerfold. Instead of eliminating female sex objects, the exploitation of male sex objects has become the latest marketing device. The article ends with descriptions of ads projecting positive image of women.

0207
     Verna, Mary Ellen. "The female image in children's TV commercials," *Journal of Broadcasting*, 1975, 19:301-309.

A study of 182 television commercials aired during Saturday morning children's programs revealed over 50% male dominated ads and 14% female dominated ads (the rest being sexually neutral). Female children were not seen competing with one another at games, as male children did, however female adults were seen competing with one another to be sexiest, most beautiful and best housekeeper. When playing with dolls, girls were portrayed as potential mothers, but boys playing with action dolls were not portrayed as future fathers. Males were used to sell food in children's commercials while females sold food in adult food ads.

0208
     "'Vulgar' sex ads demean all, insult consumer, panel finds," *Advertising Age*, March 24, 1975, 46(12):67.

Although sex is a powerful selling force and is considered appropriate in advertising, sexist ads which exploit women's bodies and portray men as sexual fools have no place in advertising. Specific examples of sexist airline, whiskey and cigar ads are compared to tasteful ads showing sex appeal among sexual equals.

0209
     Wagner, Louis C. and Janis B. Banos. "A woman's place: a follow-up analysis of the roles portrayed by women magazine advertisements," *Journal of Marketing Research*, 1973, 10:213-214.

In a follow-up study to the 1970 Courteney/Lockeretz findings (see 0132) the authors studied the ads in January, 1972 issues of seven general interest magazines. The 1972 study indicates an increase of portrayal of working women from 9% in 1970 to 21% in 1972. Although the percentage of working women doubled in two years, women were still shown infrequently interacting with other women, purchasing big ticket items independent of

men, and participating in activities involving banks or
industry. Women as decorative object in advertising increased in 1972.

0210

Webb, Marilyn Salzman. "Woman as secretary,
sexpot, spender, sow, civic actor, sickie," *The
New Woman; A Motive Anthology on Women's Liberation*, ed. by Joanne Cooke, Charlotte Bunch-Weeks,
and Robin Morgan. NY: Bobbs-Merrill, 1970. pp.
117-141; also in *Roles Women Play: Readings
Towards Women's Liberation*, ed. by Michele Hoffnung Garskof. Belmont, CA: Brooks/Cole, 1971.

Popular advertising copy is quoted and placed within
the context of a brief history of capitalism. With the
advent of a consumption culture woman's function became
limited to certain roles: secretary, sexpot, spender,
sow, civic actor, and sickie.

0211

Wensberg, Peter. "Dubious battlemarks," *Boston;
Published by Greater Boston Chamber of Commerce*,
September, 1970, 62:56-57.

An advertising man blames women advertisers for projecting the stereotyped sex roles, but justifies the
stereotyped ads for their wit, imagination and entertainment value.

0212

Winick, Charles. "Sex and advertising," *Sexual
Behavior*, April, 1971, 1:36-40+; also in *Mass
Media: The Invisible Environment Revisited*,
ed. by Robert J. Glessing and William P. White.
Chicago: Science Research Associates, 1976.
pp. 122-127.

Sexual connotations abound in advertising, thus providing a form of sex education. The conduct of adults
seen in television commercials possibly influences an
adolescent's attitudes toward sex roles more than the sex
education taught formally in school. Advertising teaches
sexual fantasies (the maidenform bra dreamer, and I'm
Cheryl - fly me) plays on sexual inadequacies, and stereotypes the typical marriage with an unglamorous housewife
whose laundry soap brings forth "peak experiences" comparable to those her husband finds with his younger,
mannequin-like woman. Television ads also stereotype men
as Sadists and sexually appealing people of both sexes
leading antiseptic, odor-free, erotic lives.

0213
"Women, kids vulnerable to TV ads, Adams says,"
Advertising Age, November 22, 1971, 42(47):61-62.

Whitney Adams' testimony for NOW at FTC hearings on
advertising dealt with unfair and deceptive advertising
as related to women. All their lives women have been
trained to acquire a husband and satisfy family needs.
By playing on the anxieties and fears of these two goals
advertising deceives the viewer by leading her to believe
that certain products will lead to matrimony or family
happiness. Ads promise mouthwash users that they won't
become golf widows, and soap users that their hands will
appear younger as well as cleaner. A survey revealed that
11.6% of the ads analyzed played on women's anxieties
about appearance, while only 0.5% showed the same theme
for men. Stereotyped ads have detrimental effects on
women by giving them false insecurities about themselves
and their abilities, and further convince their husbands
and male employers that disorienting, dominating and confining women is acceptable behavior.

0214
"Women: nine reports on role, image, and message," *Journal of Communication*, 1974, 24(2):103.

The introduction to this special issue pictures a
role reversal in advertising with the juxtaposition of
two Tabu perfume ads: in one version a nineteenth century
romanticist throws aside his violin to passionately kiss
his female student; in the other contemporary living room
scene a twentieth century music teacher flings aside her
violin to passionately kiss her male student.

0215
Wortzel, Lawrence H. and John M. Frisbie. "Women's
role portrayal preferences in advertisements: an
empirical study," *Journal of Marketing*, October,
1974, 38:41-46.

In order to determine the types of role portrayals
most women would like to see associated with certain
products, 100 women in all degrees of sympathy or antip-
athy towards the women's movement were given the opportunity to "build" ads for appliances, household products
and food. Regardless of feminist involvement, the study's
participants overwhelmingly placed these household products within family settings, hence the authors concluded
that "women positive in their attitudes towards women's
liberation preferred traditional family roles" in advertising.

0216

"You've come a long way, baby; and other lies they hand us," *Kaleidoscope,* June 26-July 9, 1970, 3(7):7.

Women and blacks in the 1960's suffered opposite media problems: while blacks fought for recognition, women were pictured everywhere. The female deodorized, atomized, baby machine/Barbie dolls sensuously fondled automobile upholstery, then went home and delighted in waxing the floor, according to advertising.

AIRLINE ADS

See 0117. "Advertising."

0217

"Airline flap stirring little official response," *Advertising Age,* July 1, 1974, 45(26):6.

Because the Civil Aeronautics Board and Federal Aviation Administration ignored stewardess and feminist complaints about airline ad themes, NOW planned alternative strategy with action through the American Civil Liberties Union, National Advertising Review Board, and protest petitions signed by female advertising professionals.

0218

Donath, Bob. "New national ads spark attacks against 'sexist' airline campaigns," *Advertising Age,* June 24, 1974, 45(25):2.

Stewardesses for Women's Right's denounce sexist airline promotion on the grounds that they demean women, impair safety and promote situations whereby male passengers refuse to take safety-related orders from the objects of their fantasies. The ads also breed hostility among female passengers who regard stewardesses as "man-stealers."

0219

Kane, Paula. "The flying geisha girls," *Sex Objects in the Sky,* by P. Kane. Chicago: Follett, 1974. pp. 52-63.

Madison Avenue is credited with having created the flight attendant's geisha girl image of exotic subservience. The sexual invitations implicit in airline ads give male passengers supposed license to grab at their bodies and otherwise harrass them while in flight. Such advertising denies the stewardess the authoritative image necessary to exercise her ability and courage in times of emergency.

See 0319. M. Leonard, "Art thou sexist, fair adman?"

See 0199. D. E. Sexton and P. Haberman, "Women in magazine advertisements."

0220
    "Stewardess group sets counter to 'sexist' ads," *Advertising Age*, September 23, 1974, 45(38):62.

A television commercial filmed by Stewardesses for Women's Rights explains that the airline stewardess's primary function is the enforcement of safety regulations and acquiring lifesaving skills.

0221
    "Stewardesses protest sex-sell airline ads," *The Spokeswoman*, August 15, 1974, 5(2):2.

Flight attendants are protesting sexy television airline ads that have caused more consumer complaints to the Civil Aeronautics Board than any other facet of airline operation.

0222
    "Texas International ads upgrading image get critical perusal," *Advertising Age*, July 1, 1974, 45(26):60.

An airline ad uses a pun to draw attention to passenger leg room and stewardesses' legs.

0223
    Van Gelder, Lindsy. "Coffee, tea or fly me," *Ms.*, 1972, 1(7):86-91+.

According to the Madison Avenue brand of pimping, airline stewardesses are hired to perform the "Air Strip" (peeling down to hot pants on board) to "Make you [the customer] feel good all over" and to be "flown." Advertising's sexual promise fails to reflect the reality of the stewardess's profession. Stewardesses more often nurse epileptics, calm psychotics and deliver babies than deliver sex. They are also trained annually in first aid, emergency signaling, underwater rescue and hijacking precautions.

See 0206. C. Ventura, "Impact of women's liberation movement on advertising trends."

See 0208. "'Vulgar' sex ads demean all, insult consumer, panel finds."

See 0212. C. Winick, "Sex and advertising."

PRESCRIPTION DRUGS AND PERSONAL PRODUCTS

See 0116. D. Aaron, "About face: towards a positive image of women in advertising."

0224
    Berg, Roland H. "The over-medicated woman," *McCall's*, September, 1971, 98:67+.

    Typical medical journal advertising copy encourages MD's to prescribe tranquilizers and antidepressants for women who are 35 and unmarried; those who are anxiety ridden by young children, dirty dishes and unpaid bills; or who merely need calming so that life for their *husbands* will be more pleasant.

See 0128. J. Cappo. "Advertising - its own worse enemy?"

0225
    Chamber, Carl D. and Dodi Schultz. "Women and drugs," *Ladies' Home Journal*, November 1, 1971, 88(11):130-131+.

    The authors deny accusations that America's highly trained physician is duped by drug ads that offer barbiturates as valid substitute for dealing with teenage problems or marital discord. They blame prescription drug dependency on the American woman's refusal to follow doctor's instructions and on getting drugs illegally.

0226
    Christenson, Susan J. and Alice Q. Swanson.

"Women and drug use: an annotated bibliography,"
Journal of Psychedelic Drugs, 1974, 6:371-414.

Psychotherapeutic drug ads typically stereotype
women as people who cannot cope with their feminine role,
or who irritate doctors with complaints.

0227
Christopher, Maurine. "American women to spend
bundle on problem never knew existed," *Advertising Age,* July 26, 1971, 42:27.

The "problem" is solved with vaginal sprays. While
chemical companies spent a total $13 million in advertis-
ing for a corner of the market, the Federal Trade Commission was planning an investigation into the legitimacy of
the product.

0228
Delaney, Janice, Mary Jane Lupton and Emily Toth.
"The menstrual products industry, rags to riches,"
Women's Almanac, 1974, 2:48-63.

Advertising of menstrual products was taboo until the
1930's, and even then the language was extremely euphemis-
tic, stressing protection. During World War II the advertising changed to reflect women's role in the workforce.
Ads referred to "women" rather than "girls" and pictured
women punching time clocks. In the 1950's ads reflected
the feminine mystique, showing women's faces but not their
bodies, and describing tampons in terms of "daintiness."
The 1960's theme was female activity especially in water
sports while the 1970's ads dispel myths about menstru-
ation.

0229
The doctor's bag," *Scarlet Letter,* September,
1971, 1(3):6.

Ads for tranquilizers illustrate the attitude that a
woman's complaint does not deserve serious consideration
because it is based on nervous tension rather than legiti-
mate physical illness.

0230
"Effect of promotion and advertising of over-
the-counter drugs on competition, small business
and health and welfare of the public," *Advertising of Proprietary Medicine,* hearings by US Senate. Washington, DC: US Government Printing

Office, 1971. pp. 517-556. (Y4. SMI/2.
M46. pt. 2).

The testimony of Dr. Richard I. Feinbloom, MD includes the image of women in Geritol ads. The alternative
to over-the-counter drugs and prescribed psychotropics to
relieve the "tired mother syndrome" is increased political
activity for women. Lobbying for day care centers will
free women of the "tired mother syndrome" as well as ac-
tivate thought processes which have been dulled by drugs.

Psychiatrist Robert Seidenberg's testimony outlines
the prevalent images of women in medical journal drug ads:
the chronic, always female complainer, the woman who can't
get along with her daughter-in-law, the women who are distressed by washing dishes, ironing, or giving a child a
bath. These distraught housewives are drugged with Rita-
lin so that washing dishes will again become a joy.
Women are also portrayed as "sleep cripples" who verge on
nervous breakdown if averaging less than eight hours
sleep per night. With medical intervention sleep cripples
become drug cripples. Seidenberg blames the AMA for not
carefully screening ads appearing in its journals. *Good
Housekeeping* and *Parents Magazine* more effectively protect their reader-consumers from harmful advertising than
does the AMA.

Dr. Natalie Shainess, psychiatrist, testifies on the
tactic of degradation when advertising "female" drugs and
aids. The marketing of feminine deodorant sprays, an unnecessary and harmful product, carries the implication
that women are dirty and smelly, which damages both a
woman's self-esteem and a man's view of her. So-called
"ethical" drug ads further this contempt of women in their
image of women as either "girlish beauties" under age 25,
or "old uglies" over age 25, while men appear as well-
dressed, confident people. This distorted image of women
as irrational beings is not only a dishonest representation of reality, but irresponsibly promotes a product by
appealing to misogynistic prejudices. If aversion to washing dishes is a sign of mental illness requiring psychotropic drugs, then this must be the dark age of psychiatry.

0231
Ephron, Nora. "Dealing with the, uh, problem,"
Crazy Salad, by N. Ephron. NY: Knopf, 1975.
pp. 79-103.

An essay commenting on the euphemisms surrounding
the advertising and marketing of vaginal sprays, and the
Federal Drug Administration concerns about health damage
associated with the sprays.

0232
    Fidell, Linda. "Put her down on drugs: pre-
    scribed usage in women." Available from KNOW,
    Inc., PO Box 86031, Pittsburgh, PA. 15221.
    #226.

A content analysis of drug ads in leading medical
journals revealed, among other findings, that ads for
psychoactive drugs most often pictured female patients
while ads for non-psychoactive drugs pictured mostly male
patients. This differential treatment implies that men
have "real"illnesses while women have mental problems.

0233
    Frankfort, Ellen. "The drug industry," *Vaginal
    Politics*, by E. Frankfort. NY: Quadrangle
    Books, 1972. pp. 107-124.

In the area of non-prescription drugs advertisers use
sophisticated marketing techniques to convince women to
buy products that they not only do not need, but are potentially dangerous to their health. Research proves that
vaginal sprays mask infection, irritate mucuous membrane
and cause brain damage in monkeys. The author contends
that a product causing genital irritation to men would
neither be manufactured nor advertised.

0234
    Frankfort, Ellen. "Drugs and consumer
    rights, the media," *Vaginal Politics*, by E.
    Frankfort. NY: Quadrangle Books, 1972. pp.
    101-106.

A patronizing image of woman abounds in medical
journal drug ads while the popular press shows ads with
cutesy punctuation: exclamation points and asterisks
decorate ads for women's personal products. Advertising
for vaginal sprays and other products promote sexual insecurity in women, and ads for tranquilizers distort
women's fears and needs, yet the scholarly journals who
print these ads refuse ads for a book which depicts male
therapists in a sexually negative light.

0235
    Hartman, Sylvia. "Princess Valium meets Shrink-
    think: cashing in on sexism in psychiatry,"
    Radical Therapist, October/November, 1970,
    1:16-17. Also available from KNOW, Inc.,
    PO Box 86031, Pittsburgh, PA 15221.

A former psychologist demythologizes a Valium ad in

which a psychiatrist declares a female patient "neurotic", and therefore requiring tranquilizers, based on her drawing of a person. The advertising psychiatrist interprets buttons drawn on the dress as "symbolizing dependent, infantile tendencies." Hartmen counters with "How [is] this woman in the drawing supposed to get into her dress? It's buttons down the back that really make a woman dependent."

0236
    Larned, Deborah. "The selling of Valium," *Ms.*, November, 1975, 4(5):32-33.

    The ad copy for Valium pictures women as the sicker sex. While men require medication to relieve gastrointestinal symptoms of psychic tension, women require medication to relieve "persistent complaints." The ads don't mention specific sources of the female "complaints" such as persistent uterine pain, but rather stereotype women as chronic complainers.

0237
    Kunnes, Richard. "Poly-drug abuse: drug companies and doctors," *American Journal of Orthopsychiatry*, July, 1973, 43:530-532.

    Dr. Kunnes charges the pharmaceutical industry with using sexism to promote poly-drug abuse. Not only are scantily clad female models used in the advertising, but the social conditioning of women to have slim figures is exploited by drug companies who manufacture "new improved" diet pills. The improved pill is a highly addictive amphetamine/barbiturate fixed-drug combination. The advertising in professional medical and scientific journals in turn lead the physician to believe that the patient needs the combination of amphetamine to lose weight with barbiturate to counteract possible amphetamine jitteriness, whether the patient actually has "jitters" or not. Even if nervousness is produced, separate prescriptions are much less expensive than the combination pill.

0238
    Landsberg, Michele. "Your gynecologist," *Chatelaine*, August, 1973, 46:42+.

    Gynecological drug ads stereotype women as shrieking shrews, sex objects, silly and/or naturally neurotic people, and never portray them in respected occupations.

0239

McRee, Christine, Billie F. Corder and Thomas Haizlip. "Psychiatrists responses to sexual bias in pharmaceutical advertisements," *American Journal of Psychiatry,* 1974, 131:1273-1275.

A survey of psychiatrists' attitudes toward the image of women in drug ads indicates that drug companies would sell their products just as readily by using male as well as female patients in advertisements. The survey's 12 questions and response percentages follow the article.

0240

Mant, Andrea and Dorothy Broom Darroch. "Media images and medical images," *Social Science and Medicine,* 1975, 9:613-618.

A content analysis of 487 drug ads in Australian medical journals revealed that 70% of ads for mood-modifying drugs picture patients, 68% of the ads for mood modifying drugs picture female patients. Sixty three percent of Australia's general practitioners graduated from school before 1960, and therefore had little formal training in the use of mood modifying drugs. They must rely on pharmaceutical ads for a great deal of their drug information. Use of female patients in drug ads reinforces the doctor's expectation that the patient requiring mood modifiers will be female.

Drug ads picture nude women as sex objects to sell products, portray women as helpless or foolish, and present women as incapable of following doctor's instructions. Men pictured in drug ads were rarely ridiculed. No female doctor's were pictured though Australia's MD's are 13% female.

0241

"Men get cured, women get drugged," *her-self,* April, 1974, 3(1):12-13.

Illustrated with three drug ads showing anxious, neurotic women, this article describes copy from other ads and discusses the effect of their freudian overtones on the doctors who read them for educational purposes. Women are prescribed tranquilizers when their depression actually stems from hormonal imbalance or low blood sugar.

Mosher, Elissa Henderson. "Portrayal of women in drug advertising: a medical betrayal," *Journal of Drug Issues,* 1976, 6:72-78. Not reviewed.

0242
"New complaint directed to William Ewen at National Advertising Review Board," *Media Report to Women*, March 1, 1974, 2(3):10.

After the Food and Drug Administration's ruling that vaginal sprays have no hygiene value and carry the risk of physical danger to women, NY NOW filed a complaint with NARB concerning the psychological damage done to women when advertising repeatedly tells them of a supposed need for such a product. Advertising copy from six ads support the charge of "severe psychological damage" to women, followed by copy from four additional ads making harmful, false and deceptive claims.

0243
Off Our Backs, November 8, 1970, 1(13):8-10.

The centerfold "ad" for Butter Balls, a fictional product for men, is a reaction to advertising of vaginal deodorant sprays. The double spread "ad" is followed by an explanation of the problems faced by the publisher in finding a printer for the issue containing the "ad."

0244
Park, Lynn. "Advertisements," *Psychiatric News*, October 3, 1973, 7:2.

A letter to the editor reveals the findings of an informal survey of the sex role stereotypes in pharmaceutical ads found in one issue of *Psychiatric News:* 78.5% of the ads depicted depressed and passive women, as opposed to a 21% male need for medication. Such an imbalance surely affects the unconscious attitudes of the psychiatrists reading the magazine and its ads. The author asks if the editor plans to alter the advertising policy.

0245
Paulsen, Virginia M. "Women in drug ads," *Psychiatric News*, September 19, 1973, 7:2.

A letter to the editor comments on the prevalence of drug ads depicting women as "sick" and therefore requiring drug therapy. Because 90% of US psychiatrists are men, this image of the dependent woman who is sick more often than men becomes a means of protection of male doctors' power and privilege.

0246
Prather, Jane and Linda S. Fidell. "Sex differences

in the content and style of medical advertisements," *Social Science and Medicine*, 1975,
9:23-26.

Women receive 60% of prescriptions for drugs in all
categories, and 67% of psychoactive drug prescriptions.
The authors suggest that advertising influences physicians'
attitudes toward prescribing these drugs to women. The
ads found in four leading medical journals were examined
for drug name, manufacturer, symptoms or disease, pic-
torial accompaniment, verbal description of complaint, as
well as age, race and social class of all people pictured
in the ads. The results indicate "that women tend to be
shown as suffering from primarily emotional illness while
men are shown as having primarily organic illness" in drug
advertising. The article is illustrated with advertising
copy that "seems further to reinforce the notion that
women have less serious organic health problems than do
men." The authors found six recurring themes in four leading medical journals: 1) common use of sex stereotyping,
2) women were more often associated with psychotropic
symptoms than with nonpsychotropic symptoms, 3) reasons
for prescribing psychotropic drugs to men were different
than reasons for prescribing them to women, 4) female
symptoms were often presented with clever puns while male
symptoms were given straightforward approach, 5) women
were often portrayed as chronic complainers who should be
tranquilized to relieve family and doctor of her complaints, 6) women were never portrayed as physician.

0247
    Ris, Hania. "What do women want?," *Journal of
American Medical Women's Association*, 1974,
29:446-456.

According to Ris women want more respect from their
physicians. She discusses the relation of woman to the
male gynocologist-obstetrician, the image of women in
gynocology textbooks, and sex role stereotyping in drug
advertisements. The latter section is an overview of the
Prather and Fidell study. See 0246.

0248
    Seidenberg, Robert. "Advertising and abuse of
drugs," *New England Journal of Medicine*, 1972,
284:789-790.

A ten year survey of ads in medical and psychiatric
journals shows women requiring psychotropic drugs when
distressed by washing dishes and bathing children, when
they are chronic complainers who upset husband's sleep,
when they have trouble making friends in new cities or

can't get along with daughter-in-law. Men are pictured as potential patients of psychotropic drugs when irritated by environment noises and can't accept retirement. These common annoyances should not be treated as psychiatric diseases. Seidenberg proposes that the US drug pandemia be controlled by changing journal policies from dependence on drug advertising.

0249
Seidenberg, Robert. "Drug advertising and perception of mental illness," *Mental Hygiene*, 1971, 55:21-30.

If ads "not only sell products but also mold opinion and form attitudes ... toward women [then doctors] can be influenced by an inordinate use of pictures of them as 'sick' or disturbed." According to drug ads, women are the sicker sex. The advertising copy from 11 ads is discussed by sexist themes: the person distressed by tedious tasks (a woman is tranquilized in order to do the dishes), the person bothersome to family (sleeping pills for wife relieve husband of her nightly "squawks"), and other themes in which drugs rather than change of lifestyle or development of inner strength are offered as solutions.

0250
Seidenberg, Robert. "Images of health, illness and women in drug ads," *Journal of Drug Issues*, 1974, 4:264-267.

The American Medical Association standards allow misleading and deceptive advertising to appear in medical and psychiatric journals. Most of the ads depict women as shrewish people "irrationally" discontented with the female role, who are treated with chemicals rather than a new lifestyle. The ads also consistently picture women as patients rather than as the treating physician. Medical journals should take a lesson from *Good Housekeeping* and accept only those ads which they can endorse.

0251
Seidenberg, Robert. "Rx: legal addiction," *Do It Now*, August, 1976, 9(7):3.

Common themes recurring throughout drug advertising include the theme of woman as chronic complainer whose complaints keep her husband awake at night as well as upset her doctor's office routine. The ads reason that these irritations to husbands and doctors can be relieved by prescribing sleeping pills to women. The implications of an overly tranquilized female society are examined.

0252
Stimson, Gerry V. "The message of psychotropic drug ads," *Journal of Communication*, 1975, 25(3): 153-160.

Examination of a one month supply (37 issues) of controlled-circulation medical magazines, journals and newspapers supported by advertising directed at doctors revealed that ads for psychotropic drugs picturing women outnumbered those picturing men 15:1. The message implicit in these ads suggests that women are more likely than men to require sedative tranquilizers and antidepressant drugs. The most common images of women depicted in drug ads are the harassed housewife unable to cope with her role and the lonely spinster or widow who has no husband or child to care for.

0253
Stimson, Gerry. "Women in a doctored world," *New Society*, 1975, 32:265-267.

Medical ads for birth control pills are compared with ads for tranquilizers and anti-depressants. Birth control ads rarely show working class women, but most frequently picture leisure class women in park settings. The ratio of women to men in anti-depressant and tranquilizer ads is 15:1. Most frequent characters found in tranquilizer ads are harried housewives, widows, women whose children have grown up, female students or working women whose occupations conflict with the desire to be feminine.

See 0206. C. Ventura, "Impact of women's liberation movement on advertising trends."

Marketing

0254
"Advertising to women," *Madison Avenue*, December, 1976, 20(2):33-34+.

The publishers of 23 women's magazines and broadcasting executives discuss the necessity to avoid insulting stereotypes when advertising to women.

0255
    Baltera, Lorraine. "Sex stereotypes belong in
    ads, retailers advised," *Advertising Age*, Oc-
    tober 4, 1976, 47(40):44.

Although 46% of all women over age 16 work, their
impact on the work force has not yet been felt, according
to a National Merchant's Association speaker. Men still
control the outside world. Successful advertising in
which men display active behavior and women appear as
decorative objects reflects this.

0256
    Baltera, Lorraine. "The working woman's come
    a long way, but can advertisers find her?,"
    Advertising Age, July 22, 1974, 45(29):2+.

With American working women totaling 32 million, advertisers would do well to upgrade the demeaning image of
women in ads. The career oriented female consumer spends
more money entertaining, attending sports events, dining
out, buying alcoholic beverages, cars and clothes than
does the non-wage earner. Unless advertisers project a
positive image, their ads are likely to arouse an avoid-
ance response among working women.

0257
    Cadwell, Franchellie. "Shifting female market
    will kill some products," *Advertising Age*,
    August 16, 1971, 42(33):1+.

Women now have wider lifestyle options. Careers,
fewer marriages and fewer children have created a change
in female consumer habits. In order to promote products
in this shifting female market, advertisers must speak to
women as equals rather than looking down at them.

0258
    Christopher, Maurine. "P&G in major spot TV
    shift to reach more women," *Advertising Age*,
    March 26, 1973, 44(13):1+.

Procter and Gamble buys spot advertising on nightly
news programs and television specials in order to appeal
to working women and other active women who don't watch
daytime television.

0259
    Crask, Melvin R., Dianne Lanier, Fred Trawick,
    Charles Woodliff, and Fred D. Reynolds. "The

modern masculine life style," *Advances in Consumer Research*, v. 4, ed. by William D. Perreauld. Atlanta: Association for Consumer Research, 1977. pp. 242-246.

A measure of attitude differences between modern men and traditional men to determine ramifications for consumer research reveals a 54:46 ratio of traditional to modern marriages. Marketing techniques should appeal to both spouses who share consumer decisions in egalitarian marriages.

See 0136. F. Danzig, "Sales execs panel tells feminists ad obstacles."

0260
"Detroit pays lip service to women: doesn't really see their importance," *Advertising Age*, January 25, 1971, 42:3.

Because women influence more car buying decisions than men, automobile ads should be directed toward women as car driver or as potential customer, rather than confining women to the image as passenger or decorative object within the ad.

0261
Dooley, Janet L. *Effects of the Feminist Movement on Magazine Ads*. M.S. thesis, University of Tennessee, 1975.

Married female students, with both feminist and non-feminist leanings, completed questionnaires pertaining to the image of women in selected ads. Respondents of both philosophical leanings indicated a need for feminist advertising appeals, and indicated personal preference for ads with feminist appeal.

See 0141. J. Doolittle and R. Pepper, "Children's TV ad content: 1974."

See 0145. S. Ewen, "Consumption and the new woman."

0262
Foster, Anne Tolstoi. "Ad lib takes cue from women," *The New York Times*, November 28, 1971, F-13.

A more modern approach to the image of women in ads is financially expedient for advertisers. They cannot afford to insult the female consumer by portraying her as an incompetent driver or infatuated with her floor wax.

0263
    Foster, Anne Tolstoi. "Commercials tend to ignore working women," *Advertising Age*, April 10, 1972, 43(15):44.

Although almost half of the American women over 16 work, and 21 million of them are working wives, advertisers still appeal to the woman behind the sink. Even housewives identify less with that image than with the image of the married career women her husband talks to at parties. Advertising should fill the gap between television and reality.

0264
    Frye, Jerry K. "Using television commercials as an instructional strategy to teach persuasion," paper presented at the annual meeting of the International Communication Association, 1976. ERIC (ED 120 868).

Sexploitation of women in television commercials ignores the sizeable audience markets comprised of beer drinking women, female insurance policy holders and automobile purchasers. Communications professors should teach advertising students the negative effects of sexploitation of women.

0265
    Grant, Don. "Women's lib dialog tells adfolk: mend ad implications," *Advertising Age*, January 25, 1971, 42:3.

At a 1971 meeting between National Organization for Women members and representatives from leading ad agencies, several suggestions were made for an improved image of women in ads: 1) avoid showing women as stupid or incompetent, 2) avoid showing women as sex objects, 3) show women in roles besides housewife/mother, 4) have a better balance between male and female characters when advertising children's products to avoid placing artificial limitations on children's images of themselves.

0266
    Green, Robert T. and Isabella C. M. Cunningham. "Feminine role perception and family purchasing

decisions," *Journal of Marketing Research*, 1975, 12:325-332.

An increase in family purchasing decisions made by women, especially liberal women, should be reflected in the marketplace where women should present new opportunities for marketers.

0267
　　Hall, Jane. "Discovering Ms. America," *TV Guide*, December 18, 1976, 24(51):26-27+.

Many television advertisers are discarding the blatantly sexist approach. Now that 47% of all American women over 16 work outside the home, advertisers cannot afford to appeal only to the housewife target market. The image of woman as simple-minded slob and simpering idiot has given way to ads showing women in a variety of career roles, and showing married men sharing household responsibilities with wives. Although sexism in advertising still exists in more subtle forms, advertising researchers seem to be working toward its elimination.

0268
　　"Is marketing to women a hit or miss affair? An all-star panel responds," *Madison Avenue*, December, 1976, 20(2):52-54+.

Fourteen advertising and marketing women discuss the question, "Does today's advertising talk to contemporary women?" Most say no. Whether working outside the home or within it, advertising does not show a woman's pride in her breadwinning or homemaking abilities. The reliability of marketing tests is questioned as is the traditional demographic breakdown when researching ads that attempt to appeal to women.

0269
　　Johnson, Nicholas, "The talkin' blues: television, corporate greed and women's liberation," *Federal Communications Commission News*, March 2, 1970; also in Readex print non-depository US Documents, 1970, #7080. (CC1.15.J62/4).

A humorous speech by FCC Commissioner Nicholas Johnson to American women in Radio and TV ends with a description of the image of women in television programming and advertising. He calls on women in the broadcast media to help change the image.

See 0161. J. Klemesrud. "On Madison Avenue, women take stand in middle of the road."

0270
    Kovacs, Midge. "Are your ads reaching those millions of women who work?," *Advertising Age*, December 4, 1972, 43(49): 48+.

    In order to encourage advertising to bring women "out of the kitchen and into the mainstream" a list of statistics are offered to prove that working women comprise a major market. Among women in the 18 to 64 age group, 50% work. Advertising efforts to woo the working woman could include selling headache remedies in the office, showing women driving cars, and men shopping at the supermarket. Working women will also be impressed by female voiceover of authority in television advertising.

0271
    Kovacs, Midge. "Where is woman's place? Home, says ads," *Advertising Age*, July 17, 1972, 43(29):48.

    An overview of the Courteney and Lockeretz study (see 0132) is directed to advertisers in order to encourage a change in the image of women in advertising.

0272
    Kovacs, Midge. "Women simply don't recognize themselves in many ads today," *Advertising Age*, 43(24):48.

    Kovacs advises advertisers to pay attention to the feminist movement. Marketing approaches will change for families in which both partners are wage earners. Advertising will have to reflect the fact that 43% of all women work.

0273
    Kovacs, Midge. "Women's lib: do's and don'ts for ad men," *Marketing/Communications*, 1971, 299:34-35.

    Portrayals of women as idiot child-women, sex objects and kitchen slaves are among the "don'ts." Role reversals with men using kitchen cleansers, and intelligent women using products for their efficiency are two suggestions for ads in which women are not demeaned or demoralized.

0274
Kreinik, David. "Women: a growing force to be reckoned with in advertising financial services," *Broadcasting*, April 19, 1976, 90:12.

Because women are becoming breadwinners, their habits of consumption are changing. Advertising should reflect as well as appeal to this demographic change by showing more female scientists, mechanics and athletes, and eliminating the stereotype of women as "check-bouncing financial lost sheep." Kreinik suggests a selective use of television programming to appeal to active women who watch television.

0275
"Marketing to the 'new woman'," *Industry Week*, April 21, 1975, 185:40+.

Marketers are beginning to revamp their approach to female consumers. A greater number of working women in a variety of fields and income levels are included in the market research samples. Advertisers are also learning to be more conscious of sex roles and are attempting to avoid stereotypes. Women are recognized as more sophisticated consumers who are interested in product information. As more female marketing majors graduate from universities, the female influence on marketing and advertising approaches will continue to increase and become more widely accepted among companies who don't currently believe in the "new woman."

0276
Martin, Judith. "Washing the sexism right out of those ads?," *The Washington Post*, March 28, 1975, p. B-1.

A report of the National Advertising Review Board recommendations and checklist mentions that "Advertising and Women" was written because of the many letters sent to NARB protesting female incompetence and guilt portrayed in ads for household cleaning products. NARB cannot force an advertiser to meet its standards nor does it force ad agencies to read the report. Agencies do not even see it unless they specifically request copies.

0277
Miles, Virginia. "The new woman: her importance to marketing," *Annual Editions: Readings in Marketing*, Guilford, Conn: Dushkin, 1973-1974. pp. 148; also in *The American Woman: Who Will She Be?*, ed. by Mary Louise McBee and Kathryn A.

Blake. Beverly Hills, CA: Glencoe Press, 1974.
p. 152.

Because most women today under age 35 reject traditional values, Dr. Miles advises marketers to change their
approach by appealing to women as well as men when marketing hotels, gas stations and convenience foods. She
emphasizes focus on a duel audience, especially in the advertising of liquor where women "buy 40% of all liquor and
in many cases make the brand selection."

0278

National Advertising Review Board. *Advertis-
ing and Women.* Available from NARB, 850 Third
Ave., NY, 10022. $1.00; also in *Advertising
Age,* April 21, 1975, 46:72+.

NARB, self-governing body of four national advertising associations, outlined the reasons why advertising has
a social responsibility to portray women more realistically as people who have other interests besides fighting
dirt in the home; women should be portrayed as vibrant,
talented people and therefore sexually appealing. The
image of sex object/mannequin-like being should be eliminated. NARB recommendations include a checklist of destructive portrayals of women and a list of constructive
portrayals.

0279

O'Brien, Sally Ann. "Colgate looks with a new
eye at women," *Broadcasting,* October 7, 1974,
87:13.

In market research for a television special on
women's sports, Colgate Palmolive tested female respondents for recall of program events and commercial messages.
Recall was 61% for commercials seen on the women's television special, and 34% for the same commercials advertised on "The Rookies."

0280

"P&G stockholders rebuff attempt to change role
of women in TV commercials," *Broadcasting,* October 20, 1975, 89:40.

The United Presbyterian Church, a Procter and Gamble
stockholder, proposed a resolution to study the role of
women in P&G advertising. Most women do not secretly
squeeze toilet paper in the grocery store, or fear that
divorce is imminent if they do not make good coffee, as
P&G ads imply. Although the stockholders voted against

the resolution, company officials promise gradual change.

0281
"Poll finds most women favor efforts to strengthen role," *Advertising Age*, October 14, 1974, 45(41): 80.

Results of the poll indicate that American women favor equal partnership in marriage including financial, homemaking and child-rearing responsibilities. Intelligence is rated as the most admired quality in both sexes, followed by sex appeal, sensitivity and sense of humor.

0282
Santi, Tina. "Today's woman explodes yesterday's ad dream world," *Advertising Age*, March 18, 1974, 45:49-53.

Written by a Colgate-Palmolive female PR executive, this article compares the realistic 1974 advertising appeal to the 1963 fantasy approach of doves and knights. Photographs of the actual ads are used to compare female passivity of 1967 to female activity in the 1974 ad campaigns.

0283
"Savvy marketers will improve women's ad roles: JWT execs," *Advertising Age*, March 3, 1975, 46(9):53.

J. Walter Thompson agency is improving the image of women in its ads. An early Clairol headline, "If you're not young and blonde, you might as well bury yourself," is compared to the current "For Brunettes Only" campaign. Advertising's aim should be letting women free themselves from being "less than women have a right to be."

0284
Scott, Rosemary. "Media woman - the stereotype," *The Female Consumer*, by R. Scott. NY: Wiley, 1976. pp. 203-255.

A study of the female consumer and her relation to the marketer and advertiser who insist on portraying and communicating to women on their terms rather than on hers. The chapter, dealing specifically with media stereotypes, examines the grain of truth in every stereotype, and provides a total picture of each type. The conclusion offers 16 plausible situations which could be used in television advertisements.

0285
   Stuteville, John R. "Sexually polarized products
   and advertising strategy," *Journal of Retailing*,
   Summer, 1971, 47:3-13.

   Having saturated the female market with hair spray,
marketing experts and advertisers now appeal to the male
market by packaging the same product in bold colors, em-
blazoning the packaging with shields, swords and accoutrements of war, and adding pine scent to the product. The
author foresees a more androgynous future where "masculinity will have less status relative to femininity."

0286
   Thorpe, Dara. "Hearings find corporations promote
   stereotypical images of women," *CIC Brief*. Available from Corporate Information Center, Rm 566,
   475 Riverside Dr., NY, 10027. 60¢.

   Public hearings sponsored by Interfaith Center for
Corporate Responsibility covered advertising values; sexist, racist and ageist stereotypes, and social and corporate responsibility concerning stereotypes and the
media.

0287
   Wasson, Hilda C. "The Ms. in magazine advertising," *Proceedings:* Southern Marketing Association 1973 Conference, ed. by Robert L. King.
   pp. 240-243.

   An assessment of the differences in advertising approach for similar products by traditional magazines
(*Ladies Home Journal*, *McCall's* and *Redbook)* and liberal
magazines (*Ms.*, *New Woman* and *Cosmopolitan)* led to four
hypotheses: 1) Advertising in liberated women's magazines is perceptually different from that carried in
magazines appealing to traditional women, 2) most ads in
liberated magazines have favorable images of women, 3)
neutral advertising appeals more toward liberated than
traditional women, and 4) ads which overlap traditional
and liberated philosophies less effectively communicate
with liberated women.

0288
   "What's a sexist ad? NARB offers guides," *Advertising Age*, March 17, 1975, 46(11):3.

   A summary of the National Advertising Review Board's
report, "Advertising and Women" (see 0278) explains that
changed conditions of society warrant a changed image of

women in advertising in order to avoid offending female
consumers. Included are examples from the checklist of
questions and mention of studies revealing that working
women are underrepresented in both print and broadcast advertising.

0289
    Willett, Roslyn. "Do not stereotype women - an
    appeal to advertisers," *Journal of Home Economics*,
    October, 1971, 63:549-551.

    Advertising should reflect the diversity of con-
temporary American women's experiences and aspirations
rather than continue to stereotype woman as she does not
exist. The importance in eliminating the sex role stereotypes lies in the fact that advertising's public images
of "reality" are accepted as partial truths by people who
learn to see themselves as intellectually stupid and as
objects rather than as real people. Women are not all
housewives, as advertising implies. Women also function
as corporation presidents, stock brokers, engineers. In
1968 women comprised 38% of the labor force and almost
50% of the student body in American colleges. Ads show
female grocery shoppers almost exclusively, when in reality men shop for food and launder clothes. This form of
personal maintenance is no more sex related than brushing
teeth, yet advertising chooses to ignore this aspect of
reality. By expanding to non-stereotyped sex roles, advertisers will be free to explore more creative approaches
to selling.

0290
    Wilvers, Francine Wexler. "The female image in
    ads: time for a change?," *Broadcasting*, Septem-
    ber 20, 1971, 81(11):14.

    A feminist advertiser calls on her peers to discon-
tinue the practice of portraying idiotic women enthralled
by their reflections on shiny floors and begin portraying
women behind a desk instead of in the kitchen. She also
advises them to discontinue the cheap cop-out of associat-
ing naked women with men's grooming products.

0291
    "Woman as person emerges: D-F-S study," *Adver-
    tising Age*, April 5, 1976, 47(14):34.

    A Dancer-Fitzgerald-Sample study on women's atti-
tudes and expectations showed that women's liberation has
influenced most women. No longer the typical television
woman, most women today want to be defined as people

rather than by a family role, they want equal opportunity as well as equal pay, and prefer to have "doors opened to them, not just held for them."

0292
    "Women's ad guides pegged good start, but no panacea," *Advertising Age*, May 12, 1975, 46(19: 58.

A debate among advertisers over the NARB report (see 0278) aired opinions on the strength of its recommendations. Betty Harragan would have preferred a stronger directive approach advocating the advertising community's participation in NARB guidelines rather than the wishy-washy questions approach. Nancy Giges added that ads using cutesy phrases to soft pedal women in working roles purposely negate the social effect of the working woman.

0293
    "Working wives become major marketing force," *Advertising Age*, April 5, 1976, 47(14):34.

Opening the following markets to women have been suggested when appealing to working wives: labor-saving appliances, insurance, credit cards, rental cars and airlines. The 55.3% female labor force could be reflected in advertising by shifting emphasis from the guilt-ridden housewife image to husband-shared housekeeping.

0294
    "Working women no monolith, admen told," *Advertising Age*, November 3, 1975, 46(44):22.

At a *Woman's Day* National Business Conference seminar ideas were bandied for reaching the working woman through advertising.

Classified Ads

See 0304. M. Akamatsu, "Liberating the media: advertising."

See 0122. I. P. Bell, "The double standard."

0295
   Bem, Sandra L. and Daryl J. Bem. "Does sex-biased
   job advertising 'aid and abet' sex discrimination?," *Journal of Applied Social Psychology*, 1973,
   3:6-18.

   An emphatic "yes" is the answer to the question posed
by the title. The first of two studies reported here indicates that sex segregated want ads written in sex biased
language discourage women and men from applying for
"opposite-sex" jobs. When the sex bias is lifted from the
same job advertisement, women apply for outdoor jobs on
telephone lines and men apply for jobs as telephone oper-
ators. For a summary of Experiment II, see 0296.

0296
   Bem, Sandra L. and Daryl J. Bem. "Sex segregated
   want ads: do they discourage female job applications?," *Psychology and Social Issues*, ed. by
   J. Herbert Hamsher and Harold Sigall. NY: Macmillan, 1973. pp. 261-265; also as Experiment
   II in *Journal of Applied Social Psychology*, 1973,
   3:6-18. See 0295.

   This study was conducted for use as legal testimony
in order to prove that sex-segregated want ads aid and
abet employment discrimination. Female job hunters ex-
plicitly stated that they do not pursue jobs listed in
"Male Interest" columns, regardless of their qualifications for the jobs.

0297
   Boyer, Elizabeth. "Help-wanted advertising -
   every woman's barrier," *Hastings Law Journal*,
   1971, 23:221-231.

   Sex segregated want ads perpetuate the entrance of
women into traditionally female occupations. Less than
one percent of employed women are found in positions not
listed in female help wanted columns (i.e. physicians,
judge, professor, college president). Women who are
qualified for traditionally male occupations are effectively barred from jobs posted in male help wanted columns.

0298
   "Discrimination," *The New York Times*, June 24,
   1973, p. E-3.

   In a 5:4 decision the Supreme Court prohibited newspapers from publishing sex segregated want ads on the
grounds that they encourage sex discrimination in

employment. Because of their commercial nature, want ads are not protected by First Amendment freedom of the press provisions.

0299/0300
    Meade, Marion. *Bitching*. Englewood Cliffs, NJ: Prentice-Hall, 1973.

    Help wanted advertising characteristically uses sexist language.

0301
    "NOW vs. *The Pittsburgh Press*, Revolution in microcosm." Available from KNOW, Inc., PO Box 86031, Pittsburgh, PA 15221.

    Based on the premise that segregated want ads continually present low aspirations to women, NOW charged *The Pittsburgh Press* with violating the city's Human Relations Ordinance for segregating want ads when bona fide occupational qualifications did not exist. Details of the long court battle and NOW's victory are reported.

See 0108. L. C. Pogrebin. "Women on the tube: four insiders report."

0302/0303
    Skotzko, Eugene, "Significant decisions in labor cases: Sex in job advertisements," *Monthly Labor Review*, September, 1973, 96:81-85.

    An account of the US Supreme Court 5-4 ruling prohibiting sex segregated job announcements in newspapers.

Advertising Employment

0304
    Akamatsu, Muriel. "Liberating the media: advertising," *Freedom of Information Center Report*, #290. Columbia: University of Missouri School of Journalism, 1972; also available from KNOW,

Inc., PO Box 86031, Pittsburgh, PA 15221. #290.

The image of women in print and broadcast advertising as well as the status of women in classified advertising are examined. Change can be facilitated through EEOC, Title VII and personnel restructuring within the agencies.

0305
   "Betty Harragan wins her case; EEOC finds J.
   Walter Thompson had sex bias policy," *Media
   Report to Women*, February 1, 1977, 5(2):7-8.

Excerpts from Betty Harragan's 1971 charges of sex discrimination against J. Walter Thompson and her 1976 settlement discussions. EEOC table indicates that the average salaries paid employees of Thompson's Public Relations Department were $13,900 for women, $20,000 for men.

0306
   Callan, Maureen. "Women copywriters get better,
   but male chauvinism in ads rolls on," *Advertising
   Age*, October 4, 1976, 47(40):75-76.

Callan wonders why the new women entering the advertising field are not overthrowing the image of foolish dirt chasers. Interviews with female copywriters relate experiences where their more modern ideas were overruled by men who truly believe that sexism sells.

0307
   Donath, Bob. "Can agency fire to protect account?
   McGee ruling calls it 'retaliation'," *Advertising
   Age*, November 1, 1976, 47(44):10+.

An advertising senior account executive was fired after filing charges with NY Human Rights Commission when her request for equal pay for equal work was denied. She has subsequently been blacklisted from employment with other ad agencies, but won her court case: $100,000 in back pay and a year's salary.

0308
   "Honored gals discuss ad opportunities." *Advertising Age*, June 5, 1972, 43(23):35.

Although job opportunities for women are increasing in the advertising field, most award winning ad women interviewed here agree that men are still most often hired for the more important jobs in the industry.

0309
    Levere, Jane. "Portrayal of women in ads defended
    by top ad women," *Editor and Publisher*, June 8,
    1974, 107:11+.

    Six award winning female advertisers are interviewed
on two basic subjects: the image of women in advertising;
the effect of their womanhood in the field of advertising.

0310
    Louie, Elaine. "Rare birds in adland," *Art Direc-
    tion*, November, 1974, 26(8):62-65.

    The salaries, ages and accounts of female Art Direc-
tors in leading ad agencies are revealed along with an
account of the sexist treatment of women and the rarity
of female executives. However, most women claim that they
don't want executive responsibility.

See 0060. D. Saperstein, "Your time, your station:
changing woman's thinking through the great communication
revolution."

0311
    "Slow improvement in status our fault," *Adver-
    tising Age*, April 5, 1976, 47(14):22.

    Essentially a consciousness raising speech, Joan
Levine and Adrienne Hall encouraged their female colleagues
in the advertising industry to raise their professional
status by competing with male advertisers rather than always being judged against other women.

0312
    Yanow, Jo. "But baby, still a long way to go,"
    Madison Avenue, July, 1971, 14:8-9.

    Top women in the advertising field discuss profes-
sional discrimination they've faced in hiring, promotions,
and day-to-day remarks made by men. The attitude toward
women projected in the ads themselves also reflect ad
men's conceptions of ad women: "Can a woman be pretty -
and smart?"

See 0070. "Your daughter's education."

Advertising Counterbalance

See 0304. M. Asamatsu, "Liberating the media: advertising."

0313
Baltera, Lorraine. O&M and NOW rap about ads that lib group finds 'demeaning'," *Advertising Age*, July 10, 1972, 43(27):3+.

NOW representatives Joyce Snyder and Shere Hite led a workshop for Ogilvy and Mather advertising agency where they exposed sexist points in television and print advertising, and offered examples of ads showing women in favorable light. Most advertising executives enthusiastically agreed with many of NOW's points and hissed at the more blatantly sexist ads shown. The workshop ended with NOW calling for a more realistic presentation of women in advertising.

0314
Butler-Paisley, Matilda. *Image of Women in Advertisements: A Preliminary Study of Avenues for Change*, ed. by Butler-Paisley, Matilda, with chapters by Sheridan Crawford, Jinnet Lewis and Sonya Sokolow. Stanford: Stanford University, California Institute for Communication Research, 1975. ERIC (ED 118 107).

After interviewing feminists actively promoting advertising change, and interviewing advertisers to learn the function of an ad campaign, the Stanford University Institute for Communication determined five avenues for change: 1) national women's organizations should approach major advertisers and agencies with suggestions for change, 2) stockholders should demand more accurate presentations of women, 3) organize nationwide boycotts of products advertised with sexist presentations, 4) advertisers should pay more serious attention to NARB recommendations, and 5) raise consciousness of the Federal Trade Commission.

0315
"Brickbats, laurels for ads with women," *Broadcasting*, August 30, 1971, 88:41.

NOW presented ten "old hat" awards to advertising agencies whose ads present demeaning images of women, and five awards to agencies whose ads show women as intelligent, active, professional people.

See 0149.   A. T. Foster.   "Is that really me?"

See 0151.   L. J. Friedman, *Sexism in Advertising, A Humorous Portrayal of the Image of Women.*

0316

Friedman, Leslie J.   "A quick and easy guide to limiting sexism in advertising."   Available from author, 1704 Stonybrook Dr., Cincinnati, Ohio 45237.   35¢.

One of the most effective means of limiting sexist advertising is to send letters to the presidents of manufacturing companies responsible for offensive ads.   This pamphlet details how to write the protest letter and where to find the names and addresses of corporate presidents.

See 0264.   J. K. Frye, "Using television commercials as an instructional strategy to teach persuasion."

See 0265.   D. Grant.   "Women's lib dialog tells adfolk: mend ad implications."

0317

"Joyce Snyder: FTC should apply its standards to women," *Media Report to Women,*   February 1, 1975, 3(2):7.

Ads which deceptively imply that women are obsessed with cleanliness should be governed by the same FTC standards that rule against deceptive advertising for cleaning products.

See 0163.   L. Komisar, "Image of women in advertising."

0318

Kovacs, Midge.   "Women's rights drive gets off the ground," *Advertising Age,* September 25, 1972, 43(39):73-74.

Midge Kovacs tells the story behind the public service ad campaign, "Woman Power, it's much too good to waste," which offers women inspiring female role models as well as debunking several sex role myths.

See 0274.   D. Kreinik, "Women: a growing force to be

reckoned with in advertising financial services.

0319
    Leonard, Mary. "Art thou sexist, fair adman?"
    The National Observer, November 9, 1974, 13(45):
    1+.

    Stewardesses for Women's Rights have made public
service announcements countering the "Fly Me" campaign
which they find detrimental to their image and unnecessarily jeopardizing to passenger safety. Other countering strategy include NOW petitions with the FTC regarding
ads that are deceptive and harmful to women, and NOW petitions filed with the FCC to deny license renewals to
stations who do not operate in the best interest of women.
While women do in fact work in varied occupations, are
intelligent consumers, and are resourceful homemakers and
mothers, advertisers insist on portraying them as dumb
blondes employed in serving occupations or as hapless
homemakers who are rescued by Mr. Clean, the White Knight
or other fantasy men.

0320
    "NOW salutes P&G, Lanvin, Wards, slaps at Wayen-
    berg's," *Advertising Age*, August 28, 1972, 43(35):
    3.

    NOW's 1972 "positive image of women" awards in ad-
vertising went to Procter and Gamble for the Pampers-clad
girl whose headline read "The future President of the
United States deserves a drier bottom." Positive image
awards and negative "keep her in her place" awards went
to the best and worst television and radio talk shows,
magazine publishers and book authors.

0321
    "NOW visits workshop to attack sexist ads,"
    Advertising Age, August 5, 1974, 45(31):39.

    At a NOW-staged counter forum during an *Ad Age* work-
shop, advertisers' consciousness were raised concerning
ads which portray women as passive, submissive and empty
headed (human characteristics not unknown among men) while
men are portrayed as compassionless, macho beings. These
stereotyped sex roles become believable models for people
who "feel they're being shown their true nature." A number of ads were denounced or praised depending on their
sexist or positive portrayals of people.

0322
    "NOW's awards score whiskey and two airlines,"
    The New York Times, August 26, 1974, p. 48.

    The 1974 "Hall of Shame" awards went to Black Velvet
Whiskey and "Fly me" ad campaigns. Positive Image Award
went to bank ads headlined "We give women a lot of credit"
and "We love women drivers."

See 0050. New York NOW, "Images of Women in the mass
media."

0323
    Papachristou, Judith. "Social change," *Women
    Together, A History in Documents of the Women's
    Movement in the United States*, ed. by J. Papa-
    christou. NY: Alfred Knopf, 1976. pp. 246-248.

    The National Organization for Women has opposed the
image of women in the media and in children's literature
by pressuring advertisers, publishers and educators to
project a non-stereotyped image. Examples of two ads are
shown: one portrays a strong woman, the other a man as
butt of a joke.

0324
    Pingree, Suzanne, Robert Parker Hawkins, Matilda
    Butler and William Paisley. "A scale for sexism,"
    Journal of Communication, 1976, 26(4):193-200.

    The authors devised a consciousness scale with which
ads may be qualitatively rated for sexist content. Level
I (most stereotyped) shows women and men as two dimensional decorations, Level II shows woman's place in the
home or in womanly occupation, while man's place is at
work or manly activities at home, Level III shows professional women whose first place is in the home and professional men whose first place is at work, Level IV shows
women and men as equals, while Level V shows women and
men as individuals without the dogmatism of Level IV.
The researchers measured the consciousness level of advertising in four types of magazines: *Playboy* had 54% of
its ad content for one year in Level I, 10% in Level IV,
Time and *Newsweek* both had approximately 60% in Level II
and 20% in Level IV, while Ms. had 40% of its ads at Level
II and 37% at Level IV. All four magazines had a preponderance of ads showing women as decorative objects or
engaged in "womanly" activity designed to keep woman in
her place. Advertising's repeated portrayal of women in
roles as housewife, mother, secretary, and nurse is not a
reflection of reality, but rather a stereotypical

distortion of reality.

0325
   Peck, Ellen. "Advertisers, unite! Strike a blow
   against motherhood," *Advertising Age*, January 24,
   1972, 43:33-34.

   TV advertising glorifies Woman as Breeder. Alternative ads are offered which could effectively sell dis-
posable diapers without glamorizing motherhood, and sell
laundry aids using independent, self-respecting husbands
and wives.

0326
   Pogrebin, Letty Cottin. "Toys: bad news/good
   news," *Ms.*, December, 1975, 4(6):60-63+.

   Advertising copy and package illustrations still
promote most toys by sex, but at least ten manufacturers
of toys have eliminated the sexist approach. The Public
Action Coalition on toys presented awards to manufacturers
whose products are imaginative but safe, inspire non-
violent activity, have non-sexist, multi-racial package
illustrations and use non-exploitive merchandising techniques.

0327
   "Public service ad campaign goes over the $3
   million mark," *Media Report to Women*, February
   1, 1974, 2(2):2.

   "Hire Him. He's Got Great Legs" and other Woman
Power ads have been successful both financially and in
terms of public recognition. They are seen in junior
high to college level English literature and social studies textbooks as well as in national magazines.

0328
   "Sex change for savings ad satisfies feminist complaint," *Advertising Age*, April 12, 1976, 47(15):
   36.

   A radio ad for life insurance drew feminist complaints
for making the wife look impractical and foolish. A
simple role reversal was employed whereby the wife buys
the insurance and the husband is reticent on matters concerning life insurance. Includes radio copy.

0329
   Sloane, Leonard. "Advertising: Women's lib to

give awards," *The New York Times*, August 26, 1971, p. 63.

Ten old fashioned straw hats were the awards given by NOW to ad agencies responsible for most outdated, degrading portraits of women in their 1971 ads. The negative ad stereotypes depicted women as not marriage material, as subservient lovers and overmanipulative mothers. "Breakthrough" awards were given to agencies whose ads showed positive portrayals of women including those with active women in athletics and professional roles.

See 0220. "Stewardess group sets counter to 'sexist' ads."

See 0763. "'Tear open the boxes' is new program in toy packaging and ads."

See 0206. C. Ventura, "Impact of women's liberation movement on advertising trends."

See 0115. "Women's proxy pressure."

BROADCAST MEDIA

Television in General

See also CHILDREN'S TELEVISION, 0907-0949.

0330
Aronoff, Craig E. *Age and Aging in Television Drama: Symbolic Functions and Images.* M.A. thesis, University of Pennsylvania, 1974.

Female televised characters most frequently appear in young and early-settled adulthood age groups, while male, televised characters most frequently appear in the middle-settled adulthood age group.

See 0907. J. R. Baris, "Study concludes that TV promotes stereotypes that adversely affect children."

See 0003. K. Barrett, "Daughters."

0331
Bird, Caroline. "What's television doing for 50.9% of Americans?," *TV Guide*, February 27, 1971, pp. 5-8.

Television rarely offers bright 13 year old girls be-lievable role models who are more appealing than the ecstatic floor waxer on ads. The black television image is reflecting the excitement previously reserved for white men, but women are still portrayed as housecleaners or sex objects. Television can more easily make a white charac-ter black than a male character female. Women older than 37 are rarely shown on television and women under 37 ap-pear primarily as props to be rescued by male colleagues.

See 0715. J. C. Bond, "The media image of black women."

0332
   Bruce, Elaine. "To see ourselves as others see us:
   Television and its portrayal of the female." Mon-
   treal: Sir George Williams University, 1974. ERIC
   (ED 103 010).

   A comparison of the image of women on television in
North American, Communist and Third World countries reveals that a distorted reflection of womanhood is presented by television almost worldwide. The author applies
the results of another study to her theory that television
has the power to pressure viewers to behave according to
the sex role standards projected on the screen. In this
case a reversal to non-stereotyped portrayals of the sexes
could be as successful in instilling confidence and independence in American women as the Cuban Revolution was
successful in changing the attitudes of Cuban women.
Television can become a significant force in helping women
change society's generalizations of the female.

See 0015. L. J. Busby, "Sex role research in the mass
media."

0333
   "CPB study finds women underused and underserved,"
   Broadcasting, November 24, 1975, 89:31-32.

   The women's task force of the Corporation for Public
Broadcasting performed a study revealing that the exclusion of women in adult programming implies women's unim-
portance to economic and public life. Children's
programming in CPB also degrades women by showing more
male characters in higher status positions. Statistics on
sex discrimination are also listed. For the entire study
see 0434.

See 0716. C. C. Clark, 'Television and social controls:
some observations on the portrayals of ethnic minorities."

0334
   Cole, Barry G. "Women on the screen," *Television*,
   by B. G. Cole. NY: Free Press, 1970. pp. 265-
   266.

   The image of women on television stifles women's
struggle for equality.

0335
   "Creating a stage for boys," *Media Report to*

Women, February 1, 1974, 2(2):5.

When ABC filmed a National Geographic special program documenting 19 teenagers climbing the Peruvian Andes, not one female teenager was filmed by the cameramen who decided that filming "girls reaching the top would make the ascent look too easy." A storm of protest concerning the sexist invisibility of actual female participants in this "news" documentary precipitated a last minute verbal dubbing that young women also reached the Andes peak.

See 0026. J. Faust, "Testimony before the NY City Commission on Human Rights."

0336
    Franzwa, Helen H. "The image of women in television: an annotated bibliography." US Commission on Civil Rights, 1976.

False images of women are found in television's entertainment programming, broadcast news, commercials and children's programs. Television's stereotyped women are most likely to be housewives in their twenties with passive, weak personalities. The entries in the 21 page annotated bibliography suggest that the portrayal of women on television has an impact on female career goals and vulnerability to violence.

0337
    Friedan, Betty. "Television and the feminine mystique," *TV Guide*, February 1, 1964 and February 8, 1964. Also in *Television*, by B. G. Cole. NY: Free Press, 1970. pp. 267-275.

Television's "glamorous" housewife image of women is the high school girl's role model and therefore her most clearly defined aspiration.

0338
    Frueh, Terry and Paul E. McGhee. "Traditional sex role development and amount of time spent watching TV," *Developmental Psychology*, 1975, 11:109.

A correlation exists between strong acceptance of traditional sex roles and high amounts of televison viewing. This correlation is true for both sexes and does not change with age. See 0932 for an extended report of this study.

0339
    Frum, Barbara. "The social problem of women,"
    Saturday Night, June, 1967, 82:41+.

    Three television documentaries look at women "from
the womb out" by dealing with hormonal whims and "feminine
inadequacies," and mocking those women who managed to break
the feminine stereotype. Television would never dare to
espouse such platitudinous views about blacks.

See 1005. J. Garbarino and S. Turner, "Television and vocational socialization."

0340
    Gerbner, George. "Violence in television drama,
    trends and symbolic functions," *Television and
    Social Behavior*, V. 1, ed. by George A. Comstock
    and Eli A. Rubinstein. Rockville, Md: National
    Institute of Mental Health, 1972. pp. 28-187.
    (HE 20.2402/T23^2).

    Analysis of 762 leading characters of violent pro-
gramming during the television seasons 1967, 1968, and 1969
reveals that women typically represented love or family interest while men were typically unmarried. Male perpetra-
tors of violence had 6.9:1 odds for getting away with
crime, while violent women getting away with crime met odds
of 1.6:1. Women, especially unmarried women, were most
likely to be victimized. Married women were more likely
than single women to be violent. Tables include violence
index for three commercial networks, children's cartoons
and prime time programming.

See 0028. E. Goldfield, "A woman is a sometime thing."

0341
    Gross, Larry. "The 'real' world of television,"
    Today's Education, January-February, 1974, 63(1):
    86+.

    Woman's role on television is either that of a young,
attractive, romantic figure, or victim of violence while
men are sometimes in the role of victim, sometimes murderer.
Nurses are usually portrayed by young women while doctors
and teachers are usually mature men. A questionnaire, ad-
ministered to sample groups of heavy and light television
viewers of similar educational backgrounds, determined
that the heavy television viewer perceived reality and sex
roles in terms of television reality rather than in terms
of the world structure as it actually exists.

0342
"HEW study to determine the impact of television
on sex discrimination and sex-role stereotyping,"
"...*To Form a More Perfect Union...*" *Justice for
American Women*; Report on the Observance of International Women's Year, 1976. (Y3.W84 1/976)
pp. 253-254.

Although content analyses concerning sex role stereotyping on television have been made, few studies have researched the effects of sexism on the airwaves. The IWY
Commission recommends a study by US Department of Health,
Education and Welfare to determine the impact of television
programming and advertising on sex discrimination in American society.

See 0724. J. L. Hinton, et al., "Tokenism and improving
imagery of blacks in television drama and comedy."

0343
"The image of women in television," *Intellect*,
1975, 103:424-425.

Television commercials, soap operas and prime time
programs all stereotype women in the few accepted roles as
housecleaner and cosmetic purchaser, with passive, subservient and dependent personalities. Two prime time
television characters, Amy Prentiss and Mary Richards,
deviate from this norm as independent women in positions of
authority.

0344
"An incredible lack of 'good taste'," *The New
York Times*, January 20, 1974, p. D-17.

Letters to the editor comment on television's rape
theme as discussed by Beth Gutcheon (see 0410), the need
for a convincing teleplay about rape, and an explication
of television series "Owen Marshall" as a study in misogyny.

See 1007. N. Kaniuga, et al., "Working women portrayed
on evening television programs."

See 0924. E. Kaye, "Sexism."

0345
Keller, Suzanne. "The future role of women,"

American Academy of Political and Social Science, Philadelphia. *Annals*, 1973, 408:1-12.

When interacting with the female sex, boys of the future will learn to compete with girls, men will learn to lose as well as win to women and will be free to throw off the artificial, obsolete superiority to women. This eventual overthrowing of unnatural sex roles could become reality much sooner if the powerful medium, television, would eliminate the idealized, outdated sex roles in its programming and advertising.

With the present decreased emphasis on maternity, the female role will necessarily change in the future. Housework will become an adjunct of life rather than its central purpose, women will no longer be economically dependent on men, and women will enjoy greater self-esteem.

0346

Levan, Kathryn. *Television and Sex Roles*. M.A. thesis, University of Pennsylvania, 1974.

Examination of the relationship between television viewing and the sex role attitudes of viewers indicated that television reinforces sex stereotyped behavior among viewers.

0347

Liebert, Robert M. "Modeling and the media," *The School Psychology Digest*, 1975, 4:22-29.

The sex role socialization of children is facilitated by television's exposure, acquisition and acceptance of these values. Liebert supports his theory with research from a number of studies concerning sex roles and televised aggression.

0348

Liebert, Robert M., John M. Neale, and Emily S. Davidson. "Television content: stereotyped and social roles," *The Early Window: Effects of Television on Children and Youth*. (Pergamon General Psychology Series, 34). NY: Pergamon, 1973. pp. 18-22.

Television is more than an entertainment medium; it describes the present social structure and shapes attitudes about ourselves, others and society in general. In so doing television perpetuates a biased reflection of the sex roles. The most powerful group, the white

American man, is portrayed as young, middle-class and unmarried, aggressively violent, and least likely to be punished for aggressions. Women are stereotypically found in the sexual context of romantic or family role and are married, divorced, widowed or engaged. Women are least likely to be involved in violence, but when confronted by violence, are most likely to be victims. Unlike men, women who participate in aggression are usually unsuccessful. Single women are most often victimized; employed women are most often villainous. A "cement" metaphor is employed to describe television's rigid adherence to a conservative status quo that doesn't reflect the current accelerated social change.

See 0928. M. L. Long and R. J. Simon, "Roles and statuses of women on children and family TV programs."

See 0932. P. McGhee, "Television as a source of learning sex role stereotypes."

See 0507. S. MacLaine, *You Can Get There From Here.*

0349
    McNeil, Jean C. "Feminism, femininity, and the television series: a content analysis," *Journal of Broadcasting*, 1975, 19:259-271.

    A study of 43 television programs, of which average inter-coder reliability was 92%, revealed the following results: male characters outnumbered female characters by over 2:1, marriage and parenthood were considered more central to women's lives than to men's, traditional division of labor in marriage prevailed with 78% of married men and 21% of married women employed. When women did work, they were assigned to low prestige positions under male supervisors. Television plots most often centered around female characters' personally oriented problems and male characters' professionally oriented problems. Female characters, who were more passive than male characters, often left their problems for other people to solve. Television programming does not acknowledge the existence of the feminist movement. By presenting no alternatives to traditional sex roles, television implies that these behavior patterns are the only appropriate roles for women.

0350
    McNeil, Jean C. "Imagery of women in TV drama: some procedural and interpretive issues,"

Journal of Broadcasting, 1975, 19:283-288.

McNeil counters the charges and questions the research validity of John F. Seggars preceding article (see
0395). She also takes issue with his comments on the
relationship between women's anatomy and women's roles.

See 1009. A. L. Manes and P. Melnyk, "Televised models
of female achievement."

See 0047. "Media in Montana."

0351
    Meyer, Karl E. "Sexism and sadism," *Saturday
    Review*, November 29, 1975, 3(5):41.

Women are usually projected as ninnies in television
advertising and swooning housewives on game shows. Although contemporary American feminism has been dealt with
in television's "Woman Alive!", no inspiring American
series has been produced about pioneer American feminists
comparable to the rare positive image of women seen on the
BBC "Shoulder to Shoulder" series.

0352
    Miller, M. Mark and Byron Reeves. "Dramatic TV
    content and children's sex-role stereotypes,"
    Journal of Broadcasting, 1976, 20:35-50.

Two content analyses, one evaluating the types of sex
role stereotypes on television programming and the other
surveying children's reactions to television stereotypes
revealed that television helps shape children's sex role
perceptions. Children tend to model themselves after
televised characters. When exposed to televised portrayals
of women in counter-stereotypic occupations, children were
more likely to endorse those occupations as appropriate
for women, than were those subjects who did not see the
program.

0353
    National Organization for Women, Kalamazoo Area
    Chapter. "A week with Merv Griffin," available
    from Kalamazoo Committee for Children's Television,
    5228 Ridgebrook Dr., Kalamazoo, MI 49002.

Though aimed clearly at adults, "The Merv Griffin
Show" is broadcast from 4:30 - 6:30 PM, during children's
prime viewing hours. The program was monitored to

determine its suitability for children who may watch it with their parents. Findings reveal the show's dependence on highly stereotypic sexual and ethnic slurs for humor, as well as reinforcement of sex role stereotypes for the sake of humor, even when women intend to counteract these attitudes. The program was found to be unacceptable viewing fare for children.

0354
National Organization for Women, National Capitol Area Chapter. *Women in the Wasteland Fight Back, A Study of the Treatment of Females and Males in WRC-TV Programming Aired During a Composite Week.* Washington, DC: NOW, 1972.

A commercial Washington, DC television station, WRC-TV was monitored during a composite week from 7 AM to 1 AM, May 30 to June 17, 1972, in order to determine statistical discrepancies between male and female appearances and treatment of the two sexes in programming. Summaries of each article appear separately in this bibliography.

0355
"National sisters communication service tells ABC its opinion of show on rape of nuns," *Media Report to Women,* June 1, 1976, 4(6):4.

Reprint of a letter to ABC-TV president expresses concern for the stereotyping of nuns as more tragic rape victims than any other woman. The letter offers advice concerning the image of all women including minority and elderly women who are too often stereotyped and voiceless.

0356
Northcott, Herbert C., John F. Seggar and James L. Hinton. "Trends in TV portrayal of blacks and women," *Journalism Quarterly,* 1975, 52:741-744.

From 1971 to 1973 the appearance of black men and women on television decreased while the appearance of white women increased. White women were more often seen in the workforce than black women who have almost disappeared from the screen. Television seems to be responding more to the women's liberation movement of the 1970's than to the black civil rights movement of the 1960's.

See 0279. S. A. O'Brien, "Colgate looks with a new eye

at women."

0357
O'Connor, John J. "Be mad, ladies, but don't
be muddleheaded," *The New York Times,* July 1,
1973, p. D-13.

In response to Judy Klemesrud's article (see 0386)
O'Connor argues that people don't watch television for
role models. Even if finding role models were motivation
for watching television, the portrayal of a female judge
is little more than the female equivalent of male action/
adventure roles, and is therefore a chic fantasy symbol
which doesn't promise much in the way of satisfactory role
models.

0358
Peck, Ellen. "Television's romance with repro-
duction," *Pronatalism, the Myth of Mom and Apple
Pie,* ed. by Ellen Peck and Judith Senderowitz.
NY: T. Y. Crowell, 1974. pp. 78-97.

Television's soap opera plots, pre-game show chatter,
detective show and sit-com plots all equate womanhood with
motherhood. Television commercials exploit pronatalist
bias even further by using large families as product sales
tools, idealizing family situations, sentimentalizing the
image of children, and promoting the "madonna image" of
women.

0359
Press, Tina. "News woman in a man's world," *Public
Telecommunications Review,* February, 1975, 3:28-30.

The conclusions one would draw about American women if
television were the only source of data, would not include
the following realities: 44% of US women over age 16 work,
63% of all working women are married, 50% of American
mothers whose children are ages 6-17 work. Television
distorts reality by depicting 88% of its advertising women
as housewives, by hiring only men as game show hosts, and
depicting women primarily as sexy, dull people on dramatic
programs. A major reason for the stereotyped portrayal of
women is the preponderance of male writers and corporate
executives. However broadcasting license challenges and
discrimination suits are helping to raise the consciousness of broadcasters.

See 0519. G. Rock, "I can't believe I watched the whole
thing."

0360

Rosen, Diane. "TV and the single girl," *TV Guide,* November 6, 1971, pp. 13-14+.

Young single women find no soulmates on television. "The Dating Game" offends, "That Girl's" incompetence presents a bizarre view of single life, and "The Mary Tyler Moore Show", though offering a more realistic portrait of the unattached, self-sufficient woman, nevertheless presents her work responsibilities as more accurately reflecting those of secretary than associate producer. The image of the young single woman on television offers no better role model than any other television woman.

0361

Rossi, Alice S. "Equality between the sexes: an immodest proposal; institutional levers for achieving sex equality," *The Woman in America,* ed. by Robert Jay Lifton. (The Daedalus Library, 3). Boston: Houghton Mifflin, 1965. pp. 119-139; also in *Roles Women Play: Readings Toward Women's Liberation,* ed. by Michele Hoffnung Garskof. (Contemporary Psychology series). Belmont, CA: Brooks/Cole Publishers, 1971. pp. 145-164.

Pre-school age boys see active role models in the working class men who drive trucks and pave roads. This image is reinforced by television's cowboys, baseball players and Indians who shoot guns, swing bats and sling arrows. The pre-school girl sees as her less active role model, her own mother and television mothers, women whose domestic roles are in parenthood, but who defer to men in all other situations. If exposed to professional women with drive and dedication outside the home, then when grown, these women will not feel threatened by an egalitarian relationship with a husband who shares in parenthood and home maintenance.

0362

Saturday Afternoon, 16mm, 11 mins., color, rental, $15, purchase, $150. Teleketics, 1229 S. Santee St., Los Angeles, CA 90015.

Through mime technique and make-up, and robot-like motions, the film comments on the influence of television programming and commercials on the sex role rituals of a husband, wife and son.

0363

Seggar, John F. "Imagery as reflected through TV's cracked mirror," *Journal of Broadcasting,*

1975. 19:297-299.

Should television reflect society as it presently exists, or reflect a different model in terms of women's roles?

0364

   Seggar, John F. "Women's imagery on TV: feminist, fair maiden, or maid? Comments on McNeil," *Journal of Broadcasting*, 1975, 19:289-294.

   Seggar defends the research questioned by Jean C. McNeil, supports her contention that female occupational roles on television are limited and stereotypic, then cautions against the value judgments implicit in her study. (See 0350.)

0365/0366

   Seggar, John F. and Penny Wheeler. "World of work on TV: Ethnic and sex representation in TV drama," *Journal of Broadcasting*, 1973, 17: 201-214.

   Occupational stereotypes were studied in a sample of 250 half-hour television units. Of the 1,830 portrayals, 81.7% were male and 18.3% female. Female characters included white and black women and two Chicana women but no American Indian women. Minority women were generally portrayed in occupations of higher prestige value than were white women, although the reverse was true for men. Women of all ethnic groups were most often limited to five traditional occupations while men had much greater variety. Women tend to be grossly underrepresented on television, and when visible, are limited to stereotyped occupations. A more comprehensive occupational picture of career opportunities might enlighten viewers of career opportunities available.

See 0045. Ellen Sherman. "Femme scribes cop top jobs."

0367

   Smythe, Dallas W. "Reality as presented by television," *Public Opinion Quarterly*, 1954, 18: 143-156.

   Sex role stereotyping was evident in the earliest

years of television. In 1954, female villains were most often working women, while housewives were rarely portrayed as villainous. Male villains were usually non-American, while the character of female non-Americans often approached the heroic magnitude of white American male protagonists. American women fell short of this model. Housewives were the most stereotyped of all female characters.

0368
Sprung, Barbara. "Involving parents - television," *Non-Sexist Education for Young Children, A Practical Guide*, by B. Sprung. NY: Citation Pr, 1975. pp. 14-16.

Teachers may raise the feminist consciousness of students and their parents by facilitating discussion of the unrealistic sex roles seen on television. Mothers, grandmothers, aunts and babysitters do not discuss soap and floor wax all day. Neither do men exclaim over glossy floors or dirty rugs. Children are encouraged to write letters to networks protesting television programming and advertising.

0369
"Statement of Ms. Jane Hoback, Cochairman, Media Task Force, Denver Chapter, National Organization for Women," *Sex and Violence on TV*, Hearings before the Subcommittee on Communications of the Committee on Interstate and Foreign Commerce, House of Representatives. Washington, DC: US Government Printing Office, 1977. pp. 25-29. (Y4.In8/4.94-140).

Television programming deals with rape as a sexual matter rather than as the crime of violence that it is. Television's rape victims are invariably young and beautiful women who "ask for it" by walking dark streets alone, opening doors to anyone, and remaining ignorant of self-defense techniques. The "woman as victim" theme becomes a ploy facilitating an "inevitable glorious capture of the rapist by our hero. Rape as a crime is just another way to make the male star look good." Woman's role as sex object, used as a means to rescue a poorly written, mundane plot, is a violation of woman's integrity. if television would cease the portrayal of woman as sex object and portray her more realistically as the intelligent, capable, competent human being she is, then "the image of women in the public eye would change drastically."

0370
Wolfe, Morris. "Television: a propaganda machine for male supremacy," *Saturday Night*, April,
1974, 89:43.

Male television screen appearances outnumber female
3:1 in television interviews, voiceover announcements,
and talk show hosts. When women do appear on television,
they sing songs in celebration of their submissiveness,
play supporting roles to male co-hosts, and serve coffee.
One network is considering establishing minimum guidelines in improving its treatment of women, following a
feminist group's attempt to block license renewal.

Prime Time Programming

0371
"Analysis of WRC-TV entertainment talk show,
public affairs and sports programming aired during the composite week," *Women in the Wasteland Fight Back*, by National Organization for
Women, National Capitol Area Chapter, 1972.
pp. 118-138.

Results of the 43 non-dramatic hours monitored
showed 80% of the programs hosted by men, 20% by women.
Of the guests or participants, 28% were female in spite
of the fact that 53% of the population and a high percentage of the viewing audience is female. Topics of conversation relating to women included homemaking and fashion
while the changing role of women (which does interest a
segment of the viewing audience) was disregarded.

0372
Arenstein, Howard Leigh. *The Effect of Television
on Children's Stereotyping of Occupational Roles*.
M.A. thesis, University of Pennsylvania, 1974.

Interviews with 60 children, aged three through six,
revealed strong stereotyped attitudes toward the roles of
doctor, teacher and police officer. When the stereotyped
responses were challenged, the children accepted television characterizations as evidence for non-sex related
occupations. Examples of female doctors on television,
then, could further influence a child's acceptance of
women in male-dominated professions.

0373
Arlen, Michael J. "Three views of woman,"
New Yorker, December 8, 1975. 51:154+; also in
The View from Highway 1: Essays on Television,
by M. J. Arlen. NY: Farrar, Straus and
Giroux, 1976. pp. 264-277.

I. Many television commercials feature a housewife
who resembles "simpering, brainless jelly" and is pathologically obsessed with the state of cleanliness of her
kitchen floor or bathroom bowl. The Wisk commercial
however employs unusual brutality in its Cinderella-in-
reverse tale of one woman's embarrassment in the hotel
corridor.

II. "Rhoda" and "Phyllis" are two television programs
featuring the Modern Woman as protagonist, but they are
actually just modernized versions of standard sit-com
heroines. Rhoda is the wise-cracking husband-manipulator
while Phyllis is the scatterbrained, meddlesome widow.

III. The PBS account of George Sand on "Notorious
Woman" places disproportionate emphasis on the rhetoric
and costuming that appeal to its modern feminist audience.

0374
Aronoff, Craig. "Old age in prime time,"
Journal of Communication, 1974, 24(4):86-87.

Television's age/sex stereotypes follow a pattern:
Young adult females outnumber young males 2:1, while
television's elderly are 5% of both sexes. Aging, especially for women, is associated with increasing evil,
failure and unhappiness.

0375
Bond, Jean Carey. "Flip Wilson, The Mod Squad,
Mission Impossible: Is this what it's really
like to be Black?" *Redbook*, February, 1972,
138(4):82-83+.

Flip Wilson's character, Geraldine, offends black
women who regard the transvestite image as a stereotype of
black woman as domineering, castrating and, literally, a
man in woman's clothing.

0376
Cameron, Sue. "Police drama: women are on the
case," *Ms.*, October, 1974, 3(4):104+.

Three prime time weekly dramatic series, "Police

Woman," "Get Christie Love," and "Amy Prentiss," each have positive female leads whose diverse roles take them beyond the television stereotypes of police women handling only juvenile and rape cases. The series also have female writers and story advisors.

0377
    Christ, Carol. "Marcus Welby or Archie Bunker: will the real chauvinist pig please stand up?," *Christian Century*, March 12, 1975, 92:260-262+.

Jim Anderson ("Father Knows Best") is compared to an omniscient God the Father while Mike Kiley, Marcus Welby's protege, becomes a Divine Son and product of virgin birth with Welby as his sole parent. The sex roles on "Marcus Welby" define men/doctors as saviors and women/patients as people who need saving. This true chauvinism in the guise of a good, kind father figure who condescendingly guides women to their true, unselfish role is more subtly sexist than Archie Bunker's treatment of Edith. Exorcising television of a father who knows best would liberate the medium further than would the humiliation of a blatant Archie Bunker.

0378
    "Comparison of treatment of females and males in dramatic programming and variety shows aired by WRC-TV," *Women in the Wasteland Fight Back*, by National Organization for Women, National Capitol Chapter. Washington, DC: NOW, 1972.

Monitoring of prime time dramatic programming during a composite week revealed the following recurrent themes: of 200 characters on 17 programs, 30% were female. No program listed a female name in the title. Forty percent of all male characters were over age 40 while only 15% of the female characters were in this older age group, therefore 85% of the female characters were in the more sexually desirable age classification. Of all characters with occupational roles, the 21% working women most often had low status positions and were frequently portrayed as emotionally unstable, alcoholic, bitter or thrice-divorced. Men who were portrayed as emotionally unstable totaled 1.7%. Although most variety shows had an equal balance of male and female guests, women were frequently dressed scantily, referred to as "honey" or "baby" rather than by their names, and were often the butt of jokes. While the women's bodies were emphasized both physically and verbally on programming with dual sex audiences, men's bodies were always covered and never discussed.

0379
Conklin, George, Sandra Gess and Gail Joralemon.
Sex Role Stereotyping in Prime Time Television:
the United Methodist Women Television Monitoring
Project, 1976. Available from Methodist Service
Center, 7820 Reading Road, Cincinnati, Ohio
45237. $1.00.

An extensive study of 17 family programs and 18 adult
programs from the 1975-76 season includes ten graphs and
charts which measure the ratio of male to female characters by network; the major, supporting and minor roles by
sex; age of characters by sex; character occupations by
sex; occupational authority by sex; and aggression/
victimization by sex of character.

0380
Donagher, Patricia G., Rita Wicks Poulos, Robert
M. Liebert, and Emily S. Davidson. "Race, sex
and social example: an analysis of character
portrayal on inter-racial television entertainment," *Psychological Reports*, 1975, 37:1023-1034.

Viewers learn attitudes from television by recognition (blatant underrepresentation of women facilitates
attitude of female insignificance), through occupational
roles (female unemployment strongly contrasts the professional, prestigious and powerful male occupations) and
portrayals of individuals (competent male police officers
rescue threatened female police officer). Analysis of
the 60 characters from 139 prime time television episodes
reveals subtle lessons about character portrayal of 29
white male characters, 13 white female, 11 black male,
and seven black female characters.

0381
Edgar, Patricia, *Sex Type Socialization and Tele-*
vision Family Comedy Programs. (La Trobe University. School of Education. Technical Report,
2). Bundoora, Australia: La Trobe University.
1971.

Twelve Australian prime time television shows from
the 1972 season are examined for stereotyped female behavior. Seven themes emerged: the single woman, marriage,
women's interests, occupations, sex role behavior, behavioral characteristics of women, and sex education. In
each theme women were commonly acquiescent toward men,
and were self-deprecating. When unfortunate situations
befell women in sitcoms, canned laughter was common, however no canned laughter followed the same situations be-
falling men. The audience was led to laugh at women's

unfortunate predicaments and sympathize with men's. Television socializes women to behave a certain way and teaches men to regard women as less significant.

0382
Efron, Edith. "Is television making a mockery of the American woman?" *TV Guide*, August 8, 1970, pp. 7-9; also in *Mass Media: The Invisible Environment Revisited*, ed. by Robert J. Glessing and William P. White. Chicago: Science Research Association, 1976, pp. 143-145.

In a discussion with the group, Media Women, Shulamith Firestone commented on advertising's psychological effects which create a blurred distinction between sexuality and individuality among women. Susan Brownmiller found Emma Peel to be the only heroic woman on television. This 1970 article in which feminists criticize television for its insulting, demeaning stereotypes of women, has a 1976 introduction in the Glessing title, which acknowledges the prevalence of the same 1970 stereotypes on television six years later. In 1970 Ti-Grace Atkinson called commercials "legal pornography" in which women are seen only as sex objects or reproducers. Besides protesting women's image on television the feminists also protested television's news coverage of the movement which ignored serious content while focusing on lunatic fringe non-issues like bra-burning and violence. The author foresees a gradual "humanization" of television's portrayal of women both in programming and news coverage. The introduction indicates that "eventually" has been only minimally realized by 1976.

0383
Gross, Leonard. "Why can't a woman be more like a man?" *TV Guide*, August 11, 1973, pp. 6-8+.

Several reasons are offered for shelving plans to use female leads in prime time dramatic series: writers tend to write for men; the 52% female population prefers to see men; the male audience feels discomfort at the sight of strong women, media men are threatened by female dramatic leads.

See 0410. B. R. Gutcheon, "Look for cop-outs on prime time, not on 'soaps'," *The New York Times*, December 16, 1973. p. D-21.

0384
Harrington, Stephanie. "Women get the short end

of the shtick," *The New York Times*, November 18, 1973, p. D-21.

A comparison of three television variety/comedy specials about women show two attempts at liberated chic with jokes that still essentially insult women, while the third, a Lily Tomlin special, shows the absurdity of situations rather than poking fun at women themselves.

0385
"How to make a show on hysterectomies be men's programming," *Media Report to Women*, November 1, 1975, 3(11):6.

A letter to NBC President analyzes the roles of five female sex objects in one prime time drama.

0386
Klemesrud, Judy. "TV's women are dingbats," *The New York Times*, May 27, 1973, p. D-15.

The only liberated role model on television is Miss Kitty, a 19th century saloonkeeper. Television's other prime time women are ding-a-lings, sex kittens, lovable widows, or detectives' secretaries. With television recognized as a powerful force in shaping people's attitudes, the repetition of television's birdbrained women makes it hard to believe that some true life women have become successful doctors, lawyers, executives and cops.

0387
Kopecky, Gina. "You're under arrest, Sugar," *The Village Voice*, December 9, 1974, p. 106.

Impressions of a television monitor after spending the first week gathering demographic statistics for a NOW survey concerning the image of women on television. The author notes black female detectives surrounded by white men, "evidence of the male-bonding phenomenon" in "The Rookies," Planet of the Apes," and women primarily cast in roles of subservience for whom the promise of pleasing men is the only motivation.

0388
Kreigsman, Alan M. "Desperation in NBC 'sneak preview,'" *The Washington Post*, August 28, 1971, p. C-7.

A television pilot stereotypes women as representatives from the over-20, over-30, and over-40 slots of womanhood.

0389
> Lindsey, Karen. "Gene Kelly's wonderful world of girls," *Women: A Journal of Liberation*, 1970, 1(3):39.

The prime time television special portrayed women as catty, male-oriented, castrating bitches. In each skit women were stripped of dignity and condescendingly treated as "stupid, subordinate, social inferiors." She compares this treatment of women to the out-of-vogue condescension of blacks.

0390
> Mariani, John. "Women in jeopardy: plot line of the year," *New York*, April 14, 1975, 8:40-43.

The "woman in jeopardy" theme proliferates prime time television with a new twist - women are no longer helpless damsels in distress but are able to avoid murder without male assistance.

0391
> "The medium is macho," *Human Behavior*, August, 1975, 4(8):71.

On prime time television Maude Finley sits when her husband tells her to, Fred Sanford grimaces at the sight of an unattractive stewardess and Frank Cannon thanks male informers with a $20 bill and thanks female informers with a pat on the cheek. The imagery gives child viewers a negative impression of womanhood. Viewers are urged to use their power to complain, praise and pressure the networks to change the image of women in programming and to teach children to be critical of stereotypes.

0392
> "NBC compulsion to re-air 'Born Innocent' is seen; portrays women as rapists," *Media Report to Women*, December, 1975, 3(12):10.

At a Senate hearing members of Lesbian Feminist Liberation, Inc., testified against television stereotyping of lesbians committing violent, though hypothetical, rape with a broomstick when the more common form of rape by male perpetrator is rarely portrayed as brutal.

See 0728. "NFBO lists TV complains and protests 'That's My Mama'."

0393
    Pincus, Ann. "Shape up, Bionic Woman!," *News-week*, November 15, 1976, 88(20):15.

    Prime time television characters are examined for a larger-than-life heroine who might make a worthy role model for American girls. Mary Richards functions as the newsroom's Ann Landers, Rhoda is neurotic, Phyllis is dumb and Maude verges on hysteria, while Police Woman is a flirt who must be rescued from the villains by police-men. Wonder Woman rescues only her beau from harm and the Bionic Woman is weaker than her $6 million counterpart even though both are made from the same machines. Even the most bigoted, clumsiest men on television perform as decision makers and problem solvers - a function denied television women. An adequate female role model should also make these difficult decisions. Television should reflect the lifestyle of American women who are simultan-eously wives, mothers and working women. A realistic character like this could be called the "Three-Dimensional Woman."

0394
    Rock, Gail. "Same time, same station, same sexism," *Ms.*, December, 1973, 2(6):24-26+.

    Of the 62 prime time programs with regularly appear-ing leading performers, in 1973, 48 had sole male leads and 6 (9.5%) had sole female comedy leads. These six characters ran the gamut from zaniness to frustration to grotesquerie. In the 48 male-dominated programs women were portrayed as male appendages: housewives, secretar-ies, nurses, mothers and daughters. On the 26 crime shows, women were increasingly victimized. Behind the scenes of these 62 programs women were found in one position as ex-ecutive producer, one script consultant, three writers and no regularly scheduled female director.

0395
    Seggar, John F. "Imagery of women in television drama: 1974," *Journal of Broadcasting*, 1975, 19:273-282.

    A descriptive analysis of five weeks of prime time viewing yielded the following results: of 946 female roles, 9% were major roles, 65% were bit parts, 9% were black women, and 6% women of other minority groups. A study of sex related factors showed photographic references to female anatomy to be 13%, as opposed to feminist charges of sex symbol orientation of camera men. Feminist charges of television's overabundance of passive women was countered by the 33% statistic of women directing men. Other changes in female imagery on television include the increase of women in major roles from 18% in 1971 to 38% in 1974, and a decrease in stereotyped female occupations from 50% in 1971 to 30% in 1974. The author recommends higher representation of minority group women on television and reflection of female occupational competence in television drama.

0396
    Tedesco, Nancy S. "Patterns in primetime," *Journal of Communication*, 1974, 24(2):119-124.

In prime time dramatic television programming from 1969-1972, women had 28% representation. In comparison to male characters, females were more often cast in comic or light roles, were more often married, and more often killed. Female victims outnumbered female killers 3:1 while the ratio of male victims to male killers was 1:2. The stereotypical female character was younger and less likely to be employed than the stereotypical male character. Such stereotypes repeatedly projected on television make it difficult for the viewer to recognize equality between the sexes.

See 0422. J. Turow, "Advising and ordering, daytime, prime time."

0397
    "We're not 'Muddleheaded'," *The New York Times*, July 15, 1973, p. D-13.

Letters to the editor by Judy Klemesrud and Midge Kovacs answer O'Connor's editorial response (see 0357) to Klemesrud's initial article (see 0386). The letters deal with television's dearth of professional women on television when numerous sitcom men own businesses or are successful lawyers, writers, psychologists and photographers. Female characters are rarely employed in sitcoms and are usually portrayed as emotional cripples in television drama.

0398
    "Why have men writing women's shows?," *Media Report to Women*, November 1, 1975, 3(11):6.

Excerpts from several letters and articles attacking

the role stereotyping on "Shoulder to Shoulder," a television program about British suffragists written by men.

0399
    "Women on Words and Images." *Channeling Children*,
    1975. Available from author, PO Box 2163, Prince-
    ton, NJ 08540. $2.50; also in ERIC (ED 110 068).

Every episode of 16 top Nielson rated prime time television shows of the 1973 and 1974 seasons were reviewed.
Although considered primarily adult entertainment, each
show is commonly watched by children. Because children
model their behavior after that observed on television,
the purpose of the study was to determine the types of
sex stereotyped role behavior children learn from television. The results indicate that more males than females
appeared on all shows examined. Most women, especially
mothers were economically dependent on men, women exhibited more negative behavior than men, especially on adventure series where negative behavior was evidenced in
82% of the female and 27% of male characters. Women were
also more than twice as likely to show incompetence as
men, while men were twice as likely to cleverly employ
sarcasm in put-downs.

Children, by virtue of age and limited experience,
are unable to separate truth in advertising from environment while a male voice of authority summarizes the
product's virtues. The 214 ads examined show men in
twice as many different and varied occupations than
women. Women were most often seen doing housework or caring for a sick adult. Suggestions for counteracting the
effects of television's stereotypes on children are
offered.

Daytime Programming

0400
    "Analysis of male and female participation on WRC
    'Quiz Show' programming," *Women in the Wasteland
    Fight Back*, National Organization for Women,
    National Capitol Chapter, Washington, DC: NOW,
    1972. pp. 139-146.

The seven quiz shows examined were hosted by seven
men. Even though female contestants outnumbered male
contestants, when moderators, announcers, celebrities and
prize exhibitors were all counted, the ratio of men to

women was 150:112. Hosts often discussed male contestants'
occupations while 33% of the female contestants occupations were never mentioned. Women were often called
"honey" or other inappropriate terms of endearment while
men were called by their names. Women as a group were
commonly the butt of jokes while, during the composite
week, generic man was never the butt of a joke.

0401
    Bart, Pauline B. "Depression in middle-aged
    women," *Woman in Sexist Society: Studies in
    Power and Powerlessness*, ed. by Vivian Gornick
    and Barbara K. Moran. NY: Basic Books, 1971.
    pp. 99-117; also *Readings on the Psychology of
    Women*, ed. by Judith M. Bardwick. NY: Harper
    and Row, 1972.

A common theme in soap opera and women's magazines
is woman's devotion to husband and children, and her vi-
carious living through their achievements. This article
examines the types of depression common to women who live
the feminine ideal taught them by the media. "There is
no bar mitzvah for menopause." To avoid these serious
depressions in middle age, women should be supported and
encouraged to fulfill their *own* potentials, rather than
poking fun at them in Sophie Portnoy caricatures when
they get older.

0402
    Bethel, Elizabeth R. "Evaluation of traits of fe-
    male characters on daytime TV soap operas," *Sis-
    com '75, Women's (and Men's) Communication*; Pro-
    ceedings of the Speech Communication Association's
    Summer Conference XI, 1975. pp. 63-71. Also
    in ERIC (ED 127 643). pp. 69-77.

An exploration of soap opera figures as role models
for female viewers.

0403
    "Comparison of treatment of females and males
    in soap operas aired by WRC-TV," *Women in the
    Wasteland Fight Back*, by National Organization
    for Women, National Capitol Chapter. Washing-
    ton, DC: NOW, 1972. pp. 52-90.

Of the four soap operas monitored, male characters
outnumber female 52:45. The total number of appearances
of characters was 54.5% male, 45.5% female. Eighty-
eight percent of the male characters held jobs while 46.6%
of the female characters were employed, mostly in lower

status jobs rather than professional. Men were shown at
work during 52% of their appearances, women 17%. Appearances in family roles were 15% male, 50% female. The
average ages were 40 years for men, 31.9 years for women.
Advice was given 30 times by men, nine times by women.
Advice was received eight times by men, 31 times by women.
Men advised women on seven broad subjects such as health
and legal problems; women advised men on two subjects:
marriage and love life. Ten percent of female lead characters had mental problems, while no men had mental problems.
The article lists characters and plot summary for each
program monitored, and tables which break down characters
by race, sex, occupation, age and subject of advice.

0404
     Downing, Mildred. "Heroine of the Daytime Serial,"
     Journal of Communication, 1974, 24(2):130-137.

     Even though the serial is a male-dominated genre,
female characters have equal representation, are intelligent, self-reliant and articulate, and grow old grace-
fully and without diminution of effectiveness in ability
to help those in need.

0405
     Durdeen-Smith, Jo. "Daytime TV: soft soaping
     the American woman," *Village Voice*, February 8,
     1973, pp. 19+.

     After watching nine soap operas on three consecutive
days the author noted the following trends: the people
are not characters, but rather embodiments of problems.
All crises are personal rather than political, social or
moral. The women control and direct the emotional trans-
actions while the more passive men are compared to the
"inert, meddled decency that dogs have." She notes three
types of women: one is the wise confidante, one has a
highly developed tactical ability that is used solely to
manipulate events of the heart (i.e., male possession),
and the third is the sweet woman blinded by suffering,
over whom the other two types compete (when they're not
competing for men).

     The danger of this "dream America" depicted in soap
opera is that women learn that their role exists in a
society overwhelmed with personal crises but devoid of
social and political problems.

0406
     Efron, Edith. "The Soaps - anything but 99-44/100
     percent pure," *TV Guide*, March 13, 1965; also

in *Television* by B. G. Cole, NY: Free Pr,
1970. pp. 156-162.

Soap opera women are usually typed as "good" (coy,
baby-worshiping women) or "villainous" (heavily made-up,
career oriented women who lure the husbands of "good"
women into adultery).

0407

"Ellen Peck proposes countering soap opera's pronatalism," *Media Report to Women*, February 1,
1976, 4(2):8.

By altering daytime television's irresponsible emphasis on reproduction, a public service action could be
initiated in a new stress on the image of women who are
socially aware and reproductively responsible.

0408

Gade, Eldon M. "Representation of the world of
work in daytime television serials," *Journal of
Employment Counseling*, 1971, 8:37-42.

Women represented 32% of the total work force shown
on daytime serials. Leading occupations were secretary,
physician and nurse.

0409

Goldsen, Rose K. "Throwaway husbands, wives and
lovers," *Human Behavior*, December, 1975, 4(12):
64-69.

The "antifamily antidramas" commonly known as soap
operas, examined during the first half of 1975 revealed a
preoccupation with incest, adultery and sickly children.
These themes, coupled with the caricatures of humanity
found in the commercial interruptions, have a harmful effect on the 15 million pre-school age children for whom
daytime serials provide consciousness forming experiences.

0410

Gutcheon, Beth R. "Look for cop-outs on prime
time, not on 'Soaps'," *New York Times*, December
16, 1973, p. D-21.

While prime-time fare insults women along with everyone else, soap opera avoids patronizing women by casting
them as doctors, lawyers, writers and nurses. The author
contrasts soap opera's sympathetic handling of the theme
of rape with prime time handling involving the rapist's

mistaken identity and other non-victim related subplots
that avoid the actual issue of rape.

0411
Gutcheon, Beth. "There isn't anything wishy-
washy about soaps," *Ms.*, August, 1974, 3(2):
42-43+.

Soap operas are valuable in that they expose the
viewers to ideas and information not readily available
elsewhere. Viewers learn the sign language of the deaf
while exposed to discrimination facing the handicapped,
they see a black orderly save the life of a wealthy
bigot, and see a female lawyer whose male lawyer husband
supports her decision to foster a career instead of children.

0412
Katzman, Natan. "Television soap operas: what's
been going on anyway?," *Public Opinion Quarterly*,
1972, 36:200-212.

Because of the soap opera's large audience and
limited themes, they are "potentially a major force in
the transmission of values." These values include occupational roles of the sexes. A week of monitoring determined that 60% of the male characters were doctors, lawyers or businessmen while less than 5% of the female
characters held professional positions. Working women
were nurses, secretaries and employed in other stereotyped
forms of female labor. The soap opera world is one of
male professionals, in which a woman's place is in the
home or at the typewriter.

0413
Kilguss, Anne F. "Using soap operas as a therapeutic tool," *Social Casework*, 1974, 55:525-530.

The twentieth century problem of myth deprivation may
be satisfied, at least for the daytime television viewer,
by the soap opera genre. This myth teaches implicitly
that a woman's place is in the home and her raison d'etre
is fulfilled by helping others, i.e., giving advice.
Television soap operas and confession magazines both tend
to socialize their audiences toward accepting certain attitudes. With the emphasis on procreation, pregnancy
becomes a great source of joy. Modern birth control techniques do not exist here. The author, a social worker,
uses soap opera as a point of reference with her patients.
When soap operas begin showing women owning businesses and
acquiring advanced degrees, as networks have announced,

the author expects her patients to be affected by the
shift in mythology toward role models with more realistic,
contemporary lifestyles.

0414
Kinzer, Nora Scott. "Soapy sin in the afternoon,"
Psychology Today, August, 1973, 7:46-48; also in
Mass Media and Society, ed. by Alan Wells. Palo
Alto: Mayfield, 1975. pp. 78-81.

The female value system reinforced by the writers of
daytime serials includes fostering pronatalist attitudes
whereby female doctors and nurses ignore contraceptive research and are continually pregnant. Serials also foster
female passivity whereby women are raped, divorced, aban-
doned, or given drugs, but rarely initiate action
themselves. Women are often stereotyped as chronically
ill. They suffer from exotic maladies but never acquire
realistic diseases such as cancer.

0415
Klemesrud, Judy. "Soap operas: same time, same
station, but a new boss," *The New York Times*,
October 11, 1972. p. 38; reprinted as "NBC's
daytime schedule now in woman's hand," *The Provi-
dence Sunday Journal*, October 22, 1972. p. D-2.

The new female director of NBC daytime programming
discusses plans for independent, financially successful
heroines on daytime serials.

0416
Lopate, Carol. "Daytime television: you'll
never want to leave home," *Feminist Studies*,
Spring/Summer, 1976, 3(3/4):69-82.

The predominant values taught on daytime television
are the importance of consumption and the sanctity of the
family. The game show MC functions as a sexy rich uncle
who distributes cash and prizes to the female contestants
who resemble "preadolescent Lolitas" as they enthusiastically kiss the powerful uncle after acquiring a commodity.
Married contestants often play the accepted game show role
of self-mocking wives and powerless, infantilized husbands who defer to the MC/uncle.

The family motif operates more overtly in the afternoon serials. Within each family is a bond of love, kin-
ship and equality between spouses, though interaction
among several families often borders on incest.

0417
   Mannes, Marya. "Everything's up-to-date in soap
   operas," *TV Guide*, March 15, 1969. Also in *Television*, ed. by B. G. Cole, NY: Free Pr, 1970.
   pp. 163-168.

   Serials' women may wear modern pantsuits but they
still have only one proper role - non-thinking housewife/
mother. Emphasis on this role implies that so long as
the housewife is "enthroned as the single highest good,"
housewives are encouraged to maintain their status as
consumers.

0418
   Miksch, Ingrid. "Sudsville - the cleanest and
   warmest place in the world: an analysis of soap
   operas." Available from author, 201 E. Walton,
   apt 609, Chicago, IL 60611.

   Soap operas typically portray men as doctors, lawyers
and professors while portraying women as nurses, housewives and mothers. Contrary to reality where one in three
marriages terminate, the domestic serials woman finds
happiness in the home and creativity in the kitchen. So
long as she's a Good Mother, the soap woman lives a secure
and happy existence, but as soon as she decides to leave
the home for career or other activity, disaster strikes in
the form of abortion, sterility and divorce.

0419
   Poverman, Marion F. "Suds get in your eyes,"
   Women's Almanac, 1974, 2:177-187.

   One of the values of television soap opera is its
exposure of a primarily blue-collar audience to the necessity of annual pap smears and the problems of child abuse.
Daytime serials also further a feminist goal: the elimination of predetermined sex roles, where the male
characters are as emotionally expressive as the female.

0420
   Ramsdell, M. L. "The trauma of television's
   troubled soap families," *Family Coordinator*,
   1973, 22:299-304.

   After 600 hours of soap opera viewing, Ramsdell perceived the following stereotypes: male occupations include doctors and lawyers but no plumbers, carpenters or
truck drivers. The primary female occupation is "mommy".
When women do pursue careers, they become either villainous or emotionally unstable. Token blacks appear in

respectable occupations but racial pride is never promoted.

The daytime serials are designed to sell sponsors' household and baby products. The scripts conform to the consumption ethic by reassuring the housewife/viewer that she too can become Cinderella if she consumes well and performs as a fulltime housewife and mother. In order to promote consumerism among viewers, soap opera glorifies the consumption-oriented family with aggressive, achieving husbands married to at-home wives. Ramsdell questions the ultimate social value of such a family structure when real-life sex roles are so drastically changing.

0421
   Stewart, Linda. "TV money shows: the shame game," *Ms.*, June, 1973, 1(12):10-12.

The image of wives and husbands on game shows and daytime television commercials.

0422
   Turow, Joseph. "Advising and ordering: daytime, prime time," *Journal of Communication*, 1974, 24(2):138-141; also ERIC (ED 093 003).

Men gave 90% of all directives in prime time television and 56% in daytime television. According to the author the selection of characters, assignment of occupations and plot development are all written in a manner which minimizes female opportunity to display superior knowledge.

Broadcasting Employment

See also News Media, 0071 - 0100.

See 0072. American Association of University Women, "The image of women in television, a survey and guide."

See 0077. W. W. Bowman, "Distaff journalists: women as a minority group in the news media."

See 0719. L. A. Elliot, "Black women in the media."

0423
    Abel, John D. and Phyllis L. Rogowski. "Women
    in television station management: the top 50
    markets," paper presented at the annual meet-
    ing of the Broadcast Education Association,
    1976. ERIC (ED 120 878).

Television has the power to change the negative,
often false image of women it has created but not without
promoting women to positions of management and decision-
making levels in the broadcast industry.

An examination of *Broadcasting Yearbook* indicates
that of 1,743 persons employed in management and decision-
making position, 4.8% are women. This severe underrepresentation of women in high level positions indicates that
women have little impact on station policy and are therefore blocked from improving the image of women in
television content. The authors also call for revision of
Federal Communications Commission (FCC) form 395, whose
present format offers an ambiguous picture of the broadcast industry's female work force.

0424
    Brown, Les. "TV's minority employment on
    rise, survey shows," *The New York Times*, Oc-
    tober 17, 1973. p. 95.

The United Church of Christ, who uses its broadcast
funds for "watchdog" purposes rather than to air denomi-
national programming, has studied employment reports filed
with FCC. Although the broadcast industry is overwhelmingly white and male, some progress was shown in the hiring of minorities, but no such progress was made in the
hiring of women. Of the 127 non-commercial stations, ten
had no full-time female employees. By hiring women and
minorities to introduce new tastes and values, television
will be able to overcome its present homogenization of
culture and distortion of self-images.

0425
    "CBS and its women: a dialogue. *Columbine*
    (special supplement), September, 1973, v. 2;
    also in *Rooms with No View*, by the Media Wom-
    en's Association, NY: Harper and Row, 1974.
    pp. 298-330.

CBS Women's Group presented grievances to CBS president and corporate executives. Grievances included inequities in promotion, training, salaries, and benefits.
Suggestions for affirmative action plan implementation
and an improved image of women in programming were offered.

Monitors of CBS programming found that television's portrait of the American woman more closely resembled an unflattering and unrealistic caricature. The daytime serials' few strong women worthy of emulation, usually ended up in jail or a hospital bed. CBS official response to the Women's Group indicates amenability toward improved professional conditions for women. They did not respond to the issue of women's image in programming, feeling that it should be kept separate from the equal opportunities issue.

0426
    "Canada: CBC management accepts recommendations of task force on women employees," *Media Report to Women*, July 1, 1975, 3(7):7.

Success story upgrading women's status at Canadian network.

0427
    Cantor, Muriel G. "Women and Public Broadcasting," *Journal of Communication*, 1977, 27(1): 14-19.

A summary of the *Report of the Task Force on Women in Public Broadcasting* (see 0484) dealing with women's image on the screen and in employment situations.

0428
    Del Colliano, Jerry. "Women in radio: an 'or else' situation," *Madison Avenue Magazine*, December, 1976, 20(2):30.

In order to avoid Federal Communications Commission pressure, radio broadcasters should actively recruit women immediately. Kathleen Bonk, National chairperson of NOW Media Reform Task Force offers three suggestions for broadcasters to support women's radio needs: 1) schedule access days for community women to discuss unique problems with broadcasters and to learn to use radio effectively, 2) put women on the air; national and local women's groups may suggest qualified women, 3) put women in management positions; sales is a good starting point for beginners.

See 0080. G. E. Diliberto, *Profiles of Three Newswomen*.

See 0562. L. A. Elliot, "Black women in the media."

0429
"Few minorities and women found in better jobs
of cable business," *Broadcasting*, August 9, 1976,
91:45.

The Federal Communications Commission issued an Equal
Employment Opportunity (EEO) ruling for active promotion
of women to top decision-making positions in cable television industry when a cable television bureau study found
that women constituted 2% of the officials and managers,
4% of the professionals, and 9% of its sales workers.
Members of other minority groups were found to be represented in even fewer numbers.

0430
Gelfman, Judith S. *Women in Television News*.
NY: Columbia University Press, 1976.

Interviews with 30 female broadcast news reporters
explore their perceptions on career discrimination or
career tokenism, emphasis on their appearance and image,
job satisfactions and dissatisfactions and the impact of
the women's liberation movement on the increased number of
women in news. The book combines the frank, open interviews with a statistical analysis of the measurable data
gathered from the interviews.

0431
Harwood, Kenneth. "Earnings and education of
men and women in selected media occupations,"
Journal of Broadcasting, 1976, 20:233-238.

The median annual earnings and years of education of
men and women are compared for people employed as authors,
editors and reporters, photographers, radio and television
announcers, and in public relations, advertising and
sales. Although the educational background is basically
equal, men make twice, and in one case, nearly three times
the salary of women in the same fields.

0432
Hennessee, Judith. "What progress women at CBS?,"
Personnel, July-August, 1975, 52:33-44.

The status of women employed at CBS is improving by
raising the collective consciousness of male executives
through role-playing, by rewriting the secretarial manual
in a more intelligent and professional style, by training
women for jobs with more career advancement opportunities,
and by giving female news reporters more television exposure. Shortcomings to this reversal of women's place

131

at CBS include male bosses who continue to resist the change, the "locker room" outlook of some areas of the industry, and the slow progress of management's "persuasion" technique.

0433
      Hobson, Sheila Smith. "Women and television," *Sisterhood is Powerful*, ed. by Robin Morgan. NY: Random House, 1970. pp. 70-76.

Personal testimony of the race and sex barriers encountered by a talented, educated, qualified black woman when seeking a job in the television industry.

0434
      Isber, Caroline and Muriel Cantor. *Report of the Task Force on Women in Public Broadcasting*. Washington, DC: Corporation for Public Broadcasting, 1975. Available from CPB, 111 16th St. NW, Washington, DC 20036; also in ERIC (ED 118 153).

Public radio and television were monitored for the employment visibility and image of women, and interviews of personnel were made to identify attitudes concerning employment and visibility of women. It was found that female characters comprised 15% of the monitored programs and 26% of the jobs. The concluding policy recommendations concern programming, employment and the inclusion of women on boards of trustees.

0435
      Jennings, Ralph M. *Television Station Employment Practices: the Status of Minorities and Women*. NY: United Church of Christ, 1972; also in ERIC (ED 107 304).

In 1972 minority employees comprised 10% of the full-time staffs of 609 commercial television stations; 22.5% of the stations had no full-time minority employees, 75% of all women employed by television stations were in office and clerical positions.

0436
      Jennings, Ralph M. and Allan T. Walters. *Television Station Employment Practices*. NY: United Church of Christ, 1976.

The most recent annual update shows less than 40% of the 641 commercial stations monitored increasing the

number of female managers, professionals, technicians and
sales workers.

0437
    Klever, Anita. *Women in Television*.   Phila-
delphia: Westminster Pr, 1975.

Women employed at every level of the production,
technical and "on-air" facets of broadcasting from secretary to superstar describe the types of television jobs
they've had, how they started in television, and explain
the routines and responsibilities of each job.

0438
    Kustow, Lis. "Television and women," *The Body
Politic, Writings from the Women's Liberation
Movement in Britain*, 1969-1972, ed. by Michelene
Wandor. London: Stage One, 1972. pp. 66-71.

A BBC director tells of her fight to token woman
status even though mediocre men were promoted to director
level without the added personal struggle that she en-
dured. Her suggestions for eliminating such female exploitation include employee unionization, opening technical, administrative and creative jobs to women, female
representation at all decision-making levels, flexible
working hours for people with children, and protests of
sex role brainwashing in ads.

0439
    Landsberg, Michele. "TV women: how they're
doing in male-chauvinist tv-land," *Chatelaine*,
May, 1974, 47:39+.

Women in Canadian network news face discrimination
when aspiring toward powerful executive positions. The
promotion criteria are simple: men are promoted, women
are not. Several Canadian performers, interviewers, female sportscaster, weekend anchor and others are interviewed for attitudes toward the problem.

0440
    Naegel, Lana. *Women in Radio*. M.S. thesis,
University of Wisconsin, 1973.

A study of sex discrimination in radio employment revealed greater perceptions of personal discrimination by
women content in jobs than by those discontented. Women
employed in smaller markets perceive more discrimination
than those in larger markets.

0441
    Nash, Abigail Jones. "Minorities and women in
    broadcast news: two national surveys," ERIC
    (ED 095 557).

An examination of the types of discrimination faced
by women and minority newspeople.

0442
    Nash, Abigail Jones. *The Status of Women in
    Broadcast Journalism: A National Survey*. M.A.
    thesis, University of Wisconsin- Madison, 1974.

National samples of female broadcast news reporters
and news directors were surveyed concerning working conditions for women and job satisfaction. Data indicated
that newswomen received lower pay and less promotional
opportunity than male colleagues, even though job satisfaction was high.

0443
    "Olivetti girls aren't forever," *Broadcasting*,
    August 7, 1972, 83(6):39-44.

In 1971, 24% of the radio and television jobs were
held by women. Most of these positions were clerical,
although women did comprise 1.1% directors of commercials,
1.4% newscasters, 2% program managers, 1% unit managers.
A number of successful women in broadcasting and advertising discuss the best way for women to establish successful careers in broadcast media.

0444
    "Public TV reported lagging in minority hearings,"
    The New York Times, January 31, 1973. p. 82.

Although employment discrimination for women is not
as widespread in public television as in commercial television, over 18% of US public television licencees had
no women in top three job categories, while over 50% of
female employees were placed in office and clerical positions, according to a study by the United Church of
Christ.

See 0394. G. Rock, "Same time, same station, same sexism."

See 0059. *Rooms with no View*.

See 0452. S. D. Ross, "Mass media - radio and television."

0445
      Sherman, Ellen. "Femme scribes cop top jobs,"
      Ms., December, 1974, 3(6):84+.

      Television programming's stereotyped image of women
will most effectively be changed as more scriptwriters
appear. The "femme scribes" who won most of the 1974
Emmy awards for writing are interviewed here about their
personal careers and scripts featuring strong female protagonists.

0446
      Stone, Vernon and Abigail Jones Nash. "A survey
      of women in broadcast news," *RTNDA Communicator*,
      March, 1975, 5:4-5.

      A national survey of women working in broadcast news
revealed 68% admission of discrimination in pay, promotion and story assignments, a higher median salary level
for minority employees than for women, 85% job satisfaction among women, and 92% rejection of special protection
from danger and violence.

0447
      Stone, Vernon. "Surveys show younger women be-
      coming news directors," *RTNDA Communicator*,
      October, 1976.

      Some results of a survey of female news directors
show that many are under age 30, operate in smaller markets, receive lower salaries than male news directors,
and have no trouble supervising men or women.

See 0732. B. Wood, "Black women in television news."

                        Legal Action

See 0423. J. D. Abel and P. L. Rogowski, "Women in television station management: the top 50 markets."

See 0424. L. Brown, "TV's minority employment on rise,

survey shows."

See 0078.   E. Chacon, "Women journalists on TV should be
positive role models for other women."

See 0021.   A. K. Daniels, "The mass media and social
change."

See 0428.   J. Del Colliano, "Women in radio: an 'or else'
situation."

See 0429.   "Few minorities and women found in better jobs
of cable business."

0448
        Komisar, Lucy.   "Turning off the tube," *Ms.*,
        August, 1972, 1(2):4-6.

        Rather than complain among friends about offensive
television programming, Komisar proposes action with a
step-by-step approach to monitoring and then filing an
FCC license challenge to deny television station petition
to renew broadcast license.

0449
        "Los Angeles women's coalition asks denial of
        KNXT-TV (CBS) license," *Media Report to Women*,
        December 1, 1974, 2(12):12+.

        Excerpts from the petition to deny KNXT license re-
newal include evidence of bias against women in employment,
news programming, public affairs programming as well as
programming where women are primarily shown as non-pro-
fessional while male stars are doctors, detectives and
psychiatrists.   In advertising women clean bathrooms and
kitchens but never sell cars, on game shows they are sex
object assistants who rarely speak, and in children's cartoons girls are less visible than the boys who are forced
to live up to a "superman" image.

0450
        McNeil, Jean C.   "Whose values?," *Journal of
        Broadcasting*, 1975, 19:295-306.

        McNeil expresses the hope that continued dialogues
such as that between herself and John F. Seggar (see 0349
0350, 0360, 0364) along with NOW broadcast license challenges and other pressure tactics will facilitate

constructive change from present sex role stereotyping on
television.

0451
    Mills, Kay. "Fighting sexism on the airwaves,"
    Journal of Communication, 1974, 24(2):150-153;
    also *Mass Media and Society*, ed. by Alan Wells.
    Palo Alto: Mayfield, 1975. pp. 403-406.

Representatives from the National Organization for
Women challenged the US Congress, the Federal Communications Commission, and the National Association of Broadcasters to improve the image of women in television
programming and advertising and to hire and promote female
talent.

See 0107. "New media reform task force."

See 0359. T. Press. "News woman in a man's world."

See 0059. *Rooms with no View.*

0452
    Ross, Susan Deller. "Mass media - radio and tele-
    vision," *The Rights of Women; the Basic ACLU
    Guide to a Woman's Rights*. NY: Avon Books,
    1973. pp. 148-163.

Women's roles on television have been consistently
limited to children's caretaker, men's servant and sex
object. This biased image coupled with discriminatory
employment practices in broadcasting can be overcome when
women petition to deny license renewals. The author explains the Fairness Doctrine in simple language and outlines a step-by-step line of attack.

0453
    Stanley, Nancy E. "Federal communications law and
    women's rights: Women in the wasteland fight
    back," *Hastings Law Journal*, 1971, 23:15-53.

Three legal arguments women may use when petitioning
the denial of broadcast license renewals are: 1) inadequate service to needs of the (female) community, 2)
unequal employment between the sexes, 3) and abuse of the
Fairness Doctrine by presenting a biased and distorted
televised view of women and women's role. Feminist
challenges should compel the licensee's programming to
meet the needs of women; to counter the negative image

of women by also presenting them as independent, active and intelligent; to present women outside traditional roles; to hire and promote women into policy-making positions; and to report the feminist movement fairly. Women will be treated fairly when programming reflects women's problems of unemployment, as heads of households and when free public service announcements tell locations of child care facilities, job training programs and women's rights meetings.

Television commercials and variety programming continually spoof women's struggle for equal rights but abide by the Fairness Doctrine in abstaining from spoofs of black persons as railroad porters or advocates of civil rights. The news distorts and ridicules the women's movement, and television drama casts women in secondary and subprofessional occupations, portrays them as emotionally unfit for leadership and overly concerned with catching a husband. Broadcasters should be compelled to reform this unfairly and unrealistically negative image of women.

0454
    Wexler, Marvin and Gilbert Levy. "Women on television: fairness and the 'fair sex'," *Yale Review of Law and Social Action*, 1971, 2:59-68.

The danger of sex role stereotypes on television lies in the fact that children acquire a value system and set of appropriate behavior patterns from this sort of programming. By arguing that stereotypes defame women as a class, feminists may apply the Fairness Doctrine when pressuring the television industry to accept its social responsibility in projecting realistic sex roles. The Fairness Doctrine also concerns reasonableness of presentation, therefore the licensee must present a fair and sufficiently varied view of women.

0455
    "We are demonstrating against the unreality of television," *Media Report to Women*, January 1, 1975, 3(1):3.

A protest of unrealistic portrayal of women on KNXT Los Angeles called for female representation of all classes, ages, work roles and life styles on the station's programming. The demonstration was an effort supporting a petition for denial of license renewal because of sexist employment and programming policies.

See 0370. M. Wolfe, "Television: a propaganda machine

for male supremacy."

0456
"Women in prime time TV roles, TV commercials,
and TV production," "...to Form a More Perfect
Union..."; Justice for American Women; Report
of the National Commission on the Observance on
International Women's Year, 1976. (Y3.W84.1/976).
pp. 143-144.

Male actors are employed in over 71% of all prime
time roles and 68% of television commercial roles. Under
Title VII, EEOC has the authority to litigate broadcasting
discrimination of this type even without individual complaints. The IWY Commission encourages such litigation
considering that 67.4% of all respondents to a Screen Actors Guild survey said they wish to see women appearing on
television in positions of authority.

See 0114. "Women in the media."

0457
"Women tell FCC their criticisms of programming
on CBS station KNXT-TV," Media Report to Women,
December 1, 1974, 2(12):13.

Denial of KNXT license renewal was petitioned on
grounds that men were accorded different and more positive
treatment than women in roles, program format and content.
Many roles women fill in real life (doctor, lawyer, architect) are not reflected in television programming where
women are seen as subservient to male co-stars.

Television Counterbalance

0458
Britton, Helen Ann. "The role of women in television: avenues for change." Paper presented
at the annual Telecommunication Policy Research
Conference, 1976. ERIC (ED 122 733).

Television reinforces traditional gender related behavior. Although advertisers and programmers claim that
they cannot afford to offend the "average" viewer by
promulgating social change, researchers are concerned by
the potential effects that television's narrow portrayals

139

of acceptable social behavior may have on the next gen-
eration. The author recommends that the television industry employ women in executive positions, recognize
its role as an instrument of social control, propose programming guidelines to eliminate sex role bias, and
conduct research on social reality (including sex role
behavior) as a function of television research.

See 0428. J. Del Colliano, "Women in radio: an 'or else'
situation."

0459
     Doyle, Nancy. "The media and the message,"
     Woman's Place: A Look at Sexism, (Public
     Affairs Pamphlet, 509). NY: Public Affairs
     Committee, 1974. pp. 20-21.

The prime time television specials which show women's
place in history, and show children of both sexes sharing
human experiences have been facilitated by feminist activism. Scholarly research studies of women's image on
television, feminist group petitions to the Federal Communications Commision to deny license renewals because of
derogatory female image, and complaints regarding discriminatory hiring practices are responsible for the level
of improvement of women's image evident thus far.

0460
     "Feminist Theater produces alternative soap opera
     for 'A Woman Is...' show," *Media Report to Women*,
     April 1, 1976, 4(4):13.

Soap opera format is used for a television program
about struggles of strong women to resolve problems and
control own lives.

0461
     "Guidelines for showing women are sent to TV
     networks," *Media Report to Women*, May 1, 1975,
     3(5):12.

Guidelines of the Lesbian Feminist Liberation, Inc.
call for accurate television portrayal of all lesbian lifestyles, reflecting those who live alone, live communally
with other lesbians, and live within a traditional marriage to a man. They also call for the elimination of
stereotyped portrayals of "masculine" lesbians which distort the true physical appearance of gay women. When
portraying lesbians, television should reflect their
community involvement, tender motherhood and platonic

friendships.

0462
Guttentag, Marcia and Helen Bray. "The socialization of women and the image of women in the
media," *Undoing Sex Types*, by M. Guttentag and
H. Bray. NY: McGraw-Hill, 1976. pp. 166-167.

Consciousness-raising projects for Junior High
School students include writing and acting soap opera
plots.

See 0438. L. Kustow, "Television and women."

See 0391. "The medium is macho."

0463
National Organization for Women, San Jose Chapter,
"Sex O'Clock News," available from KNOW, Inc.,
PO Box 86031, Pittsburgh, PA 15221. #250.

A fantasy news broadcast with female anchors reporting top stories about female President, Chief Justice and
Pope, and sexy weather boy. The role reversal extends to
the commercials showing a despondent househusband whose
life loses meaning when his barbecued chicken doesn't
please his wife, and an ad for a male genital spray, Sub-
poena.

0464
"NOW asks networks to give women more positive
role," *Broadcasting*, September 22, 1975, 89:59.

Members of the National Organization for Women, National Media Task Force, met with representatives from
all three networks. NOW proposed a revision of the NBC
manual to include a section on sexist language, a more
sensitive approach to rape on television series, and a
depiction of women as emotionally stable and professionally fit for traditionally male occupations. Of the 69
prime time shows examined, the NOW image committee found
that 62% feature male leads while 13% feature female leads.

0465
"'Pull the plug,' says Wilma Scott Heide," *Media
Report to Women*, December 1, 1976, 4(12):8.

Excerpts from a speech in which Heide proposes to

liberate broadcasting by "pulling the plug" of one network. Broadcasters have socialized, legitimized, distorted and limited reporting long enough. "Feminist
consciousness raising, letter writing and meetings haven't
worked. Since all else has failed, the majority of the
public - women - must convince the media to meet women's
needs by this drastic means.

0466
   "Stop that stereotype'," *Media Report to Women*,
   March 1, 1974, 2(3):11.

A public service announcement inadvertently using a
sex role stereotype to warn people to be prepared against
fires was removed following a private citizen's letter to
the program manager. The PSA had shown a helpless woman
struggling with a fire extinguisher until a male hero appeared and successfully operated the equipment.

0467
   "Transition group formed by film executives; seeks
   better climate for women," *Media Report to Women*,
   November 1, 1976, 4(11):3.

A motion picture and television production team encourages writers to develop higher standards for women's
roles. Their 12 projects for 1976/1977 show women in
realistic, non-stereotyped positions.

0468
   Williams, Carol Traynor. "It's not so much
   'You've come a long way, Baby' - as 'You're
   gonna make it after all'," *TV: The Critical
   View*, ed. by Horace Newcomb. NY: Oxford Uni-
   versity Press, 1976. pp. 43-53.

The humanized characters on "The Mary Tyler Moore
Show" include an unmarried female protagonist who serves
neither coffee nor male egos, but rather produces programs
and hires on-camera personnel. The other characters, of
both sexes, are vulnerable, appealing human beings who
continue to learn about themselves and grow.

0469
   "The women at home also are getting a new shake
   from television," *Broadcasting*, August 7, 1972,
   83(6):40-41.

Local daytime television programming in a number of
cities includes conversational shows dealing with

informative, educational, controversial issues rather than the traditional household hints format.

Women's Image

0470
    Alexander, Shana. "Hanging out in sexual space,"
Newsweek, November 12, 1973, 82(20):48.

In a discussion of sex and violence in the movies
Alexander relates an anecdote about a film whose male
lead enjoyed shooting and killing women. When the censor
labeled it "perversion" and blocked its release, the filmmaker "argued that shooting women wasn't perversion;
shooting *men* was perversion. He got his seal." The article later mentions the prevalence of rape in the movies.

0471
    Baunoch, Joseph W. with Betty E. Chmaj. "Film
stereotypes of American women," *Image Myth and
Beyond*, ed. by Betty E. Chmaj, Pittsburgh: KNOW,
1972, pp. 275-284; also ERIC (ED 121-192).

Examination of the stars and their films for each
category: pillars of virtue, the glamour girls, the emo-
tive woman and the independent woman.

0472
    Betancourt, Jeanne. "Whatever happened to women
in film?," *Media and Methods*, October, 1975, 12
(2):28-33+.

After cataloging the early film images of women,
Betancourt questions the present convention whereby woman's
sexuality is obscured under the new definition of sex
equated with male violence. The calm acceptance of female
rape contrasted to the stunned reaction to male rape calls
for reexamination of traditional sex roles with more emphasis on maturing love, the impact of divorce on parents
and children, and the joys and loneliness of growing old
alone, in order to explore every facet of human experience.

0473
     Bronstein, Lynn. "Cinemasculinity," *Women: A
     Journal of Liberation*, Fall, 1970, 2(1):27-30.

     A three part discussion of 1) the cliches about women
in traditional westerns, war movies, adventure films and
science fiction, 2) the exceptions to these cliches in
the films of Garbo, West, Davis and Hepburn, and 3) interesting possibilities for future roles of self-sufficient
women in film.

0474
     Brownmiller, Susan. "The myth of the heroic rap-
     ist," *Against Our Will: Men, Women and Rape*,
     by S. Brownmiller. NY: Simon and Schuster,
     1975, pp. 283-308.

     The myth of heroic rapist (male) and human booty (fe-
male) is a recurring motif in James ·Bond films, Charles
Perrault's "Bluebeard", Mick Jagger's rape/murder lyrics,
and the stylized, glamorized rape scenes in *A Clockwork
Orange*, *Frenzy* and *Straw Dogs*. The common stereotypes in
these rape scenes show women either enjoying the brutality,
or as inconsequential objects in the more important theme
of man's revenge on man by defiling his wife (property).
A rare rape scene occurred in *Deliverance* where the brutality was not enjoyed and where the rapist was murdered.
Female rape victims rarely murder their rapists, the
films' protagonists. Men are raped and brutalized by "bad
guys" while female victims are raped and brutalized by
"good guys." Movie producers claim that this is the image
of people that "the [American public] wants to see."
Brownmiller claims that such depictions "perpetuate, shape
and influence our popular attitudes." She cites instances
where real life rapes have directly paralleled the rape
scenes in popular movies.

See 0615. B. E. Chamj. "It ain't me babe! or is it?
American woman through the eyes of the counterculture
music, films."

0475
     "Discrimination noted in EEOC suit filed by
     California Women against Universal Studios,"
     Media Report to Women, May 1, 1976, 4(5):14.

     Charges include discrimination in recruiting, casting
and employment in all levels of the studio, as well as
stereotyped roles for women which present a dehumanizing
image of the female sex.

0476
Ephron, Nora. "Deep throat," *Crazy Salad*, by
N. Ephron. NY: Knopf, 1975. pp. 63-70.

A description of the film industry's penchant for
sexual objectivation and victimization of women.

0477
Farber, Stephen. "The vanishing heroine," *Hudson
Review*, 1974, 27:570-576.

By eliminating women from all but token roles as
people who are raped or murdered, contemporary buddy
films retreat from the real world where men must learn to
deal with dependent, assertive women to "a childlike world
where women do not exist as challenges, and where no com-
mitment has to be intense or enduring." Farber compares
the movies discussed in Haskell's (see 0488) and Rosen's
(see 0522) books to today's movies whose only strong female models are found in films set in the past (*China-
town*, for example). Directors are either stymied or
afraid to deal with the struggles confronting contemporary
women.

0478
Farber, Stephen. "Violence and the bitch goddess," *Film Comment*, November, 1974, 10:8-11.

Cinema of the 1940's perverted the theme of success
to glorification of the violent male vigilante and the
cold-blooded and greedy female monster. Character studies of the plots of four movies reveal avaricious, success-
crazed women who are willing to marry and murder to
satisfy their greed.

See 0026. J. Faust, "Testimony before the New York City
Commission on Human Rights."

0479
Fischer, Lucy. "The image of woman as image: the
optical politics of *Dames*," *Film Quarterly*, Fall,
1976, 30(1):2-11.

With Busby Berkeley's kaleidescopic techniques women
literally became the image of Woman. They were symbols
of feminine sexuality with no personal individuality.
The women even looked alike, with little facial differences. In *Dames* organza dresses symbolized woman as pure
"fluff" on one level, when later the same dresses came
together to form a photographic jigsaw-puzzle vision of

Ruby Keeler's face - a fragmented version of woman's "image" on another level. Berkeley's optical image of woman as "ambulatory Surrealist mannequin" was also apparent in the lyrics which stressed the value of beautiful "dames."

See 0720. L. Freeman, "From servant to superchick ain't necessarily up."

0480
    Gans, Herbert J. *"The Exorcist:* a devilish attack on women," *Social Policy*, May-June, 1974, 5:7-1, 5:71-73.

If most horror films "describe the consequences of fooling with the status quo" *The Exorcist* attacks the 1970's effort of women to change society by overthrowing traditional roles. All the sick people in the film are female: a dying old woman, a young drug addict, and Regan, whose aggressive sexuality is the major manifestation of her "possession." The article describes several misogynistic points of the movie and book.

0481
    Gant, Liz. "Ain't Beulah dead yet? or images of the Black woman in film," *Essence*, May, 1973, 4:60-61.

The black woman in film has traditionally been stereotyped as the tragic mulatto, the mammy or earth mother, the innocent or ingenue, and the siren or hot mama.

0482
    Gerard, Lillian. "Belles, sirens, sisters," *Film Library Quarterly*, 1971, 5(1):14-21.

The female roles in *McCabe & Mrs. Miller, Carnal Knowledge* and *Sunday, Bloody Sunday* are examined in terms of realistic female image and strength of character. In *Carnal Knowledge* especially, women are treated as accessories, traded in the same "way a man flips cards." The solution to this unrealistic and unfair portrayal of women is to encourage more female directors and writers to enter the field.

0483
    Gilburt, Naome. "To be our own muse: the dialectics of a culture heroine," *Notes on Women's Cinema*, ed. by Claire Johnston. (Screen Pamphlet, 2).

147

London: Society for Education in Film and Television. pp. 5-13; also in *Women and Film*, No. 2, 1972.

Male cinema deals with the culture myths that delineate woman's work as reproductive or procreative while man's work is productive and creative. Within this context the male hero is immortalized while the "eternal female" becomes an aesthetic principle rather than a person in her own right.

0484
Gross, Amy. "What are they doing to women now?," *Mademoiselle*, January, 1977, 83(1):88-89+.

After a lengthy absence women are returning to the screen in 1977 cast in basically two types of films. There are the two-woman buddy films with teams like Shirley MacLaine/Anne Bancroft and Jane Fonda/Vanessa Redgrave, and there are films like *Network* which feature pathologically ambitious women who end up alone. Quotes from a number of well known actresses reveal perceptions on women's role in the motion picture industry.

0485
Gufstafson, Judith. "The declining of women among the top ten box office stars, 1931-1972. *Image, Myth and Beyond*. (American Women and American Studies, 1), ed. by Betty E. Chmaj. Pittsburgh, KNOW, Inc., 1972; also in ERIC (ED 121 192).

The "wipe out" of women from box office stardom began in the 1930's when Shirley Temple, a child, became the top female star. In 1940 only two women were among the top ten. By the 1950's male crooners were taking over and in the 1960's only two types of women, the Sweet Young Thing and the Sex Goddess, were seen with frequency on the screen. A yearly list of women in the top ten box office scores, 1932-1971 ends the article.

0486
Harmetz, Aljean. "Rape - an ugly movie trend," *The New York Times*, September 30, 1973. p. D-1.

From 1971 to 1973 there were at least 20 "rape-infested films." Movie styles of rape included supernatural, stylized, incestuous rapes, multiple violations of one woman's body, those enjoyed by the victim, and two raped men. "Raped men are allowed anguish, raped women are ignored."

See 0031. J. Harris, "A role without a script."

0487
     Haskell, Molly. "The Cinema of Howard Hawks,"
     Intellectual Digest, April, 1972, 2:56-58.

     In his silent films, dramas, and screwball comedies,
Howard Hawks didn't indulge in the sex role stereotypes of
man as subject and woman as object. He presented both
sexes in all shades of emotion, intellectual competence
and activity.

0488
     Haskell, Molly. *From Reverence to Rape: The
     Treatment of Women in the Movies.* NY: Holt,
     Rinehart Winston, 1974.

     Haskell looks at women's roles in film within the
context of film history. She defines roles not only
through well delineated trends within decades (with an eye
to political and sociological pressures), but also through
the eyes of certain key American and European directors.
She covers films and film stars who conform to and deviate
from the pattern.   Laura Bulkeley

0489
     Haskell, Molly. "Here come the killer dames,"
     New York, May 19, 1975, 8:46-49.

     The violent, castrating, black exploitation film
stars are compared to the classic white sex goddesses and
the less violent, more self-assured strong women of the
1940's.

0490
     Haskell, Molly. "Howard Hawks - masculine femi-
     nine," *Film Comment*, March/April, 1974, 10(2):
     34-39.

     A look at the films in which Hawks explored the mas-
culine and feminine instincts in all people, regardless
of actual gender.

0491
     Haskell, Molly. "What is Hollywood trying to
     tell us?," *Ms.*, April, 1977, 5(10):49-51.

     To compensate for the shortage of women in films,
Hollywood is casting female kiddies, moppets and nymphets.

Although Hollywood has always had a penchant for child sweethearts, Mary Pickford and Shirley Temple worked alongside adults while today's children are replacing the women.

0492
> Haskell, Molly. "Women in films: a decade of going nowhere," *Human Behavior*, March, 1974, 3(3):64-69.

An analysis of the decline of three dimensional womanhood in the cinema from 1963-1973. Women became merely bodies - gutless, ineffectual bodies to be raped and flogged. A few sympathetically portrayed women have been spinster schoolteachers suffering from sexual malnutrition. Women disappear from films and their places are filled by men. While men with long hair and beads take over rock music, the film industry's androgynous equivalent is the soft, sensitive, tender man who now enjoys the glamorous narcissism and filtered camera shots once ascribed to female stars.

0493
> Haskell, Molly. "Reviving what custom staled," *The Village Voice*, April 13, 1972, 17(15):81+.

Haskell suggests that the decline of women in films is partially caused by television's soap opera which meets the demand for female leads involved in tales of romance; consequently the movies are now giving themes of love, romance and seduction to the men.

0494
> Haymes, Howard. "Movies in the 1950's: sexism from A to Zapata," *University Film Association Journal*, 1974, 26:12+.

The author randomly selected 25 award winning or popular films of the 1950's whose titles each began with a different letter of the alphabet. The films were explicated according to the four treatments of "woman as other" defined by Simone de Beauvoir in *The Second Sex*. "Female-as sex" operated in 11 of the 25 films where women were raped, pawed and often murdered because of their "evil" flesh. Women who dared to be "magna mater" ended up morally broken or murdered for their non-submissive behavior. Woman as "divine guide" in *On the Waterfront* and *Ivanhoe* became personifications of truth, beauty and goodness who did not participate in the action. "Woman-as-equal" operated in only two of the 25 randomly selected films of the 1950's. The same exercise of a random

alphabetical selection of 25 movies produced during one
decade which applied the opposite approach of looking for
women of dignity, would be a much more difficult, perhaps
impossible task.

See 0725. E. Holly, "Where are the films about real black
men and women?"

0495
   Israel, Lee. "Women in film: saving an endan-
   gered species," *Ms.*, February, 1975, 3(8):51-
   57+.

If after a nuclear holocaust a band of outer space
creatures were to discover an uninhabited Earth and base
their perceptions of our civilization on our motion picture plots, their ideas of the age, lifestyle and raison
d'etre of American women would be quite distorted. Distortions exist in nearly every motion picture because there
are so few women (or sympathetic men) at influential executive levels in the film industry. Glenda Jackson, Eleanor
Perry and other women are unable to convince movie moguls
to support their ideas for movies about strong women.
Meanwhile men's speaking roles outnumber women's 12:1.

0496
   Johnston, Claire. "Women's Cinema as Counter-
   Cinema." *Notes on Women's Cinema* (Screen pam-
   phlet, 2). London: Society for Education in
   Film and Television, 1973.

Women as women have never been present in the cinema.
They have existed as fetishizations, either as the spec-
tacle of sexuality or as the symbol of motherhood. Mae
West's persona was a fetishized phallic replacement with
her masculine voice and phallic dress. Even the films of
Howard Hawks, with their seeming positive qualities of
womanhood, actually dealt strictly with the male and the
non-male. In order to be accepted into the male universe
Marilyn Monroe in *Gentlemen Prefer Blondes*, became a man.
The work of Arzner and Lupino challenge and subvert sexist
ideology while working within the male dominated Hollywood
film. Women's film collectives are another major step for
counter-cinema. Both approaches are necessary to demystify
sexist ideology.

0497
   Kaminsky, Stuart M. "Historical and social change:
   comedy and individual repression," *American Film
   Genres: Approached to a Critical Theory of Popular*

Film, by S. M. Kaminsky. Dayton: Pflaum, 1974. pp. 141-173.

In man vs. woman screwball comedies emotionally liberated women threatened the more serious men who were rigidly tied to work responsibilities and other manifestations of the traditional male role.

0498

    Kane, Joe. "Beauties, beasts and male chauvinist monsters; the plight of women in the horror film ...," *Take One*, March/April, 1973, 4(4):8.

Although most of the actresses associated with horror films have played the victim, one woman, Barbara Steele, has played the monster. Complete with fangs and expanded nostrils, Steele nevertheless exhibits beauty and sinister sexuality. Lon Chaney, Boris Karloff and the like were never expected to be handsome as well as ominous.

0499

    Kapacinskas, Thomas J. "*The Exorcist* and the spiritual problem of modern woman," *Psychological Perspectives*, 1975, 6:176-183.

The manifestation of sex roles in *The Exorcist* is analyzed in terms of Jungian Psychology.

0500

    Kaplan, Ann. "The feminist perspective in film studies," *University Film Association Journal*, 1974, 26:5+.

A proposed methodology for a feminist view of films includes: 1) women's film images and roles, 2) the historical and social context in which the film was made, and 3) the director's style and film language. When used in a "Women and Film" class this methodology provides a clear understanding of the extent of women's dehumanization in film, and allows discussion of the difference in treatment between female and male directors.

0501

    Kinder, Marsha and Beverle Houston. "Truffault's gorgeous killers," *Film Quarterly*, Winter, 1973-74, 17(2):2-10.

Though still femme fatales, Truffaut's later women are "responsible adults whose social virtues transcend the romantic illusion and selfish cruelty so pervasive in [his] earlier films."

0502
　　　Klemesrud, Judy. "Feminist goal: better image
　　　at the movies," *The New York Times*, October 13,
　　　1974. p. L-82.

With the demise of the studio system which had previously assured an adequate supply of parts for women under
contract, and with the relative absence of women in the
power structure of the film industry, male speaking roles
dominate female 12:1. The once Romantic Couple has been
replaced with prostitutes or an occasional part as someone's girlfriend. Eleanor Perry, Molly Haskell, Joan
Hackett, Phyllis Chesler and Amalie Rothschild formed a
panel at the 1974 New York Film Festival to discuss possible characterizations that would enhance the lives of the
female audience.

0503
　　　Klemsrud, Judy. "The woman who hated 'Cat Danc-
　　　ing'," *The New York Times*, July 29, 1973, p.
　　　D-1.

Eleanor Perry comments on the image of women in film:
they are confined to being pregnant, killed or raped.
Women employed in the film industry are usually secretaries, never studio heads. When they are film producers or
writers, like Perry, they regularly suffer from subtle,
and often not-so-subtle, discrimination.

0504
　　　Kopkind, Andrew. "Hollywood...under the influ-
　　　ence of women?," *Ramparts*, May, 1975, 13(8):
　　　56-60.

Some of the old Hollywood stereotypes of woman as
bitch, vamp and madonna are breaking as evidenced by the
more realistic portrayals of working class women as they
attempt to cope with day to day life in *Alice Doesn't Live
Here Anymore* and *A Woman Under the Influence*.

0505
　　　Korda, Michael. "The domestic chauvinist," *Male
　　　Chauvinism! How It Works*, by M. J. Korda. NY:
　　　Random House, 1972. pp. 151-172; also in *Sex:
　　　Male/Gender: Masculinity*, ed. by John W. Petras.
　　　Port Washington, NY: Alfred Publishing Co, 1975.
　　　pp. 149-157.

In the book and subsequent film version of Ira
Levin's *The Stepford Wives* the theme of male chauvinism is
perceived as a modern form of witchcraft and superstition.
Newspaper quotes of corporate executive wives are examined
within the context of *The Stepford Wives* credo: corporate
wives must be useful, alert, healthy and have a "sense of
humor without being witty."

0506

Kowalski, Rosemary Ribich. *Women and Film: A
Bibliography*. NY: Scarecrow, 1976.

A comprehensive annotated bibliography with 2,302
entries on women as performers, filmmakers, columnists
and critics of film, and the images of women in film. Indexed.

0507

MacLaine, Shirley. *You Can Get There from Here*.
NY: Norton, 1975.

Shirley MacLaine tells the story behind the film,
The Other Half of the Sky: A Chinese Memoir (see 0553)
in which she led an American delegation of women and feminist filmmakers through the People's Republic of China.
She also discusses her television show "Shirley's World,"
over which she had little control and had few opportunities to appear as a strong, independent woman.

0508

McGarry, Eileen. "Documentary, realism and
women's cinema," *Women and Film*. 1975, 2(7):
50-59.

Filmic realism rarely reflects true reality. Faye
Dunaway's wardrobe, makeup and hair style in *Bonnie and
Clyde* was actually more reflective of 1960's style than
1930's. She did not resemble a photograph of the historical Bonnie Parker, because certain fictional codes are
accepted where true reality would be unacceptable. These
codes, or stereotypes operate in documentary films as well.
Frederick Wiseman's *High School* deals heavily in stereotypes. The older female teachers with glasses and sharp
voices are interpreted as less interesting and less sympathetic than the younger female teachers with modern
clothes, soft voices and prettier faces. In the documentary the real woman is treated with the same stereotypes
that characterize fictional or fictionalized historical
woman in the commercial film: she is either old hag or
young chick.

0509
Martineau, Barbara. "Thoughts about the objectification of women - constructed around a series
of quotes from movies and books," *Take One*,
November/December, 1970, 3(2):15-18.

The notions of woman as object, depersonalized screen
victim, and female star as the creation of male producer
are applied to the psychology of woman's oppression in
society.

0510
Maynard, Richard A. "Women on film," *Scholastic
Teacher*, May, 1973, 102:21-22.

Six films are listed which show woman as sex object,
spinster, divorcee, bitch and happy-go-lucky, strong-
willed person. Each film raises provocative questions
about woman's role suitable for high school class discussion.

0511
Mellen, Joan. "Bergman and women: Cries and
whispers," *Film Quarterly*, Fall, 1973, 27(1):
2-11.

Rather than portray woman as an intellectual being,
Bergman presents woman only as a "creature tied to her
flesh." He does not divorce woman from a biological function in his hostile vision of women. The article is a
chapter from *Women and Sexuality in the New Film*.
See 0512.

0512
Mellen, Joan. *Women and Their Sexuality in the
New Film*. NY: Horizons Press, 1974.

Several of the film images of women examined include:
Bergman's and Bertolucci's self-hating women, the Hepburn
and Crawford "mannish" types, the sexual manikins of Monroe and followers, Karen Black's disintegrated, alienated
contemporary woman, and lesbianism in film.

0513
Michener, Charles and Martin Kasindorf. "Year
of the actress," *Newsweek*, February 14, 1977,
89(7):56-66.

Although 73% of the featured and supporting roles
have gone to men in recent years, the American Film

Institute projects a greater concentration of "women's pictures" in 1977. The decline of the studio system, television's soap operas providing dramatic roles for actresses and the present unacceptance of women's stereotyped sex roles are given as reasons for the lack of good acting parts for film actresses.

0514
Minton, Lynn. "Will Hollywood ever discover women?," *McCall's*, April, 1976, 103:150+.

Motion picture plots do not reflect the changes women are making in today's world because, according to male producers, women prefer television to movies. Midge Kovacs of NY-NOW says, "The moviemakers have totally wiped out the changing roles of women from 1968 to the present as though it never happened ... we're the vanishing species."

See 0727. J. P. Murray, "Diahann Carroll and female singers take the lead."

0515
Orth, Maureen. "How to succeed: fail, lose, die," *Newsweek*, March 4, 1974, 83(9):50-51.

While in reality American women are becoming aware of their full capacities, the film industry is reflecting America as a monosexual culture - all male. Male speaking parts outnumber female 12:1. Women in films either don't exist or play victims, losers, or extensions of male libidoes whose necklines are dropped to distract attention from a poorly written scene. This attitude will continue so long as men control the industry. The 3,060 male producers are unwilling to relinquish any control to their eight female counterparts.

0516
Patrick, Robert and William Haislip. "Thank Heaven for Little Girls," - An examination of the male chauvinist musical," *Cineaste Magazine*, 1973, 6:22-25.

The movie musicals are steeped in unattractice stereotypes of both sexes. Women are infantile and stupid but beautiful objects who can dance. Men are vulgar, brutish juveniles for whose marital devotion women sacrifice careers and wealthy suitors.

0517
    Reed, Rex. "Movies: give them back to the women,"
    Vogue, March, 1975, 165:130-131+.

    While off screen American women are leading produc-
tive, purposeful, interesting lives, on screen they barely
exist. In the paltry roles offered them, women must play
either birdbrains or ballbreakers. Although Reed lists
six movies with strong female leads he admits that this is
not enough and attributes the problem of the few female
parts to the paucity of women in powerful administrative
positions in the film industry.

0518
    Reynolds, Lessie M. "The journey toward libera-
    tion for Fellini's women," paper presented at
    the annual meeting of the Speech Communication
    Association, 1973. ERIC (ED 185 812).

    Comparison is made between Fellini's films *Le Dolce
Vita*, *8½*, and *Juliet of the Spirits* and Dante's *Divine
Comedy*. In Fellini's trilogy Juliet journeys toward her
paradise-liberation from myths about herself and the traditional notions of womankind as shown in the first two
movies.

0519
    Rock, Gail. "I can't believe I watched the
    whole thing," *Ms.*, August, 1973, 2(2):27-29.

    Several well known actresses have formed Creative
Women of America to protest the scarcity of women on televison where men outnumber them 7:1. The film industry
also needs the impetus of a group who will demand not only
quantity of female roles, but quality. One-dimensional
hookers and nagging housewives are the most visible adult
women on the screen.

0520
    Rosen, Marjorie. "Isn't it about time to bring
    on the girls?," *The New York Times*, December 15,
    1974, D-19.

    Film industry executives air their excuses for the
lack of strong female roles in current movies: no bank-
able female stars, little demand for macho women, and most
female character-types appear on television, free. Some
women in the film industry feel that strong parts will
soon be available. Dynamic actresses will then inspire
the female audience to leave theaters feeling good about
themselves.

0521
    Rosen, Marjorie. "Popcorn venus, or how the movies have made women smaller than life," *Ms.*, April, 1974, 2:41-47+; also in *University Film Association Journal*, 1974, 26:6-10.

A condensation of the book *Popcorn Venus*. See 0522.

0522
    Rosen, Marjorie. *Popcorn Venus; Women, Movies, and the American Dream.* NY: Coward McCann and Geoghegan, 1973.

Within the framework of women's history in America Rosen discusses Hollywood's various stereotypes of womanhood: the Victorian sweetheart, predatory vamp, flashy flapper, money-hungry chorine, wise-cracking women, underworld moll, Rosie the Riveter, marriage-hunter, mammory woman, professional virgin, sex object, rape victim and today's omitted woman. The last two chapters provide an upbeat ending in which 1970's few movies featuring strong women and the work of female directors and scenarists since 1915 are shown to have broken the stereotypes.

0523
    Sarris, Andrew. "From soap opera to dope opera," *The Village Voice*, August 14, 1969, p. 35.

The trend in movie themes has shifted from the tear-jerking "soap opera" in which wives were misunderstood by husbands, to the "dope opera"where alienated youths, misunderstood by parents, hustle heroin.

0524
    Secrist, Meryle. "The male chauvinist flicks," *The Washington Post*, November 1, 1971, p. K-1+.

The American Film Institute's women's film festival explored deeply rooted attitudes toward women. Typical images of women in film are Myrna Loy as the docile and domesticated wife, Katherine Hepburn as career woman bested by a man, and Marilyn Monroe epitomizing the sex object. "Emancipated womanhood [is] equated with the Communist Menace" though occasionally women like Rosalind Russell do keep both their jobs and their men.

0525
    Shevey, Sandra. "Down with myth America," *The New York Times*, May 24, 1970, p. D-13; also in *The Other Half: Roads to women's Equality*, ed.

by Cynthia F. Epstein and William J. Goode. Englewood Cliffs, NJ: Prentice-Hall, 1971. pp. 62-64.

Myths about womanhood evident in religion and folklore also function in film: women are evil temptresses who seek to destroy men. In order to survive men must therefore subjugate women. Female subjugation, male chauvinism and male homosexuality are three themes most evident in current films.

0526
Siegel, Esther. "Molly Haskell: women in the movies," *Off Our Backs*, May, 1974, 4(6):19-20.

Haskell blames directors for the lack of strong female roles in contemporary movies when contemporary reality, which movies supposedly reflect, is enjoying a steady increase of professionally and economically successful women. Most films about strong women are produced in the narrative genre by independent female filmmakers.

See 0731. B. Smith, "Black women in film symposium."

0527
Sommers, Tish. "The compounding impact of age on sex, another dimension of the double standard," *Civil Rights Digest*, Fall, 1974, 7(1):2-9.

The film *Harold and Maude* shows a bizarre symbol: love between an old woman and a young man, though a May/December wedding with sexes reversed would not be considered bizarre at all. The same billion dollar film industry promotes women from sex object to obsolescence when she reaches a certain age.

0528
Talbert, Linda Lee. *Images of Women in Three Ingmar Bergman Films: Through a Glass Darkly, Persona and Cries and Whispers*. M.A. thesis, Arizona State University, 1975.

An examination of Bergman's treatment of women reveals many provocative images, although his overall attitude is disparaging and destructive. While the male psyche is explored philosophically as well as in terms of sexuality, women are rarely shown divorced from their sexuality. Bergman's double standard involves an ethical realm for his men and a biological realm for his women.

0529

Thornburg, Linda. "The creation of a new mythology," *University Film Association Journal*, 1974,
26:13-15.

The value system of every age is supported by that
age's mythology. Twentieth century mythology is trans-
mitted through the socializing powers of the mass media,
particularly film. Women find very limited role models
among female film characters, who are most often defined
solely by their relationships to men as wives, mothers,
lovers, or prostitutes. Those servile women who live for
men usually win male love while independent women die by
the end of the film. Women are often portrayed as powerless pawns of men, however director Mai Zetterling offers
alternative images of women. Three of her films are reviewed in terms of their independent heroines who defy
the stereotypes. Directors of this nature are creating a
new mythology.

0530

Trumbo, Sherry Sonnett. "A woman's place is in
the oven," *Notes from the Third Year*, NY, 1971, pp.
90-92; also in *Radical Feminism*, ed. by Anne
Koedt, Ellen Levine, Anita Rapone. NY: Quadrangle Books, 1973. pp. 419-424.

Treatment between male and female characters varies
considerably in popular movies. Male characters in
"system" movies like *Five Easy Pieces* are aware of their
conflict with society, and actively seek to change their
situations. Female characters, however, do not seek change
but pursue a stereotyped search for security which often
frustrates the male lover's search for change. The con-
tradictory treatment of women further shows them to be
prized as objects, yet ignored as people.

See 0750. F. Ward. "Black male images in film."

0531

Weiss, Marion. "Have we really come a long way,
Baby?," *University Film Association Journal*,
1974, 26:11.

Most of the 50 top grossing movies of 1973 showed
women cast in few significant roles. Where they did have
leading roles, they played either the feminine equivalent
of Superstud, as in *Cleopatra Jones*, or else a virginal
"Mary Poppins" type. The few films directed by women or
homosexual men treated female and gay characters as if
they were "mentally disturbed idiots." American

filmmakers should follow the lead of European directors whose treatment of female and homosexual characters is much less stereotypical.

See 0115. "Women's proxy pressure."

Films By/About Women

0532
Alterman, Loraine. "Judy in disguise," *Melody Maker*, September 1, 1973, pp. 10-11.

Judy Collins discusses the making of the film, *Portrait of a Woman*, about her teacher and mentor, Dr. Antonia Brico. Collins discusses the influence of Dr. Brico's strength and independence on her early years, and talks about her own songwriting.

0533
Armatage, Kay. "Women in film," *Take One*, May-June, 1972, 3(11):45-48.

Discussion of the films and political climates of four major women's film festivals held in New York, Edinburgh, London and Toronto from June, 1972 to July, 1973.

0534
Binford, Mira Reym. "Half the sky: women's worlds on film," *International Development Review*, 1976, 18:37-40.

A review of nine films about Third World women, filmed in their environments and cultures. The final message states that until women find their own voices, they need to speak to one another. Films by and about women reveal different truths than those made by men.

0535
Dawson, Bonnie. *Women's Films in Print: An Annotated Guide to 800 Films by Women*. San Francisco: Booklegger Press, 1975.

An annotated listing of 800 16mm films produced or directed by women. Includes a directory of filmmakers.

0536
"The emerging woman," *Off Our Backs*, March, 1974, 4(4):16-17.

The making of a feminist documentary film showing today's feminists emerging from the underpaid, overworked millworkers of the early twentieth century. The article is illustrated with old photographs and woodcuts from the film, including a 1920 photo of a picketing Alice Paul.

0537
Epple, Ron. "Films by/about women," *Media and Methods*, February, 1975, 11(6):36-37.

Reviews give films dealing sensitively with the female experience.

0538
Faxon, Pookie and Mary Bolint. "Films by and/or about women, 1972: Directory of filmmakers, films and distributors, Internationally, past and present." ERIC (ED 127 217).

An annotated listing of films arranged by subject.

0539
Freyer, Ellen. "Film," *Craft Horizon*, April, 1974, 34:13+.

A review of three very different films: one documents "hip feminism," one tells of an individual struggle for independence and strength in becoming a woman, the third is a feminist political newsreel.

0540
"Films by and about women." Available from Insight Exchange, PO Box 42584, San Francisco, CA 94101.

16 mm films dealing with women's issues: art, sexuality, aging, worker's rights and sports.

0541
Grilikhes, Alexandra. "Films by women, 1928-1971," *Film Library Quarterly*, 1972/1973, 6(1):8-11+.

One of the most powerful socializing forces in our society is the film medium. Because most directors are male, it is the male image of woman as harpy, narcissist and sexual prop that prevails. Based on that premise the author created a film festival of all female filmmakers to explore female perceptions of womanhood. All films shown during the festival are discussed in terms of the filmmaker's vision and/or cinematic innovations. Grilikhes calls for more women to become filmmakers in order to change media images of women to more powerful, truer visions of womanhood.

0542
    Henshaw, Richard. "Women directors, 150 filmographies," *Film Comment*, November/December, 1972, 4:33-45.

The images of women in front of the camera and behind it are explored in the introduction to the styles of 150 directors examined.

See 0496. C. Johnston, "Women's cinema as counter-cinema."

    "Judith Chaikin: How to increase the boxoffice at Paramount," *Media Report to Women*, February 1, 1976, 4(2):1.

In order to reflect the experiences of the 53% female population, Paramount should hire women writers, directors, producers and technicians from this country's large pool of female talent.

0543
    Lindeborg, Lisbeth. "Fostering feminist films," *Atlas World Press Review*, April, 1976, 23:50.

International filmmakers Mai Zetterling, Agnes Varda, Sarah Maldorer, Liliane de Kermadec, Michele Rosier, and Nelly Kaplan describe the image and experience of women articulated in their films.

0544
    Lowell, Sondra. "Women in film," *Take One*, September/October, 1971, 3(7):40-41.

Herstory Films, a women's production company, was formed to combat the discrimination faced by women filmmakers and scriptwriters working for network news. The group works as a collective - everyone participates in shooting, editing and scriptwriting.

0545
McCreadie, Marsha. "The sex second festival of
women's films," *Feminist Art Journal*, 1976, 5(4):
16-19.

Retrospective and recent international films shown at
the women's festival include fiction films and documentaries. The article reviews the films, the filmmaker's forums
and the revealing audience reactions.

0546
Notes on Women's Cinema, ed. by Claire Johnston.
(Screen pamphlet, 2). London: Society for Edu-
cation in Film and Television, 1973.

The male created image of women in cinema articulates
women's cultural oppression. To counter this effect wom-
en's filmmaking collectives are forming in Europe and
America to emphasize women's creativity and dispel the
male media myth of woman as "one-dimensional daydream of
leisure and sexuality." The notes include several articles
and an interview with Nelly Kaplan.

0547
"Reel life at last - women and film," *Ms.*, August, 1973, 2(2):95-98.

Though rarely producing or directing films, women
have actively edited and written screenplays since the
earliest films. Today female filmmakers are taking their
places in all aspects of filmmaking, and are using the
women's film as an instrument for social change. Includes an annotated list of non-sexist films.

See 0058. J. Reichert and J. Klein. *Growing up Female.*

See 0522. M. Rosen. *Popcorn Venus; Women, Movies and the
American Dream.*

See 0526. E. Siegel. "Molly Haskell: Women in the
movies."

0548
Smith, Sharon, "Women who make movies," *Women
and Film*, July, 1973, pp. 77-90.

An annotated filmography of American, French, English,
German, Russian, Scandinavian, Italian and Eastern

European filmmakers from 1913 to the present in a condensed version of the book by the same title. See 0549.

0549
Smith, Sharon. *Women Who Make Movies*. (Cinema Studies series). NY: Hopkinson and Blake, 1975.

Chronicles the work of women filmmakers in the history of motion pictures in a worldwide survey of film since 1896, and identifies new women filmmakers working with 16mm and 35mm film.

0550
"Special report: the woman director," *Action*, *Directors Guild of America*, July/August, 1973, 8(4):7-23.

A special issue on the work of directors Dorothy Arzner, Ida Lupino and other female directors prominent in the history of film.

0551
Steed, Judy. "It's no secret that oil and gas and film festivals are related," *This Magazine is About Schools*, 1973, 7:3-5.

Injustices faced by Canadian feminist/nationalist filmmakers at the hands of those who regard Canada as an American colony include the discarding of Canadian political films in favor of American "middle class" films shown at a Canadian women's film festival.

See 0063. J. Sternburg. "Revealing herself."

See 0467. "Transition group formed by film executives seeks better climate for women."

0552
"WNET-13 Film and videocassette distribution catalog." WNET/13, 356 W. 58th St., NY, NY 10019.

Several programs from the *Woman Alive* series are available for rental.

0553
Weill, Claudia. *The Other Half of the Sky: A*

China Memoir. Available from Cyclops Films,
1697 Broadway, NY 10019.

A documentary on Shirley MacLaine's American Women's
delegation to the People's Republic of China.

0554
    Women and Film: A Resource Handbook. Washington,
    DC: Association of American Colleges, 1972; also
    in ERIC (ED 085 034).

Lists feature length commercial and documentary films
suitable for film festivals on women's roles. Also lists
16mm films and slide programs.

0555
    "Women in film issue," *Take One*, November/December,
    1970, 3(2).

The special issue includes articles, "Notes on Women
Directors," "Women on Women in Film," a filmography of
Canadian women directors, and interviews with Shirley
Clarke and Joyce Wieland.

0556
    *The Work of Dorothy Arzner; Towards a Feminist
    Cinema*, ed. by Claire Johnston. London: Brit-
    ish Film Institute, 1975. Available from BFI,
    81 Dean St., London WIV 6AA. .50p.

An examination of Arzner's contribution toward a
feminist counter cinema dealing with the female characterizations in Arzner's oeuvre, and ending with an interview
of the director.

PRINT MEDIA

Magazines

0557
   Anant, Victor. "A woman's own world," *New So-*
   ciety, January 1, 1976, 35(691):12-14.

   When compared to 1958 fiction, sex roles, themes and
plots of 1975 magazine fiction revealed that female characters were no longer bitchy towards each other, hysterical or jealous of one another. Male romantic figures in
1975 led more realistic lifestyles as opposed to the 1958
preoccupation with glamorous professions.

0558
   Bailey, Margaret. "The women's magazine short-
   story heroine in 1957 and 1967," *Journalism*
   Quarterly, 1969, 46:364-366; also in *Toward a*
   Sociology of Women, by Constantine Safilios-Roths-
   child. Lexington, Mass: Xerox College Publishing,
   1972. pp. 37-40.

   Betty Friedan's findings of the romantic happy housewife heroine predominating magazine fiction of 1958-1959
were tested for theme change in three 1967 issues of wom-
en's magazine fiction. The primary statistical change
from 1957 to 1967 indicated that happy housewives had become even happier - 93% happier - with the passing of ten
years. In 1967 the female characters had more children
and fewer romantic problems. The most significant change
was the increase of psychological problems such as grief
at a child's death. Working women were most often portrayed as "unwomanly" or as a threat to a "true" woman's
marriage. A more realistic portrayal of women in magazine
fiction was not foreseen until very definite changes are
made in the lifestyles of American women.

See 0401. P. B. Bart, "Depression in middle-aged women."

0559

Berryman, Cynthia L. "The language of women as a reflection of the image of women in a mass-circulated magazine: an analysis of *Ladies' Home Journal* fiction, 1900-1920," *Siscom '75, Women's (and Men's) Communication;* Proceedings of the Speech Communication Association's Summer Conference XI, 1975. pp. 56-62; also in ERIC (ED 127 643), pp. 62-68.

Analysis of the language used in *Ladies' Home Journal* from 1902 to 1910 and 1911 to 1920 revealed a change in woman's image. The first decade typically reflected women as married and restless, or expressing agreement with the current struggle for women's rights. By the story's end her desires were usually suppressed. The fiction of the second decade however projected an outwardly rebellious image of women who remained single, were outspoken, critical and self-sufficient. While her behavior changed drastically, her language patterns remained the same. In both decades her speech made her seem overly-talkative, emotional, non-assertive, uncertain or submissive.

0560

Binns, Catherine A. *Careers and Jobs for American Women as Reflected in the Pages of Mademoiselle,* 1935-1973. M.A. thesis, University of Missouri, 1974.

An historical approach to *Mademoiselle's* position on woman's role in society, her image in editorial content, and the influence of the women's liberation movement on editorial content. *Mademoiselle* is applauded for its treatment of careers at times when other women's magazines ignored the subject of careers for women.

See 0018. J. S. Chafetz, "Masculine, feminine or human?"

See 1003. P. Clarke and V. Esposito, "A study of occupational advice for women in magazines."

0561

Cowan, Ruth Schwarts. "Two washes in the morning and a bridge party at night: the American housewife between the wars," *Women's Studies,* 1976, 3:147-172.

Analysis of the non-fiction articles and ads from post-World War I women's magazines argues that the feminine mystique began in the 1920's and was reinforced

during the Depression of the 1930's. The advent of household technology became a major influence on the ideology
that oppresses women.

0562
   "Everything you ever wanted to know about advertising and were not afraid to ask," *Ms.*, November,
   1974, 3:56-59+.

   Most women's magazines are advertising catalogs whose
editorial pages make up a paltry 33% of each issue. *Ms.*
is different in that it has a 66% editorial policy and
accepts no advertising that demeans or condescends to
women. *Ms.* solicits advertising for all products that
women buy: insurance, airline tickets, stereo equipment
and cars, as well as makeup and food.

0563
   Flora, Cornelia Butler. "The passive female: her
   comparative image by class and culture in women's
   magazine fiction," *Journal of Marriage and the
   Family*, 1971, 33:435-444.

   An examination of 202 stories from North American and
Latin American women's magazines determined that fictional
women were more often rewarded for passive behavior than
for actively controlling their own lives. The author contends that this type of fiction shapes and reinforces
readers' values.

0564
   Franzwa, Helen H. "Female roles in women's maga-
   zine fiction, 1940-1970," *Woman: Dependent or
   Independent Variable*, ed. by Rhoda Unger and
   Florence Denmark. NY: Psychological Dimensions,
   1975. pp. 42-53.

   A thematic content analysis reveals four prevalent
female roles in 122 examples of women's magazine fiction:
1) the single, young woman whose charming incompetence,
passivity and virtue win her a husband; 2) the inherently
passive married woman who doesn't work, is devoted to her
husband, is purposely less competent than he in order to
save the marriage; 3) the widow-divorcee who cannot cope
without a man's authority; and 4) the lonely, useless,
unhappy, childless spinster.

0565
   Franzwa, Helen H. "Pronatalism in women's magazine fiction," *Pronatalism: the Myth of Mom and*

Apple Pie, ed. by Ellen Peck and Judith Senderowitz. NY: T.Y. Crowell, 1974. pp. 68-77.

Although the US birth rate has been steadily declining since 1956, the birth rate in women's magazine fiction
has steadily increased as the home-oriented mother remains
the image of the ideal woman. In a study of 122 stories
appearing in three women's magazines from 1940 to 1970,
prevalent fictional themes portray housewife-mothers leading the most fulfilling careers, babies solving marital
problems, childless women leading wasted lives, and married women not working.

See 1004. H. H. Franzwa, "Working women in fact and fiction."

0566
     Friedan, Betty. "The happy housewife heroine,"
     The Feminine Mystique, by B. Friedan. NY: Norton,
     1963. pp. 33-68; also in *A World of Her Own;*
     Writings and the Feminist Controversy, ed. by
     John N. Miller. Columbus, Ohio: C. E. Merrill,
     1971.

The changes in image of the American woman in women's
magazine fiction are traced from the emancipated "new
woman" of the 1930's and 1940's to the glorified housewife-
mother of the 1950's and 1960's who aspire to no other
lifestyle.

See 0028. E. Goldfield, "A woman is a sometime thing."

See 0031. J. Harris, "A role without a script."

0567
     Hatch, Mary G. and David L. Hatch. "Problems of
     married and working women as presented by three
     popular working women's magazines," *Social
     Forces*, 1958, 37:148-153; also in *Women in a
     Man-Made World*, ed. by N. Glazer-Malbin. Chicago:
     Rand McNally, 1972. pp. 183-186.

Three leading women's magazines were examined for a
year to determine how well the magazines met the needs of
working women. Most articles offered advice on how to
reconcile the need for familial affection with the desire
for recognition and creative expression outside the home,
and advice for managing a home after working hours. The
more recent magazines, whose editors evidently recognized

the increasing move of women into the workforce, were criticized here for not clarifying female goals and encouraging better vocational training for women.

0568
    Hoerger, Shelby. *Models of Success in Women's Magazines: An Analysis of Biographies Directed at Different Target Audiences.* M.A. thesis, University of Pennsylvania, 1975.

The approach to biographical content of career people differed in three magazines examined. *Cosmopolitan* emphasized exoticism and fortune in biographies of non-married models in popular entertainment. *Ladies' Home Journal* emphasized American values and featured middle-aged, married models in traditionally sex related occupations, while *Ms.* featured women established in serious careers, usually of non-celebrity nature, with biographical emphasis on career achievements and social contributions.

0569
    Honey, Maureen. "Images of women in *The Saturday Evening Post,* 1931-1936," *Journal of Popular Culture,* 1976, 10:352-358.

Depression age images of women in *The Saturday Evening Post* fiction often showed them in politics and facing obstacles of overt sex discrimination in employment. Successful career women were usually single ("preferably widowed") but if married, often faced conflict between marriage and career. The author wonders why career women were so common in fiction during the 1930's period of tight national economy, then changed drastically by the early 1950's.

0570
    Hynes, Teresa Mary. *The Portrayal of Woman in Selected Magazines from 1911-1930.* Ph.D. dissertation, University of Wisconsin, 1975.

Content analysis of 300 fiction and 486 non-fiction articles revealed that women in the 1920's were only slightly more emancipated than those in the 1910's. Women were concerned with politics only as an extension of the homemaker role. Careers were considered secondary to wifehood and women were liberated only in terms of individual development rather than in relationships with men and women.

0571

Ison, Susan Harte. *An Analysis of Stereotypic Male-Female Relationships in Selected Fiction Sections in Two Women's Magazines, 1924 and 1974.* M.A. thesis, University of Georgia, 1975.

While 1924 portrayals of women showed a diversity in degree of beauty, social class background and age, by 1974 women had become almost strictly middle class, middle age and average in appearance. The fiction of 1974 showed women with more aggressive personalities both in career and in influencing men's lives. Women were seen being smothered by marriage.

0572

Key, Wilson Bryan. "The gay playboy's penthouse," *Media Sexploitation*, by W. B. Key. Englewood Cliffs, NJ: Prentice-Hall, 1976. pp. 16-34.

Biologically women may have greater levels of sexual energy than most men, but the media have carefully trained women to consider themselves sexually inadequate. The purchase of clothes, cosmetics, food and other commodities and services will make her more desirable and feminine. The female self-image is further undermined in magazines like *Playgirl* who portray women as starry-eyed romantics and naive fools. *Playgirl's* articles advise women to "be an idiot" and its cartoons emphasize female disloyalty, selfishness and dominating tendencies.

0573

Kidd, Virginia. "Happily ever after and other relationship styles: advice on interpersonal relations in popular magazines, 1951-1973," *Quarterly Journal of Speech*, 1975, 61:31-39.

Non-fiction articles in popular magazines teach women how to transform themselves from Cinderella to the princess.

0574

Kline, Helen G. *The Old and the New: Ladies' Home Journal and New Woman.* M.A. thesis, Murray State University, 1972.

A comparison of the regular features and articles in 12 issues each of *Ladies' Home Journal* and *New Woman* proves a significant difference in content between the two magazines. Although the tables of contents show similarity in types of articles published (marriage, children, finances, working women and sex) the treatment differs greatly. *Ladies' Home Journal* guides its readers in running a household while *New Woman* informs readers on political and world affairs, and career opportunities.

0575

Lugenbeel, Barbara Derrick. *A Content Analysis of Good Housekeeping's Short Fiction from November 1972 - October 1973*, M.A. thesis, University of South Carolina, 1974.

Recurring themes in a 24 story analysis of *Good Housekeeping* fiction found self-sacrificing women rewarded, the wife/mother role lauded, and little encouragement for female identities to be developed outside the home. A comparison between short-length and full-length fiction revealed more liberated full-length protagonists.

0576

Mather, Anne D. *A History and Analysis of Feminist Periodicals*. M.A. thesis, University of Georgia, 1973.

A study of feminist periodicals from 1968 to 1973 revealed that they are usually run by women's collectives without hierarchical titles and salaries. A collective editorial policy features editorials written by the entire staff rather than by one editor. Feminist periodicals feature non-sexist advertising and offer free listings of other feminist periodicals. Favored non-fiction articles include feminist criticism and review of the arts, news of the women's liberation movement, and women's history. Fashion and beauty features found in traditional women's periodicals were ignored by feminist periodicals.

0577

Matkov, Rebecca Roper. *Ladies' Home Journal and McCall's in 1960 and 1970: A Content Analysis*. M.A. thesis, University of North Carolina, 1972.

Treatment of American social trends (falling birthrate, increasing female employment, rising educational level of women, and increased concern for women's rights and roles) was compared in 1960 and 1970 issues of *Ladies' Home Journal* and *McCall's*. By 1970 both magazines had begun to reflect new trends.

0578

"The *Ms. Magazine* success story: an interview with Pat Carbine," *Folio: The Magazine for Magazine Management*, April, 1975, 4(2):29-34.

Ms. Magazine operated in the black seven months after beginning publication. Success is attributed to a policy of 65% editorial pages/35% advertising. Because of an initially high subscription rate readers pay for the editorial pages as opposed to the traditional control by advertising revenue. *Ms.* solicits ads from automobile, credit card, airline and financial companies whose goods and services affect women.

0579
    Nye, Russel Blaine. "Stories for the people,"
    *The Unembarrassed Muse: The Popular Arts in
    America*, by R. B. Nye. NY: Dial Pr, 1970.
    pp. 10-40.

As the nineteenth century suffrage movement took hold, an interest in women's magazines was generated. Magazine fiction, as well as the newly-created domestic novel, questioned male-oriented society. This slant soon changed to stories of stock characters and basic plots. The characters: the Other Woman, the Handsome Seducer, the Martyred Wife, and the Dying Child, still appear in women's magazines, 130 years later.

See 0053. E. Peck, "The media trap."

0580
    Ray, Lovelle. "The American women in mass media:
    how much emancipation and what does it mean?,"
    Toward a Sociology of Women, ed. by Constantina
    Safilios-Rothschild. Lexington, Mass: Xerox,
    1972. pp. 41-62.

Both fiction and non-fiction articles in the 1965-1970 issues of *McCall's, Ladies Home Journal, Cosmopolitan* and *Playboy* were compared for their approach toward occupational role models for women and for each magazine's general image of women.

0581
    "Redbook editor sees outreach goal for women's
    magazine today," *Media Report to Women*, January
    1, 1976, 4(1):6.

Sey Chassler lists some specific practices of other media and describes *Redbook*'s attempts to teach women their potential.

0582

Rosbrow, Susan R. *Sexual Stereotyping in Magazine Fiction: A Discussion of the Romantic Myth in America.* Ph.D. dissertation, Adelphi University, 1974.

A content analysis of sexual stereotyping in fiction of 13 popular magazines from 1935 and 1971 revealed that the 1935 measure of attractive women and strong men was less significant in 1971 when both sexes were described equally in terms of strength. The romance-oriented concerns of 1935 shifted to non-romantic domestic interests by 1971. Increased sexual freedom, more available birth control, women's greater economic role and the isolation of the nuclear family account for the shift from the sexual stereotyping of 1935.

0583

Schrib, June. *Status of Women: Treatment by Selected Consumer Magazines, 1961 - 1971.* M.A. thesis, University of Wyoming, 1972.

Examination of 204 articles in consumer magazines from 1961 to 1971 revealed little attention paid to the status of women and little agreement with the aims of the women's liberation movement. By mid-1971, however, less overall emphasis was placed on the image of women as sex object and homemaker.

0584

Silver, Sheila J. "Then and now: women's roles in *McCall's* magazine in 1964 and 1974," paper presented at annual meeting of the Association for Education in Journalism, 1976. ERIC (ED 124 985).

McCall's simultaneously promotes the traditional roles of the American woman while encouraging greater self-expression within these roles. It covers the feminist issues of abortion, day care and reassessment of family responsibilities, though doesn't fully endorse any issue. It encourages a wider sphere of activity for readers while continuing to guide them in traditional roles.

0585

"Survey of women magazine editors," *Media Report to Women*, March 1, 1974, 2(3):2.

Findings of this survey revealed that women's magazines are predominately edited by men, while technical magazines in traditionally male fields are commonly edited by women. *Petroleum Today, Architectural Engineering News* and *New American Electronics* all have female editors. However only one of 25 news magazines, *Negro Reporter*, is edited by a woman.

0586
　　Stern, Paula. "The womanly image," *Atlantic*, March, 1970, 225(3):87-90.

Each stage of a woman's life is molded by five popular magazines which individually emphasize each separate life situation: adolescence, college, wedding, motherhood, and the career situation. Each magazine reinforces sex role stereotypes both in editorial policy which stress appearance, and in advertisements which sell douches and diamonds.

0587
　　Taylor, Nancy Jane. *Women in Illustrations from Ladies' Home Journal (1890-1899), Vanity Fair (1920-1929).* M.S. thesis, University of Illinois.

The image of women in magazine illustrations from 1890-1929 changed very little: *Ladies' Home Journal* portrayed women as "romantic virtuous creatures" while *Vanity Fair* portrayed them as "romantic silly creatures."

0588
　　Tilghman, Romalyn A. *A Content Analysis of Goals and Occupations of Heroines in Three Women's Magazines: 1944-1972.* M.S. thesis, University of Kansas, 1974.

A study of fictional heroines from 267 stories published in *Good Housekeeping, Ladies' Home Journal* and *McCall's* revealed little change in depiction of occupational goals during the 28 year period examined.

See 0206. C. Ventura, "Impact of women's liberation movement on advertising trends."

See 0287. H. C. Wasson, "The Ms. in magazine advertising.

See 0991. "Women beginning the sex stereotype rollback."

See 0012. S. Brownmiller, "Victims: the setting."

See 0015. L. J. Busby, "Sex role research in the mass media."

0589
    Carlson, Pamela G. "Are women's pages getting better?," *Editor and Publisher*, May 31, 1975, 108:11.

Instead of stereotyping women's interests as primarily news of births and marriages, newspapers of all sizes are shifting emphasis to feature stories on abortion, finance, nutrition and medicine. Consequently men as well as women are reading the "Lifestyle" section.

0590
    Carmody, Deirdre. "Gloria Steinem says press is failing woman reader," *The New York Times*, April 26, 1973, p. 27.

In a speech to newspaper publishers Steinem said that newspapers fail to cover women's news - ERA, sex differences in income, alimony, abortion, welfare and childcare, though the same newspapers never fail to report high school basketball scores. The women's movement is not reported accurately.

0591
    Delsman, Mary A. "Putting the ERA in context," *Everything You Need to Know about the ERA*, by M. A. Delsman. Riverside, CA: Meranza Press, 1975. pp. 13-27.

The newspaper medium is dominated by men, consequently few women have risen to top ranks in journalism. Even female reporters assigned to the women's pages are often supervised by male editors. The dominance of men in the mass media has influenced the coverage of news about the women's movement. Feminists are alternately treated as living jokes or as participants in cat fights.

0592
    Drew, Dan G. and Susan H. Miller. "Sex stereotyping and reporting." Paper presented at the annual meeting to the Association for Education

in Journalism, 1976. ERIC (ED 124 893).

Two groups of student reporters were given packets
of information about a female or a male newsmaker. The
coverage by the two groups of reporters showed that Subjects were more likely to mention qualifications when the
newsmaker was male, while noting concern for female's
capacity for combining traditional sex role with job, and
her ability to handle the job.

0593
"Equality lies in attaining top media positions,"
Editor and Publisher, May 17, 1975, 108(20):10+.

Print journalists ignore hard news about women, don't
recognize a woman's right to be called by the title of her
choice, and fail to send female reporters to cover important stories.

0594
Guenin, Zena Beth. "Women's pages in American
newspapers: missing out on contemporary content."
Journalism Quarterly, 1975, 52:66-68.

A content analysis of women's pages of six daily newspapers from various regions of the US reveals a shift in
coverage from the traditional wedding and society copy to
the more modernized general interest concerns of entertainment, and news of personalities. Further improvement
in the field of consumer news would be desirable.

0595
Guenin, Zena Beth. "Women's pages in the 1970's,"
Montana Journalism Review, 1973, 16:27-32.

Problems facing women's pages include a general re-
luctance to change from society/bridal format to informa-
tional priority, and a common salary discrepancy between
female and male journalists. The article describes some
changing attitudes.

0596
Guenin, Zena Beth. *Women's Pages in Transition*.
M.A. thesis, California State University - North-
ridge, 1973.

By expanding coverage of women's pages to include
broader interest topics, a wider audience is expected.
During the transitional period women journalists should
be given wider newsroom experience and opportunity to

edit improved women's sections. Meanwhile the working
press and journalism scholars should more carefully guide
a smooth transition.

0597
    Lachowitch, Christina. *The Photographic Portrayal
of Women in the Washington Post Now and Before
Women's Liberation Movement.* M.A. thesis, University of South Carolina, 1975.

Comparison of newspaper photographs of women in 1963
and 1975 revealed a significant decrease in stereotyped
photographs of women. The decrease is attributed to the
greater numbers of women entering traditionally male-
dominated occupations, and feminist efforts to eliminate
sexism in the media.

0598
    Miller, Susan H. "The content of news photos:
women's and men's roles," *Journalism Quarterly,*
1975, 52:70-75.

Although *The Washington Post* and *The Los Angeles
Times* have both made efforts to expand their coverage of
women, a study of 46 issues revealed that photographs of
men outnumbered those of women 3:1. Men dominated the
photo coverage in all sections of both papers except the
lifestyle sections which contained 44% of all the pictures
of women, and showed them primarily as brides and social-
ites rather than as newsmakers. The economic and social
changes in women's roles were not reflected in photo
coverage.

0599
    Morris, Monica B. "Newspapers and the new femi-
nists: black out as social control?" *Journalism
Quarterly,* 1973, 50:37.

American and English mass circulation newspapers from
1969-1970 were examined for coverage of the women's movement. For the most part news of the movement was ignored.
Newspapers were not meeting their anticipatory role by
ignoring feminist protest of women's negative image, challenges of the nuclear family's viability, and the right of
a woman to control her own body.

0600
    Richards, Carol R. "Stylebooks vs. IWY: the right
to choose Ms., Miss, or Mrs.," *American Society
of Newspaper Editors Bulletin,* September 16,

1976, pp. 6-8.

While the IWY Commission takes a conservative view
in its proposal that women quoted in newspaper articles
choose one of the three courtesy titles, Women in Communications, Inc. recommends eliminating courtesy titles altogether. These titles only perpetuate the idea that a
woman is defined by her relationship to a man. The
policies of various wire services and large metropolitan
newspapers are compared concerning use of courtesy titles
and earned titles such as Dr. or Reverend, which many
newspapers refuse to associate with female doctors, professors and ministers.

0601
Rupp, Carla Marie. "Sports editors urged to hire
more women," *Editor and Publisher*, June 19, 1976,
109:13.

Women's sports should be more heavily covered in the
sports pages, more women should be educated to become
sportswriters, sports photos of women should discontinue
emphasis on "breasts and butt" and female sportswriters
should be given passenger access on team charter flights.

0602
Sears, Marsha. *A Content Analysis of the Woman's
Pages of Five Kansas Newspapers*. M.A. thesis,
University of Kansas, 1975.

The women's pages in Kansas newspapers have increased
space allocation for "now" copy relating to non-traditional
female roles. The *Wichita Beacon* increased "now" material
from 5.1% in 1960 to 40.1% in 1972.

0603
Smith, Terry and Jack Levin. "Social change in
sex roles: an analysis of advice columns,"
Journalism Quarterly, 1974, 51:525-527.

An examination of newspaper advice columns from years
1947-1951 and 1967-1971 reveals a female-supportive trend.
The "male right/female wrong" position was given 57% emphasis in the earlier period and reduced to 41% in the
later period. Authors contend that society is slowly
shifting in its sex role attitudes by supporting the female
behavior and blaming the male behavior more than in past
years.

604
Van Gelder, Lindsy. "Women's pages: you can't make news out of a silk purse," *Ms.*, November, 1974, 3(5):112+; also in *Mass Media: The Invisible Environment Revisited*, ed. by Robert J. Glessing and William P. White. Chicago: Science Research Associates, 1976. pp. 147-150.

Newspaper women's pages may have changed their names to the slicker "Tempo" or "Scene" but the content has remained the same: serious news stories about the Equal Rights Amendment and rape legislation, which should be on pages one or two, are dumped in the women's pages along with the horoscopes and crossword puzzles. Placing the comics on the stock market page would make just as little sense, however the fact remains that the women's pages are the "dumping ground." The author suggests that "front-of-the-paper" news about women be placed in the news section along with news about men, with the trivia section kept separate from Lifestyle/Tempo/Scene pages which should explore various lifestyles and scenes.

0605
von Hoffman, Nicholas. "Women's pages: an irreverent view," *Columbia Journalism Review*, July/August, 1971, 10(2):52-54.

Poor management of the women's pages by managing editors results in sometimes shoddy reporting and missed stories concerning events (i.e., the early consumer movement) that touch people every day of their lives. The women's pages should be responsible for informing all people of both sexes on a broad range of topics.

Print Journalism Employment

See also NEWS MEDIA, 0071 - 0100

0606
Chang, Won H. "Characteristics and self-perceptions of women's page editors," *Journalism Quarterly*, 1975, 52:61-65.

A survey of 335 women's page editors revealed that female editors outnumber male editors 10:1, but male editors make significantly higher salaries.

0607

Chisholm, Shirley, "The white press: racist and sexist," *Black Scholar*, September, 1973, 5(1): 20-22.

The all-male, all-white Gridiron Club blatantly excludes female and minority members. Its industry, the press, makes only a token effort to recruit female and black reporters. Even though the Washington, DC population is 71% black, *The Washington Post* employed only 19 blacks and 34 women on its editorial staff in 1973. In the newspaper industry as a whole, only 20% of the professional reporters were female.

See 0591. M. A. Delsman, "Putting the ERA in context."

0608

"Joan Nicholson: on using employee publications for affirmative action," *Media Report to Women*, June 1, 1974, 2(6):4.

Company publications should provide visibility for women. Advertising rarely shows women in non-household related situations. On toy packages boys outnumber girls 3:1, magazines and newspapers show women's role in business as prisoner to the typewriter. In-house publications can counterbalance this stereotype by showing women doing higher level jobs and moving into previously all-male bastions of the corporate hierarchy.

0609

Lublin, Joann S. "Discrimination against women in newsrooms: fact or fantasy? *Journalism Quarterly*, 1972, 49:357-361.

An analysis of the extent and nature of discrimination against female newspaper journalists was performed by surveying 264 newspaper women. The results indicated some degree of sex bias in hiring, job status, promotability and salary, while many jobs and beats were still related to traditional sex roles rather than equal opportunity for women.

0610

Nagel, Glennis L. *A Study of the Woman Journalist Working on Daily Newspapers in Nebraska*. M.S. thesis, Kansas State University, 1974.

Some results of a study determining the status of women working on Nebraska daily newspapers indicate that she is most likely to work in the women's news department, and is basically happy with her work but would prefer higher salary, better assignments and better working hours.

See 108. L. C. Pogrebin, "Women on the tube."

0611
   Preston, Marilynn, Patricia Anstett and Glenda Sampson. "Women in the newsroom, '71: still begging crumbs," *Chicago Journalism Review*, July, 1971, 4:3-4.

Case studies of discriminatory treatment of newspaper women in story assignments and career promotion indicates that women are not treated with dignity or equality even when they have proven their writing talent and stamina.

See 0059. *Rooms with No View.*

0612
   Rupp, Carla M. "Tina Hills: a housewife in communication," *Editor and Publisher*, March 13, 1976, 109:13+.

Hills, first female IAPA Vice-President/President-elect, and President/Publisher of *El Mundo* newspaper, tells of career opportunities for women in Puerto Rico. *El Mundo's* staff is half female, with a newsroom over 50% female, and gives maternity leave.

See 0585. "Survey of women magazine editors."

THE POPULAR CULTURE

Music

See 0532. L. Alterman, "Judy in disguise."

0613
        Bangs, Lester. "They won't get fooled again,"
        Ms., August 1972, 1(2):23-26.

        The misogynistic lyrics of Cock Rock, Janis Joplin's
image as floozy, and the masochistic lyrics of female
groups are compared to the more self-respecting image of
a group called "Joy of Cooking" whose lyrics reveal the
philosophy of budding feminism and female strength.

0614
        Cavin, Susan. "Missing women: on the voodoo
        trail to jazz," *Journal of Jazz Studies*, 1975,
        3:4-27.

        Most of the pre-Jazz voodoo songs sung by slaves
celebrated the role of the Voodoo Queen. The article includes quotes from several songs and a discussion of the
crucial role held by the queens in assimilating the African, American and European traditional attitudes of
admiration and fear for good and bad witches.

0615
        Chmaj, Betty E. "It ain't me babe! or is it?:
        American women through the eyes of the counter-
        culture music, films," *Image, Myth and Beyond*
        (American Women and American Studies,2). Pitts-
        burgh: KNOW, 1972, pp. 115+; also in ERIC (ED
        121 192).

        Chmaj calls groupies the rock equivalent of the steno
pool, and discusses images of women in the songs of Bob
Dylan, Simon and Garfunkle and Janis Joplin. The image
of women in most rock lyrics is she who is destined "to
make the bed and lay in it: a return to domesticity with

the happy housewife heroine and the great American bitch."

Post-war films starring Marilyn Monroe personify the
Sex Goddess/Dumb Blonde role while Doris Day and Debbie
Reynolds personify the perpetual virgin. Marlon Brando
and several other actors become the Ordinary Guy.

0616
"Cock Rock: men always seem to end up on top,"
Rat, October/November, 1970.

Macho reigns supreme in rock from the male performer,
disc jockeys and technical personnel to the lyrics and the
male star/female groupie trip. Female performers are
limited to the more feminine folk guitar medium while the
flashy electric sound is reserved for men who use the
electronic energy to charge up misogynistic songs. Women
are most often equated with their genitals, but other recurring images of womenhood are the mysterious Ruby Tues-
day and bitchy witchy woman. When speaking to the
audience, performers make third person references to "old
ladies" and "chicks", implying that the audience is totally
male. From artist to listener women are allowed no valid
place in rock music. When women like Janis Joplin try to
find a place for themselves in rock music, they become
vulnerable symbols of pain. With only a microphone and
no instrument to separate her body from the audience,
Joplin's image became rock world sex object, even among
her friends. There is no other image for woman on the
macho rock stage.

0617
Dopp, Bonnie Jo. "The music in women," *Booklegger
Magazine*, September, October, 1975, 2(11):2-7.

Only lyrics celebrating the strength of the female
experience are accepted by producers of *Womansongs* records
and songbooks. They have no male-oriented lyrics.

See 0026. J. Faust, "Testimony before the New York City
Commission on Human Rights."

See 0665. C. W. Ferguson, "In the lighter vein."

0618
Greiner-Shumick, Betty. "Get'cher rocks off
baby, 'cause it's a man's man's man's man's
world!," *Paid My Dues*, May, 1974, 1:13.

Rock-n-roll should be revitalized by the woman's consciousness of the Blues singers who brought excitement to Rock's earliest days.

See 0492. M. Haskell, "Women in films: a decade of going nowhere."

0619
    Howe, Florence. "Feminism and literature,"
    Images of Women in Fiction, ed. by Susan K. Cor-
    nillon. Bowling Green: Bowling Green Popular
    Press, 1972. pp. 253-277.

    In the autobiographical account preceding her dis-
cussion of women in literature, Howe mentions pop music's
contribution to women's image. Being a woman is equated
with being a sex object in many lyrics.

See 0746. B. Lohof, "Higher meaning of Marlboro cigarettes."

0620
    Maccoby, Eleanor Emmons and Carol Nagy Jacklin.
    "Differential socialization of boys and girls,"
    The Psychology of Sex-Differences, by E. E.
    Maccoby and C. N. Jacklin. Stanford: Stanford
    University Press, 1974. pp. 303-348.

    Stereotyped parental attitudes towards sons and
daughters is epitomized in the musical, *Carousel*, when the
expectant father rhapsodizes about his ideal son: tall,
tough and a capable worker. When realizing the possibil-
ity of a daughter, his song takes on the theme of ribbons,
sweetness and the need for male protection.

0621
    Maccoby, Eleanor E. and Carol Nagy Jacklin.
    "Myth, reality and shades of gray; What we know
    and don't know about sex differences," *Psychology
    Today*, December, 1974, 8(7):109-112.

    Discussion of song from *Carousel*. See 0620.

0622
    Meade, Marion. "Does rock degrade women?,"
    The New York Times, March 14, 1971, p. D-13;
    also as "The degradation of women" in *The
    Sounds of Social Change: Studies in Popular*

Culture, ed. by R. Serge Denisoff and Richard A.
Peterson. Chicago: Rand McNally, 1972. pp.
173-177.

The anti-woman attitudes found in rock music range
from open contempt to sugar-coated condescension. The
Rolling Stones dehumanize women in "Stupid Girl," "Under
My Thumb," "Yesterday's Papers," and "Live With Me" where
women are equated with old newspapers and are valuable only
when between the sheets. Bob Dylan regards women as bitch,
while the Beatles and Leonard Cohen describe women as passive, spiritless and sad-eyed. The songs of Janis Joplin,
Tina Turner and Laura Nyro are the only few who capture
the spirit with which women can identify.

0623
   Meade, Marion. "Women and rock: sexism set to
   music," *Women: A Journal of Liberation*, Fall,
   1970, 2(1):24-26.

Rock lyrics of the 1950's and early 1960's starred
the virginal girl next door. Since that lyrically innocent
age Dylan, Jagger and the Beatles, among others have sung
of women as a brainless, dirty, child-whore. Her image
progresses from the level of sex object, to fantasy figure,
bitch, and finally a totally dehumanized figure in porn-
rock.

0624
   "The muses of Olivia: our own economy, our own
   song," *Off Our Backs*, August/September, 1974,
   4(9):2-3.

The woman-oriented philosophy of Olivia Records,
feminist recording collective, prohibits recording music
that is sexist, racist, classist or ageist.

0625
   "No Comment," *Ms.*, May, 1977, 5(2):98-99.

Examples of album jackets and billboard ads whose
graphics depict violence against women. Most examples were
submitted by Women Against Violence Against Women (WAVAW),
who suggests eliminating such graphics through record boycotts and public pressure.

0626
   Orloff, Katherine. *Rock 'n Roll Woman*. Los
   Angeles: Nash Publ, 1974.

The role of women in rock music is defined as performer or groupie. She is never the superstar - that's the domain of the hard rock male. Interviews with 12 female rock performers deal with their career opportunities, and perceptions of their role as "one of the boys" in rock, and the influence of the women's movement on their careers.

0627
> "*Paid My Dues* to resume publication; only journal of woman-made music," *Media Report to Women,* April 1, 1977, 5(4):8.

When it resumes publication *Paid My Dues* will provide a link between musicians, news of new recordings, and a forum for discussions about music's relationship to feminism, culture, politics and fun. Subscription information included.

0628
> Partridge, Robert. "Dialogue: Melody Maker special on women in rock," *Melody Maker,* November 10, 1973, pp. 36-38.

Six British female rock musicians and writers discussed the status of women in rock. Women have not received equal opportunity for success in the rock business: they are not given the same quality publicity that male artists receive, their music is treated less seriously by the media, and they are expected to conform to the passive stereotype, singing sweetly behind a guitar. Some female artists break from the passive stereotype to ape the male stereotype, but Joplin is the only woman mentioned who performed as herself, disregarding sex roles.

See 0056. "Really socking it to women."

0629
> "Record covers are bad, says Warner Brothers. But we can't change them; Boycott begins," *Media Report to Women,* March 1, 1977, 5(3):2.

After examining 45 record jackets whose graphics depict bruised women being further brutalized or victimized by men, Women Against Violence Against Women (WAVAW) confronted corporate executives responsible for the records. Because the executives claim to have no control over graphics, WAVAW has announced a boycott of all records produced by Warner Brothers, Atlantic and Elektra.

0630
Rennie, Susan and Kirsten Grimstad. "Women and music," *New Woman's Survival Sourcebook*, ed. by S. Rennie and K. Grimstad. NY: Khopf, 1975.

The misogyny unconcealed in popular song lyrics provided the need for woman-identified songs which express the subtleties of the female experience. The chapter includes an article about national women's recording company Olivia Records, and descriptions of women's records, music centers, music groups, songbooks and discographies.

0631
Rodnitzky, Jerome L. "Songs of sisterhood: the music of women's liberation," *Popular Music and Society*, 1975, 4:77-85.

Popular music portrays women as love objects, mothers, nags and tramps, and further demeans women when radio disc jockeys insult the female audience with "housewife jokes and stupid giveaways." The last famous female disc jockey was Tokyo Rose.

Alternate record companies are now forming to create high quality women's music which speaks honestly about women's lives. Instead of singing the heterosexual blues, women's music stresses women's needs, anger, fears, dreams and relationships with other women. *Virgo Rising: The Once and Future Woman* and other women's records prove that hard rock needn't be sexist in order to be good.

0632
Rodnitzky, Jerome L. "The Southwest unbound: Janis Joplin and the new feminism," *Feminist Art Journal*, Winter, 1976-1977, 5(4):22-25.

Janis Joplin was a "victim of sexism within a sexual revolution she helped fuel," but simultaneously and ironically she functioned as a "feminist symbol" within the sexist rock culture. She sang of womanhood's pain and paved the way for other performers to sing about preventing pain.

0633
Rosenstone, Robert A. "The times they are a-changin': the music of protest," *Sidesaddle on the Golden Calf: Social Structure and Popular Culture in America*, ed. by George H. Lewis. Pacific Palisades, CA: Goodyear, 1972. pp. 290-304.

189

When singing of love relationships male rock artists
sing of loveless marriages, American women with gritted
teeth and women who depress men by talking about sin.
Male/female relationships are seen as contests where violence is more acceptable than tenderness and where women
are constantly criticized as plastic.

0634
Shapiro, Susin. "Rock around the crotch," *Crawdaddy*, May, 1975, n48:68-69.

Best selling female vocalists sing love-lost lyrics
while flashing cleavage. As they sing of the nuclear
couple, they disregard "political visions, love of an idea,
honesty without honey, allegory, fear and frenzy." Some
female artists who do "confront themselves and convey sexual politics through song" are Phoebe Snow, Melissa Man-
chester, Bonnie Bramlett, Janis Ian and Patti Smith.

0635
Shapiro, Susin. "What once were vices aren't
even habits anymore," *Crawdaddy*, January, 1976,
n56:68-69.

Shapiro's broken habits are the recordings of pop
misogynists who sing odes to the "woman I can sock in the
jaw." She now buys the records of Meg Christian whose
words fuse sexual politics with campfire camaraderie,
Holly Near who sings of unemployment, old age and strength
of female character, and Joan Armatrading who champions
personal individuality.

0636
Shumsky, Ellen. "Womansong: bringing it all back
home," *Sing Out!*, 1974, 22(6):9+.

Personal account of a woman who experiences a cultural shock when attending integrated folk festivals after
having sung only in all-woman environments, where performers develop to their fullest potential. In the folk
festivals women are seen as adjuncts to men. Female performers defer to male colleagues who announce each song,
and when singing alone, women sing of a man-centered universe where they experience pain, humiliation and slave
status, and where male heroes advance at female victims'
expense. The author relates her rage at misogynistic
jokes and profound disappointment at low level feminist
consciousness. She had expected to hear women sing about
themselves, their growth, their strength and their sensa-
tions. She lists women's recording companies and workshops who do produce records and music celebrating

womanhood.

0637

Sims, Barbara B. "'She's got to be a saint, Lord knows I ain't':feminine masochism in American country music," *Journal of Country Music*, 1974, 5:24-30.

Basically two types of women populate country music. The long suffering woman/saint waits patiently and masochistically at home for her two-timing husband who spends his free time with the other woman, the temptress.

0638

Taylor, Fran. "Oldies but baddies, or who put the shit in the dit, dih, dit, dit dit?" *Second Wave, A Magazine of the New Feminism*, 1974, 3(2): 8-11.

The rigid sex roles defining teenage romances in 1950's and 1960's Rock and Roll portrayed men as sexual dynamos or "great balls of fire" while women were "teen angels" mercifully killed by passing trains, or blonde California girls with turned-up noses. Recurring themes included lover as property, sexually aggressive lyrics by black female groups and cuddly, cutesy lyrics by white, male, British groups. Female strength as historically personified by Emma Goldman and Cristabel Pankhurst were unknown to teenagers whose role model was "Teen Angel."

0639

Thompson, Ann. "The undaunted female," *English Dance and Song*, 1975, 37:50-51.

The folksong heroine commonly celebrated her virginity as symbolizing a husband-free time of independence, and sang of heroism whereby she defeated male aggressors.

640

Valenti, Mary Jo, Linda J. Larkin and Dorothy K. Dean. "My sister's song." Available from Woman's Soul Publishing, Inc., PO Box 11646, Milwaukee, WI 53211. $1.00.

A discography of woman-made recorded music in print. Also lists record companies who produce music by women. The discography was produced by the publishers of *Paid My Dues: A Journal of Women and Music* (see 0570).

0641
   Wilkinson, Melvin. "Romantic love: the great
   equalizer? Sexism in popular music," *Family
   Coordinator*, 1976, 25:161-166.

Two hundred songs popular from 1954 to 1968 were examined for sexism by listing descriptive adjectives and
verbs applied to both sexes. The sex role stereotypes
included pretty and heavenly women, courageous and posses-
sive men. Non-stereotyped findings included descriptions
of men crying, men needing women more often than women
needing men, male submissiveness and unfaithful women.

See 0070. "Your daughter's education."

Humor

See 0400. "Analysis of male and female participation on
WRC 'Quiz Show' programming."

0642
   Benson, Carol. *It Only Hurts When I Laugh.*
   Available from author, 427 N. Riverside Dr,
   Modesto, CA 95351. Rental, $25.

A 35mm slide documentary examining sex role stereotypes in the cartoons of *Ladies' Home Journal, Cosmopolitan, Playboy* and other mass circulated magazines. The
program is divided by theme: degrading stereotypes of
women, ridicule of the women's movement, pro-feminist
viewpoint, the "new woman". Negative stereotypes include
women as dumb broad, gossip, woman driver, golddigger,
battleax, and Supermom.

0643
   Cantor, Joanne R. "What is funny to whom: the
   role of gender," *Journal of Communication*, 1976,
   26(3):164-172.

Results of a study of female bias in humor using 68
male and 53 female college students show that sarcastic
comments made by men are perceived as clever and witty
while the same comments made by women are considered critical and cruel, hence less funny. Woman as victim is still
considered to be funnier than man as victim.

0644
"Cartoon 'humor' aimed at women," *Media Report to Women*, April 1, 1974, 2(4):12.

Cartoon cliches that stereotype women include financially irresponsible wives and other outdated domestic gags. Instead of reinforcing sexist attitudes about both sexes, cartoonists should develop more humanistic standards for themselves and their work.

0645
Chapman, Anthony J. and Nicholas J. Gadfield. "Is sexual humor sexist?" *Journal of Communication*, 1976, 26(3):141-153.

Fifteen cartoons dealing with various sexual and non-sexual themes were shown to 15 men and 15 women to indicate sex role attitudes revealed in humor. Findings reveal that men prefer female-butt jokes while women prefer male-butt jokes.

0646
Cole, William and Florett Robinson. *Women are Wonderful! A History in Cartoons of a Hundred Years with America's Most Controversial Figure.* Boston, Houghton Mifflin, 1956.

A history of women's image in the American cartoon genre, which began in the same period of history as the Women's Rights Meeting at Seneca Falls, NY.

0647
Fry, William F. "Psychodynamics of sexual humor: Man's view of sex," *Medical Aspects of Human Sexuality*, May, 1972, 6:128+.

Male fascination with sexual humor which shows overt hostility toward women may be caused by their biological inferiority to women. Women live longer, suffer fewer birth injuries, toilet train sooner and mature earlier than men. To overcome their anxieties men tell jokes which dehumanize women as sexual objects who are driven to ecstasy by his magic penis.

See 0384. S. Harrington, "Women get the short end of the schtick."

0648
Kaufman, Gloria. *Anthology of Feminist Humor.*

193

South Bend: Indiana University English Dept.
In progress.

This forthcoming anthology on humor is projected to
include both contemporary and historical examples of anec-
dotes, one-liners, movement humor, literary humor, cartoons, songs and letters-to-editors.

See 0041. L. Komisar, "The new feminism."

0649
Legman, G. *Rationale of the Dirty Joke, an
Analysis of Sexual Humor*, v. 1. NY: Grove
Press, 1968.

Although not a feminist approach, this book analyzes
examples of misogynistic jokes whose themes are "the female fool," "breasts," "the mother-in-law" and jokes about
stereotyped women in general.

0650
Levine, Joan B. "The feminine routine," *Journal
of Communication*, 1976, 26(3):173-175.

The comedy albums of four female and four male comedians were studied for evidence of self-deprecatory humor.
It was observed that women deprecated themselves 63% of
the time while men deprecated themselves only 12% of the
time. Women often mocked their bodies while men, when
dealing with appearance, mocked only non-sexual apparatus
such as beard and long hair. Evidence of women deprecat-
ing men was not reported in the study though examples are
given of women as brunt of male jokes.

0651
Nietzke, Ann. "Hostility on the laugh track,"
Human Behavior, May, 1974, 3(5):64-70.

At the root of many jokes lies a deep-seated hostility toward women. Male comedians do routines about the
ugly, nagging, frigid wife, the bad woman driver, the loose
woman, the dumb blonde, or the sex object with oversized
breasts. Female comedians have established a female anti-
woman counterpart with self-abusive humor. Phyllis Diller,
Joan Rivers and Carol Burnett are three who base their
material on personal unattractiveness and "flat chest"
jokes, although Diller's style seems to poke fun more at
the concept of the traditional woman than at herself. A
feminist comedy team, Harrison and Tyler challenge the
anti-woman humor with jokes in which men function as butt.

Penis or "weewee jokes" counter the conventional breast jokes. Feminist Lily Tomlin employs neither hostility nor self-laceration in her characters who all like themselves, and prove that people are funny without using humor as a weapon.

See 0353. National Organization for Women. "A week with Merv Griffin."

0652
Palmore, Erdman. "Attitudes toward aging as shown by humor," *Gerontologist*, 1971, 11:181-186.

In a sample of 264 jokes about aging, jokes with a positive attitude toward men outnumbered those with a positive attitude toward women 2:1. Over 75% of the women's jokes were negative, suggesting that today's society regards aging women more negatively than aging men. Most of the negative women's jokes dealt with "old maids" and age concealment among women.

See 0323. J. Papachristou, "Social change."

0653
Posner, Judith. "Dirty old women: Buck Brown's cartoons," *Canadian Review of Sociology and Anthropology*, 1975, 12:471-473.

Although jokes about dirty old men abound, lecherous old women are rarely a source of humor, mainly because society tends to deny the sexuality of older women. An exception is Buck Brown's "granny" cartoons which show a traditional grandmother with sagging physique who seduces young men.

0654
Titters, The First Collection of Humor by Women, ed. by Deanne Stillman and Anne Beatts. NY: Macmillan, 1976.

Counterbalancing the tradition of humor that assigns women's role as butt of the joke, these parodies and stories by a number of well-known comedians show women laughing at the female experience, including dieting, consumer products, women's magazines and sexuality.

0655
"Victoria Walsh and Eileen Leonard Gerrie propose

courses on women and media," *Media Report to Women*, April 1, 1977, 5(4):12.

Woman as comedic object is found on television with the Lucy character who is childish and the Rhoda character whose laughs are based on self-mockery, and in films where Marilyn Monroe and Judy Holliday portrayed comical "dumb blondes" and Barbra Streisand and Martha Ray made fools of themselves for a laugh.

0656
von Hoffman, Nicholas. "Cher: laughing all the way in a step beyond chauvinism," *The Washington Post*, February 28, 1975, pp. B 1-2.

Although Cher is not an outspoken advocate of the women's movement, the producer of her television show calls her a product of the movement. Until Cher, women have been the joke; Cher does the joke. Lucille Ball had been the butt of the joke, Carol Burnett and Mary Tyler Moore are transitional figures, but Cher is the first to carry a show in the same manner traditionally done by men.

0657
Weisstein, Naomi. "Introduction," *All She Needs*, by Ellen Levine. NY: Quadrangle, 1973. pp. 1-10; also as "Laugh? I nearly died!" Available from KNOW, Inc., PO Box 86031, Pittsburgh, PA 15221. #284.

A discussion of the political ramifications of humor as applied to the women's movement. Although feminists have been accused of having no sense of humor, Dr. Weisstein says that oppressed women have always laughed at their own victimization. When they weren't laughing, they smiled. Jews, Blacks and other powerless groups have a tradition of humor that establishes dignity and creates strength. Women don't have a comparable tradition of humor, partly because women haven't lived in strictly female ghettos, comparable to ethnic ghettos. By living with the more politically powerful men, women have learned to laugh at men's jokes. Consequently women laugh at jokes about mothers-in-law, female sex kittens and images of woman as ridiculous person.

0658
Weisstein, Naomi. "Why we aren't laughing ... anymore," *Ms.*, November, 1973, 2(5):49-51+.

Adaptation of introduction to *All She Needs*. See 0657.

0659
Zillman, Dolf and S. Holly Stocking. "Putdown humor," *Journal of Communication*, 1976, 26(3): 154-163.

A study of reactions to two types of humor - disparagement and self-disparagement - revealed that men, in keeping with machismo image, preferred the disparagement or "put-down" humor of others while the more submissive women preferred self-disparaging forms of humor.

0660
Zimbardo, Philip G. and Wendy Meadow. "Sexism springs eternal - in the *Reader's Digest*," paper presented at the annual convention of W. Psychological Association, 1974. ERIC (ED 105 318).

After having been acculturated by television and textbooks to accept sexism, children grow up and laugh at jokes in which women or ethnic groups are the butt. The article is an historical survey of the 1,069 anti-woman jokes appearing in *Reader's Digest* 1947-1948, 1957-1958, and 1967-1968. The survey revealed that "Cartoon Quips" was 15% anti-woman and "Laughter the Best Medicine" 10:1 anti-woman. The ratio of anti-woman to anti-man jokes was 6:1. The typical image of women in these jokes shows her as stupid, incompetent, foolish, domineering, exploiting men for money, catty about other women, spendthrift, gossiping, man-hunting.

Comic Strips and Books

0661
Brabant, Sarah. "Sex role stereotyping in the Sunday comics," *Sex Roles*, 1976, 2:331-337.

Even those comic strips whose family situations seem to be female-dominated, are in fact, steeped with traditional sex role stereotypes. Blondie cooks and cleans while Dagwood naps or reads. She is often apron clad while her husband never wears a symbol of domesticity.

0662
Chmaj, Betty E. "Fantasizing women's lib-stereotypes of women in comic books," *Image Myth and Beyond*, ed. by B. E. Chmaj. (American women and American studies, 2). Pittsburgh:

KNOW, 1972. pp. 311-325.

The manifestation of typical male and female fantasies about liberation are contrasted in this examination of comic books.

0663
    Coffin, Tristram Potter. "Into the ears of babes," *The Female Hero in Folklore and Legend*, by T. P. Coffin. NY: The Seabury Press, 1975. pp. 140-157.

Female folklore heroes in times past were Cleopatra, Helen, Cressida and Belle Starr. The most popular was Mother Goose. The mythical twentieth century figure, however, has been a less romantic Little Orphan Annie who outwits gangsters and sells Ovaltine. Annie functioned as an independent female crusader.

0664
    Edgar, Joanne. "Wonder Woman revisited," *Ms.*, July, 1972, pp. 52-55; also in *Sexism and Youth*, ed. by Diane Gersoni-Stavn. NY: Bowker, 1974. pp. 387-389.

The Wonder Woman of the 1940's, who combined superhuman strength with a philosophy of love, was conceived by a male feminist as a counter to the extremely violent male comic book characters. After the death of her originator, Wonder Woman's writers ascribed to her all of the stereotyped sex roles: sexier outfit, emotional nature (including increased comic book style violence), vulnerability to men, and a male advisor. A change in philosophy is expected with the newest editor who proposes to return Wonder Woman to her early feminist leanings.

0665
    Ferguson, Charles W. "In the lighter vein," *The Male Attitude: What Makes American Men Think and Act as They Do?*, by C. W. Ferguson. Boston: Little Brown, 1966. pp. 259-268.

The male attitude toward sex roles is evident in comic strips and popular song lyrics. Hard-driving, ambitious, aggressive, ravenous Maggie of "Bringing Up Father" was made appealing only by her good figure and beautiful legs. Strong, powerful Wonder Woman was kept in her place during the great deal of time she spent in chains. Spineless, acneed Clark Kent, when transformed to the magnificent Superman, could inspire Lois Lane's love and adoration. In popular song lyrics women are problems who jilt, reject,

two-time and otherwise hurt the feelings of men. The male
expectations for soft, sweet, paper doll-like women is not
met in the realistic world.

0666
    Glicksohn, Susan Wood. *The poison maiden and
    the great bitch: female stereotypes in marvel
    superhero comics.* Baltimore: T-K Graphics,
    1974.

The publisher of *Marvel* superhero comic books purports
concern for relevant issues like war, racism, drugs and
pollution, and yet continues to treat the issue of human
rights for women as a dirty joke. Women are stereotyped by
the old madonna/whore standards: as fertility goddess/
destroyer, and as virgin/hag. *Marvel's* female characters
include beautiful women who facilitate legal problems for
boyfriends when they feel compelled to steal money to buy
her presents, "liberated chicks" who wear no underwear,
scantily-clad sorcerers (or sexual objects), and "Invisible Girl" who combines marriage and motherhood with her
powers of invisibility.

See 0752. J. D. Grambs, "Books and sex bias."

0667
    Levine, Ellen. *All She Needs*. NY: Quadrangle,
    1973.

A book of cartoons which ridicules the existing sexual order. It is not the self-deprecating tradition of
female comics, but rather a new tradition which mocks the
sex roles. Feminists have not lost their sense of humor -
they're now laughing at situations rather than at themselves.

0668
    McKenney, Mary. "Mind candy for the Ms's,"
    Booklegger, September/October, 1974, 1:16-19.

Women who enjoy underground comics need no longer
settle for the sexism of R. Crumb. An annotated list of
women's comics provides "jokes that are not on us."

See 0747. H. M. McLuhan, "Blondie."

0669
    Marston, William Moulton. *Wonder Woman*, with

essays by Gloria Steinem and Phyllis Chesler. NY: Bonanza Books, 1972.

In most comic books sex roles dictate that superhuman heroes protect helpless women. Wonder Woman, however, protects Major Steve Trevor and other people in need of help. The strip is not quite a role reversal - the masculine "pow and crunch" style is replaced by the use of a magic lasso and bullet proof bracelets that require skill rather than brute force. Wonder Woman's message is always female self-reliance, strength and confidence.

See 0052. M. Nunes and W. White, *The Lace Ghetto*.

0670
Perebinossoff, Philippe. "What does a kiss mean? The Love comic formula and the creation of the ideal teen-age girl," *Journal of Popular Culture*, 1975, 8:825-835.

"Love Comics" have clearly defined sex roles: women are beautiful, fun and dedicated wives, while men are strong, protective and intelligent. Beauty is so important that even "plain" girls become beautiful when loved by men - and a man's love is the goal. Comic book women hold careers only until love evolves into marriage. The humble wife is the common role model in these basically moralistic comics.

0671
Rennie, Susan and Kirsten Grimstad. "Mind candy for the Ms's," *New Woman's Survival Sourcebook*, ed. by S. Rennie and K. Grimstad. NY: Knopf, 1975. pp. 134-137.

Male underground comics are preoccupied with violence and sex, usually showing women only as the victims of rape, beatings and degradation. Women began publishing women's comics to meet the non-sexist needs of the female comic book audience. With heroines like Petunia Pig who says, "You think *your* boyfriend is a pig!", women's comics are anti-sexist, anti-racist and non-propagandistic stories about the female experience.

0672
Spiegleman, Marvin, Carl Terwilliger and Franklin Fearing. "The content of comics: goals and means to goals of comic strip characters," *Journal of Social Psychology*, 1953, 37:189-203.

A breakdown by sex and socioeconomic status of comic book characters determines the goals and means to goals of each group. Romantic love is the female character's most common goal, with personal charm, industry and fate her most frequent means to the goal. Recreation is the most common male goal, with personal charm, industry and violence his most frequent means to the goal. Goals and means vary somewhat as class lines change.

0673
    Taylor, Fran. "A look at love comics," *Second Wave, a Magazine of the New Feminism*, 1972, 2(1): 16-19+.

In love comics women who resemble Raquel Welch viciously compete for the kiss, touch and ultimate marriage of men built like Charles Atlas. When they are not kissing or touching *him*, they're daydreaming, sighing or talking about him. In order to save young readers from the reinforcement of teenage sex role stereotypes, the author suggests balancing this anti-woman philosophy with alternatives that teach a woman's value within herself rather than in the man she catches.

See 0739. D. Trevino, "The longest running putdown; Daisy Mae doesn't speak for Appalachian Women."

0674
    Trudeau, Gary. *Joanie*. (Cartoons for new children series.) NY: Sheed and Ward, 1974.

Excerpts from the comic strip "Doonesbury" show Joanie Caucus instilling a feminist consciousness in her free-thinking, independent day care students. In an afterword Nora Ephron calls the book a perfect, painless way to introduce children to the ideas of sexual equality.

Science Fiction

0675
Anderson, Susan Janice. "Feminism and Science Fiction: beyond BEMS and boobs," *Aurora: Beyond Equality*, ed. by Vonda N. McIntyre and S. J. Anderson. Greenwich, Conn: Fawcett World, 1976.

Women's place in science fiction is generally in the kitchen, pushing buttons on the autocook. However three authors, Russ, LeGuin and Delaney, create new universes populated solely by women, or by egalitarian male/female relationships, or by an ambisexual species. Stories by these three and other authors found in the anthology, explore the future of human potential instead of relegating half the population to pushing buttons.

0676
> Clancy-Hepburn, Ken. "Sexism and Sci Fi," *Human Ecology Forum*, 1973, 4(2):28-30.

In science fiction men are brilliant, muscular studs while women are girl-friday objects of fantasy. This sex role stereotyping is defended on the grounds that the genre itself is essentially formula writing steeped in value stereotypes and dogmatic methods of problem solving.

0677
> Friend, Beverly. "Virgin territory: women and sex in science fiction," *Extrapolation*, December, 1972, 14(1):49-58.

The "what if" question in what Asimov calls "social science fiction" is applied to the theme of women and sex: What if women were treated realistically in science fiction? The works of authors Farmer, Sturgeon and LeGuin show women as more than androidal walking wombs. Within the bounds of science fiction women as complete human beings are not necessarily confined to pregnancy. Fluctuating genitalia enable everyone to give birth. A society with emotionally responsive men exists without male supremacy.

0678
> McCaffrey, Anne. "Hitch your dragon to a star: romance and glamour in science fiction," *Science Fiction: Today and Tomorrow*, ed. by Reginald Bretnor. NY: Harper & Row, 1974. pp. 278-294.

Even though science fiction has a reputation for being "more cerebral than gonadal," romance and glamour, by their traditional definitions, are important elements of the genre. Rather than being mere sexual tools, since the 1960's some well rounded female characters have appeared as romantic but capable figures in science fiction's glamorous tales of the future. The author compares these well rounded characters of popular science fiction writers to the helpless hand-wringing female caricatures of other popular writers.

0679
More Women of Wonder; Science Fiction Novelettes by Women About Women, ed. by Pamela Sargent. NY: Vintage Books, 1976.

The branch of science fiction most concerned with technical truth regards women with little importance, while the branch dealing with broader social implications explores many options for women. With the increasing emphasis on technology, female characters are no longer limited by lesser muscular strength or pregnancy. Men are given artificial wombs and breasts and lesbians are impregnated artificially. With more sexual, intellectual, career and pregnancy options, perhaps female readers will base reassessment of personal roles on more progressive attitudes learned from science fiction characters of Asimov, Heinlein, LeGuin and Russ who have all treated female characters seriously and intelligently.

0680
Moskowitz, Samuel. *When Women Rule,* NY: Walker and Company, 1972.

Science fiction writers from the nineteenth century to the present have been fascinated with the Amazon tribe of a physically and emotionally strong women. In some stories men overcome the superior women and render them slaves while in others parthenogenetic women exterminate men. In this anthology of nine science fiction stories, the theme of the strong woman predominates.

0681
Rennie, Susan and Kirsten Grimstad. "... and the new Science Fiction," *New Woman's Survival Sourcebook,* ed. by S. Rennie and K. Grimstad. NY: Knopf, 1975. pp. 131-133.

Although innovative technology and biology dazzle the reader of science fiction, the female role is still traditionally dull. Woman remains eternally Mother and Server of man. While wife, mother, and sex object live in "intergalactic suburbia" a token professional woman works as the project archeologist. She is stereotypically either slightly butchy or very curvey, but always childless.

0682
Russ, Joanna. "Image of women in science fiction, *Red Clay Reader 7 Series,* ed. by Charleen Whisnant. Charlotte, NC: Southern Review, 1970. pp. 34-40; also in *Images of Women in Fiction,* ed. by Susan K. Cornillon. Bowling

Green: Bowling Green Popular Press, 1972.
pp. 79-94; also in *Vertex*, February, 1974,
1(6):53-57.

Although the science fiction setting is in a different universe, hundreds of thousands of years in the future, the values and sex roles remain traditionally
twentieth century. The article reviews and criticizes
American science fiction novels from a feminist viewpoint.
Women are usually either prizes won by heroes or cast as
ambitious women and therefore evil, but are always super-
naturally beautiful, and often weak and passive. Men are
super heroes, and super potent. Russ also reviews science
fiction novels whose themes demonstrate equality between
the sexes or attempt role reversals.

0683
Sargent, Pamela. "Women and science fiction,"
*Women of Wonder: Science Fiction Stories by
women About Women*, ed. by Pamela Sargent. NY:
Vintage, 1974. pp. xiii-lxiv.

A description of the writing styles of female science
fiction novelists from Mary Shelley to the present is followed by a discussion of the sex roles in science fiction,
and a lengthy footnote describing both the liberated and
sexist attitudes inherent in Robert Heinlein's work. Sargent contends that science fiction, a popular art form,
will not include a more egalitarian approach to the sexes
until a wider readership provides a market demand for a
significant change in approach.

0684
Sargent, Pamela. "Women in science fiction,"
Futures, 1975, 7:433-441.

Women in science fiction have usually been portrayed
as "suffering victims, often raped, assaulted or murdered,
whose only hope lies in producing children who might
build a new world." Although science fiction is fantasy
taking place in the future, the roles of women are almost
always reflections of the past. With more women writers
this trend seems to be changing.

See 0824. J. M. Tate, "Sexual bias in science fiction for
children."

0685
Berler, Ron. "Girl copy for whatsername," *The Cincinnati Enquirer Magazine*, September 12, 1976, p. 14.

A common practice among editors of men's skin magazines is to use fictitious names, nationalities, occupations, hobbies, etc. when describing the lifestyles of the female centerfold models. The copy is literally the product of a male copywriter's fantasy.

0686
Brownmiller, Susan. "Decision, decision," *The New York Times*, August 6, 1973, p. 31.

Brownmiller applauds the Supreme Court decision on obscenity. Pornography degrades the female body and female sexual role.

0687
Gabor, Mark. *The Pin-up; A Modest History*. NY: Universe Books, 1972.

An historical approach to women and some men as pin-up/sex objects, beginning with fifteenth century woodcuts. Illustrations include magazine, film, calendar and poster pinups.

See 0723. W. H. Grier and P. M. Cobbs, "Achieving womanhood."

0688
Haskell, Molly. "The night porno films turned me off," *New York*, March 29, 1976, 9:56-60.

Porn films do violence to women in the name of eroticism. Women become nothing more than powerless bodies without dignity, destiny, hearts or minds. As objects they are only technically alive within the porn films that practice a form of necrophilia on the female bodies.

0689
Hefner, Hugh M. "On playboys and bunnies," *Up Against the Wall, Mother*, ed. by Elsie Adams and Mary Louise Briscoe. Beverly Hills: Glencoe Press, 1971. pp. 38-39.

In his "Playboy Philosophy" Hefner defends himself
against accusations of having dehumanized women by claim-
ing he offers women a more human identity than they have
historically enjoyed. Women have always been objects
rather than human beings.

0690
    Kallan, Richard A. and Robert D. Brooks. "Play-
    mate of the month: naked but nice," *Journal of
    Popular Culture*, 1974, 8:328-336.

    Playboy's nude centerfold is legitimized by her moral
admirability. The 1950's Playmate was family oriented and
was often pictured with her parents. In the late 1960's
she was a political moderate, commenting on Vietnam, hip-
pies, and other social phenomena. Her image is that of
available sex kitten who is well educated, bright, has a
responsible career, respects her parents, loves pets and
is an individualist.

0691
    Laner, Mary Riege. "Make-believe mistresses:
    photo-essay models in the candy sex magazines,"
    Sociological Symposium, 1976, n15:81-98.

    In order to determine how the types of occupations
assigned by "Candy Sex" magazines contribute to the sexi-
ness of their photo essay models, 11 magazines were examined. Occupations of 54% were not indicated. The remaining 46% were employed as beauty contest winners or in show
business related jobs, with occasional student, masseuse,
postal employee and health food store clerk. Occupations
of the models included no administrators, managers, or
craft workers who might threaten the male reader/fanta-
sizer. Most make-believe mistresses are unemployed, work
in unconventional (therefore sexy) occupations, or have
low status "accessible" jobs. These women are considered
dumb but sexy.

0692
    Marshe, Surrey. *The Girl in the Centerfold: the
    Uninhibited Memoirs of Miss January*. NY: Dela-
    corte Press, 1969.

    A disenchanted former Playboy Bunny/Playmate discusses
the image of the women who pose in *Playboy* and work in the
clubs, and the types of men who allow this corporation to
direct their fantasies.

0693
Moore, Allan J. "The Cosmo Girl: a *Playboy* inversion," *A World of Her Own*, ed. by John Miller. Columbus, Ohio: Charles E. Merrill, 1971.

Cosmopolitan magazine is the feminine equivalent of *Playboy*, which teaches women to regard men as objects and toys whom she can manipulate. Although the cosmo model's nakedness is not draped in quite the same sexy manner used by the Playmate, "peek-a-boo" covers and nude lingerie fashion spreads are equally titillating. It is as if *Cosmopolitan's* brand of "sexology" is teaching its female readers to play the role of object as prescribed by *Playboy* in order to objectify and therefore manipulate the *Playboy* reader. The author worries that this brand of objectification and manipulation denies people human expression and human dignity.

0694
Nicholson, Joan. "The packaging of rape: a feminist indictment," *The Pin-Up*, by Mark Gabor. NY: Universe Books, 1972. pp. 13-16.

An historical survey of pin-up photography from Victorian times to the present underscores a connection between the power relationship involved in rape and that in cheesecake/pornography. As defined here, cheesecake includes advertising's sexual exploitation.

0695
"Pornography is an environmental hazard," *Media Report to Women*, May 1, 1976, 4(5):11.

A member of International Tribunal on Crimes Against Women explains that pornography is a political issue for women because of the portrayal of women as sexual objects and sadistic playthings of men which legitimizes male supremacy.

0696
Richardson, John Adkins. "The shape of venus," *Art: the Way It Is*, by J. A. Richardson. NY: Abrams, 1974. pp. 68-77.

The composition of Edward Weston's well known 1936 *Nude* is quite different from the final object designed by *Playboy* artists who "treat womankind as if every bit of female flesh were made of erectile tissue and were utterly lacking of the softness more typical of the female body in repose." These erectilized women more closely resemble "male athletes with female appendages."

0697
    Richler, Mordecai. "James Bond unmasked," *Commentary*, July, 1968, 46(1):74-81; also in *Mass Culture Revisited*, ed. by Bernard Rosenberg and David Manning White. NY: Van Nostrand Reinhold, 1971. pp. 341-355.

The James Bond convention of spy writing includes a six-step plot formula as well as characterization formula. The grotesque villain (male) has an oversize, hairless head, while the good guy (Bond) is adventurous, a soldier of fortune, and a gentlemen. Sexuality is personified by women with names like Kissy, Pussy, Vesper and Mary Goodnight.

0698
    Rossi, Lee. "Whore vs. the girl-next-door: stereotypes of woman in *Playboy, Penthouse* and *Oui*," *Journal of Popular Culture*, 1975, 9:90-94.

A discussion of the two quite different varieties of female sex object in three men's magazines. Publishers of men's magazines are exploiting the "sexual liberation" aspect of the feminist movement to sell the role of woman as a sex object who is necessarily dependent on men.

0699
    See, Carolyn. "Nude times...1," *New Times*, 1974, February 22, 1974, 2(4):28-32+.

A review of the "madonna/whore/consumer" syndrome in the leading innocuous to raunchy candy-sex magazines.

0700
    Seligson, Marcia. "Nude times...2," *New Times*, February 22, 1974, 2(4):36-41.

An interview with Doug Lambert, publisher of *Playgirl*, deals with the "Playgirl Philosophy" and the macho image of men as bare hunters and nude skiers.

0701
    Stannard, Una. "What do you think of *Playboy?*," available from KNOW, Inc, PO Box 86031, Pittsburgh, PA 15221, #153.

A facetious discussion of the playboy phenomenon in

which *Playboy* is called a "boy's version of paper dolls."

See 0206. C. Ventura. "Impact of women's liberation movement on advertising trends."

0702
>"Why does Brandeis University honor publisher
>of *Penthouse* Magazine?," *Media Report to Women*,
>January 1, 1976, 4(1):7.

Brandeis student government and women's groups protested the University honoree whose publication's pornographic stories of washroom sex degrade the image of women and imply that every woman is a hooker.

Miscellaneous Pop Culture

See 0012. S. Brownmiller, "Victims: the setting."

0703
>Freese, Arthur S. "Car: a versatile sex sym-
>bol," *Sexual Behavior*, May, 1972, 2(5):53-57.

Car types are compared to women's stereotyped roles: the sedan equals the plain wife, convertible equals the thrilling mistress and the station wagon is a maternal symbol for the pregnant wife. A car's roominess is considered a uterine symbol while its speed and animal-like names are considered phallic symbols.

See 0794. J. Ginsburg, "And then there is good old Nancy Drew."

0704
>Goleman, Daniel. "Greek myths in pop fiction:
>Jason and Medea's love story," *Psychology Today*,
>April, 1976, 9:84-86.

A sexual double standard is exposed in comparing themes of women's confession magazines to men's adventure magazines.

0705

Gross, Amy. "Woman as sex object: 'I'm fragile, I'm female, I confess'.' - Life as it's lived (more or less) in the confession magazines," *Mademoiselle*, July, 1972, 75(3):128-129+.

The sex role stereotype in confession magazines is a female high school graduate and mother of three, married to an auto mechanic. They find God when one or the other sins by having extramarital sex.

0706

Jones, James P. "Nancy Drew, WASP super girl of the 1930's," *Journal of Popular Culture*, 1973, 6:707-717.

The original Nancy Drew series has been widely criticized on two counts; 1) its literary value sacrificed for the expediency of formula fiction, and 2) its abundance of racial stereotypes: shuffling Negroes, stupid Irish policemen, unscrupulous Jews. With a late 1960's revision which purged the series of damaging stereotypes, young girls once again have an exciting female role model who is the feminine equivalent of Superman, is friendly, attractive, brave and wise.

See 0413. A. F. Kilguss, "Using soap operas as a therapeutic tool."

0707

Krouse, Agate Nesaule and Margot Peters. "Women in detective fiction: why women kill," *Journal of Communication*, 1975, 25:98-104.

Agatha Christie is one of the few writers of detective fiction whose murderers are female as often as they are male. According to the authors, this liberal use of active, aggressive women is not a conscious attempt to overcome sex role stereotyping of woman as victim only, but rather to maintain the plot interest of the "whodunnit."

0708

Mason, Bobbie Ann. *The Girl Sleuth, A Feminist Guide*. Old Westbury, NY: The Feminist Press, 1975.

Written in a casual style, this first person narrative tells how one feminists's early sense of self was developed by spending her childhood with the mystery and detective series. Honey Bunch, the Bobbsey Twins, Nancy

Drew, Judy Bolton, Trixie Belden, Vicki Barr and others
are examined in terms of strength of female role model.
For forty years pubescent girls have thrived on these
books for their themes of female mobility and adventure.

0709

Mussell, Kay J. "Beautiful and damned: the
sexual woman in gothic fiction," *Journal of
Popular Culture*, 1975, 9:84-89.

Unlike the woman in Geritol commercials who attracts
and holds a man by virtue of her beauty, it is the ethereally beautiful woman in gothic novels of whom the plain
heroines must beware. While plain women uphold the traditionally feminine virtues of domesticity, nurturance
and family maintenance, their beautiful, passionate, exciting female rivals plot to destroy their domestic bliss.

0710

"Sheer bad taste and ignorance," *Media Report to
Women*, December 1, 1975, 3(12):1.

Women protest sex role stereotyping in political
cartoons in the form of an ERA advocate wearing curlers
and wielding a gun.

0711

Smith, M. Dwayne and Marc Matre. "Social norms
and sex roles in romance and adventure magazines,
Journalism Quarterly, 1975, 52:309-315.

Examination of 48 romance stories and 27 adventure
stories from one month's publications of 30 magazines revealed that quite disparate sex role expectations are
taught women in romance magazines and men in adventure
magazines. Romance stories expose female readers to re-
warding conversations between lovers and mates, suffering
caused by illicit sexual relations, the importance of
marriage and resignation to and acceptance of adversity.
Meanwhile men reading adventure magazines are exposed to
a world where women don't exist 40% of the time, where
sexual adventure is an aside from the action, marriage has
little importance, and adversity can be overcome.

0712

Sonenschein, David. "Love and sex in the romance
magazines," *Side-Saddle on the Golden Calf: Social Structure and Pop Culture in America*, ed.
by George H. Lewis. Pacific Palisades, CA:
1972. pp. 66-74.

Although illicit sex is promised in the intimate
magazine titles, photographs, story titles and contents
summaries, the overriding themes of 73 stories found in
one month's availability of confessional magazines were
themes of marriage, family, love and religion. Women's
traditional role is reinforced for working class housewives and pre-teen readers.

0713
    Zacharias, Lee. "Nancy Drew, Ballbuster," *Jour-
    nal of Popular Culture*, 1975, 9:1027-1038.

Although Nancy Drew is the epitome of superiority,
confidence and independence, her best friends, George and
Bess, play sex stereotyped roles. One is a skinny tomboy, the other plump and feminine, but both are appearance
oriented, self-abnegating and extremely loyal to Nancy
through whom they live vicariously.

THE MEDIA IMAGE OF MINORITY GROUP WOMEN

Black Women

See 0534. M. R. Binford, "Half the sky: women's world
on film."

0714
    Bogle, Donald. *Toms, Coons, Mulattoes, Mammies
    and Bucks: An Interpretive History of Blacks
    in American Films*. NY: Viking Press, 1973.

    The black sex role stereotypes in film include the
fat, cantankerous mammy, the lively pickaninny child and
the tragic mulatto among women, and the selfless Tom, lazy
coon and brutal buck among men. These stereotypes and
others are applied to the image of black characters and
the stars who played them in the history of black film
from 1903 to the present.

See 0375. J. C. Bond, "Flip Wilson, The Mod Squad, Mission Impossible: Is this what it's really like to be
Black?"

0715
    Bond, Jean Carey. "The media image of black
    women," *Freedomways*, 1975, 15:34-37.

    Although black people appear in television commercials
and are the subjects of dramatic, comedy and detective
series, racist and sexist stereotypes still persist.
Christy of "Get Christy Love!" is less a detective than a
sex object whose glossy lips and swinging hips are most
often in the camera's eye. Subtle sexism is evident in
the situation comedies where the myth of the black matriarchy is exploited in the series' family structures.
These stereotypes will change significantly only when
black people, especially black women, penetrate the decision-making positions in the television industry.

See 0831. G. E. Britton, *Danger: State Adopted Reading Texts May be Hazardous to Our Future*.

0716
    Clark, Cedric C. "Television and social controls: some observations on the portrayals of ethnic minorities," *Television Quarterly*, 1970, 8(2): 18-22.

    Television portrayals of minority group individuals of both sexes are characterized most often by invisibility or ridicule. Black men are Amos and Andy types while Oriental-American women become exotic sex objects. When pressured to upgrade the image of certain groups television writers legitimize the characters by placing them within the context of "law and order." The protagonist of the 1970 "Julia" was employed by the Department of Defense, was the widow of a Vietnam victim, had a friend employed as a police officer, and a son whose career goal was "super-spy."

0717
    Davis, Mavis Wormley. "Black images in children's literature: revised editions needed," *School Library Journal*. January, 1972, 18:37-39.

    Children's movies based on literary classics often delete the stereotyped images of blacks found in the book version. However, children who are stimulated by the movie versions to read *Mary Poppins* and *Dr. Doolittle* are exposed to the damaging stereotype of black women as watermelon-eating pickaninny.

0718
    Dieterich, Daniel J.. "Books that lie and lullaby," *Elementary English*, 1972, 49:1000-1009.

    The "lie" in the title refers to racist/sexist stereotypes, while the "lullaby" is the seemingly innocuous presentation of the stereotype. These lies and lullabies should be overthrown in educational material so that children don't develop a negative self-image from books. Although the jolly black mammies and pickaninnies have disappeared from children's literature, some of the more subtle racial and sexual stereotypes continue to damage the psyches of American youth. The article ends with a bibliography of favorable group images in children's books.

See 0380. P. C. Donagher, et al. "Race, sex and social

example: an analysis of character portrayals on interracial television entertainment."

0719
    Elliot, Linda Anne. "Black women in the media,"
Other Voices: Black Chicano and American In-
dian, ed. by Sharon Murphey. Dayton: Pflaum/
Standard, 1974. pp. 47-51.

Four black women in magazine, newspaper and newscaster positions, all advise aspiring black media women
to get good educations, acquire skills and expertise in
white publications to bring to black publications, and
be dedicated to the interests of the black audience.

See 0563. C. B. Flora. "The passive female."

0720
    Freeman, Lucinda. "From servant to superchick
ain't necessarily up," *Scene Magazine* (California
State University Journalism Dept.), Fall, 1975.

The black woman's image in film has traditionally
been white man's fabrication of black womanhood. Although
she's no longer shown as the devoted, self-effacing ser-
vant/slave, her image has not improved in black man's
films. With her "fried hair and karate chops" she now exists as another stereotype and is rarely shown as an
emotionally strong black woman.

0721
    Golden, Bernette. "Black women's liberation,"
Essence, February, 1974, 4(10):36-37.

Among the most offensive images of black women perpetuated by white men, especially in film, is the myth of
matriarchy that black women must overcome.

See 0481. L. Gant, "Aint Beulah dead yet? or images of
the Black woman in film."

0722
    Graham, Beryl Caroline. "Treatment of black
American women in children's encyclopedias,"
Negro History Bulletin, May, 1976, 39:596-
598.

Black women have traditionally been stereotyped as

the obese, domineering, uneducated mother of ten or
twelve illigitimate children. The stereotyped image of
black women in encyclopedias is slightly different in that
notable black women are omitted. The names of 23 black
women were examined in eight children's encyclopedias.
Those omitted include women considered to be heroines in
the black community but not accepted by the white community, women with black-oriented ideology and black women
who are successfully employed in traditionally white male
professions. The article ends with a bibliography of history books and biographies offering strong black female
role models for children.

0723
　　　　Grier, William H. and Price M. Cobbs. "Achieving
　　　　womanhood," *Up Against the Wall, Mother...Writ-*
　　　　ings on Women's Liberation, ed. by Elsie Adams
　　　　and Mary Louise Briscoe. Beverly Hills: Glencoe
　　　　Press, 1971. pp. 44-53.

If Miss America, the blonde, blue-eyed pin-up, is the
American ideal, then black women with dark skin and kinky
hair are the antithesis of the brand of beauty touted by
the media. Until the "Black is Beautiful" philosophy won
acceptance, black women, much more than non-beautiful white
women, were oppressed and humiliated by the media standard
of beauty.

See 0489. M. Haskell, "Here come the killer dames."

0724
　　　　Hinton, James L., John F. Seggar, Herbert C. North-
　　　　cott, and Brian F. Fontes. "Tokenism and improving
　　　　imagery of blacks in TV drama and comedy: 1973,"
　　　　Journal of Broadcasting, 1974, 18:423-432.

In 1973 eight weekly television programs regularly
featured black characters. Of these eight, only one was
female. She played a minor role. Black families were excluded from most prime time television programming of 1973.

See 0433. S. S. Hobson, "Women and television."

0725
　　　　Holly, Ellen. "Where are the films about real
　　　　black men and women?," *The New York Times,*
　　　　June 2, 1974, p. D-11.

The single formula of most black films is the action

film set in a northern urban ghetto whose characters are gunslingers, pushers, pimps and prostitutes. *Claudine* is a step in the right direction with characters and situations with which the black audience can identify.

Still needed however are films made by people who really care about black people.

See 0387. G. Kopecky, "You're under arrest, Sugar."

0726
"Monica McGuire objects to double standard on "That's My Mama," *Media Report to Women,* January 1, 1976, 4(1):7.

Excerpts from a letter to ABC President concerning sexist portrayal of black women on the television program, "That's My Mama."

0727
Murray, James P. "Diahann Carroll and female singers take the lead," *To Find an Image: Black Films from Uncle Tom to Super-Fly,* by J. P. Murray. Indianapolis: Bobbs-Merrill, 1973. pp. 36-41; also ERIC (ED 113 767).

Sophisticated black audiences are calling for more realistic roles for black actresses and actors. Although the caricatures of black maids and mammies are not recognized as such, the image of black women in the cinema has not improved significantly - black woman as slave is still a recurring motif. According to the author film roles for black actresses will not improve until comparable roles have been improved for their male counterparts.

0728
"NBFO lists TV complaints and protests "That's My Mama'," *Media Report to Women,* December 1, 1974, 2(12):16.

The National Black Feminist Organization urged the removal of "That's My Mama" because of tasteless verbal slurs against black women repeatedly made by black male characters. They called for positive and strong images of black people to replace the present stereotypic and demeaning black roles.

See 0278. National Advertising Review Board, "Advertising and Women."

217

See 0356. H. C. Northcott, et al., "Trends in TV portrayal of blacks and women."

0729

   "Reaching the black woman," *The New York Times*, December 5, 1974, p. 83.

   When advertisers appear to black women the approach is different from appeals to white women because "blacks have more children, have a more positive attitude toward homemaking than white women and do not see homemaking as drudgery."

0730

   Sloan, Margaret. "Keeping the black woman in her place," *Ms.*, January 1, 1974, 2(7):30-31.

   When the civil rights movement came of age commercial films began to reflect the new feeling of black autonomy - black male autonomy, that is. Black men acquired the cave mentality of rape and murder previously reserved for white men. The changes, struggles and growth experienced by black women were left unexpressed until movies like *Black Girl*, *Coffy* and *Cleopatra Jones* began portraying black women in all shades and situations. The roles of black women in film were no longer at the back of the "revolutionary bus."

0731

   Smith, Barbara. "Black women in film symposium" *Freedomways*, 1974, 14:266-269.

   Five well-known black actresses participated in a conference on black female images in film. Some conclusions dealt with the paucity of roles for serious black dramatic actresses, the one-dimensional treatment of black female characters in white films, and the stereotyped treatment of black women as either matriarch or whore. The role of Rebecca in *Sounder* was the one dignified portrayal of woman cited. Black children will continue to see prostitutes, drug dealers and pimps as their role models until blacks acquire more autonomy in the film industry.

See 0894. J. L. Trecker, "Woman in US history high school textbooks."

0732

   Wood, Bill. "Black women in television news,"

Essence, July, 1972, 3(3):30-31+.

Negotiations between governmental commissions and television networks for more black and female faces resulted in increased hiring of black women as news trainees. The article is a survey of training schools for minority news reporters and includes brief interviews with black women in television news.

Non-Black Minority Women

0733
"Children's books from the new China," *Racist and Sexist Images in Children's Books,* by Council on Interracial Books for Children. NY: CIBC, 1975. pp. 30-34.

Several children's books from China, translated into English, challenge traditional sex roles: a girl "doctors" a broken toy horse, a girl masterminds a clandestine mission, and a non-fiction book about the Chinese Women's Army of efficient fighters all teach the positive values that Chinese children learn to develop.

See 0716. C. C. Clark, "Television and social controls: some observations on the portrayals of ethnic minorities."

0734
Herbst, Laura. "That's one good Indian: unacceptable images in children's movies," *Top of the News,* 1975, 31:192-198.

In children's fiction Indian girls are stereotyped as dirty savages who, when bathed, become "white" girls, and are depicted as lucky when adopted by white families or are otherwise assimilated into the white culture.

0735
"How Children's books distort the Asian-American image," *Council on Interracial Books for Children Bulletin,* 1976, 7(2/3):3-5.

Analysis of the 66 books currently in print dealing with Asian-American themes indicated a racist, sexist, elitist slant to books written primarily by white, non-Asian writers. Rather than reflecting current status of

women the children's books reflected Confucianism which
sanctioned female slavery while propounding other, more
romanticized attitudes toward women. The authors established criteria for analyzing books on Asian-Americans
and list loaded words and images to avoid.

See 0798. F. Howe. "Liberated Chinese primers."

See 0937. H. Miller. "Why children's films are not rated
'R'."

0736
    Prida, Dolores and Susan Ribner. "Portrayal
    of women in children's books on Puerto Rican
    themes," *Interracial Books for Children, Quar-
    terly Bulletin of CIBC*, Spring, 1972; also in
    Sexism and Youth, ed. by Diane Gersoni-Stavn.
    NY: Bowker, 1974. pp. 272-288; also in *We'll
    Do It Ourselves: Combatting Sexism in Education*.
    Lincoln: University of Nebraska Curriculum De-
    velopment Center. pp. 13-30; also as "A femi-
    nist view of the 100 books about Puerto Ricans,"
    Racist and Sexist Images in Children's Books.
    NY: CIBC, 1975. pp. 42-48.

    Essay describes the portrayal of Puerto Rican girls
and women in 100 juvenile and teenage fiction titles.
Eighteen books are additionally reviewed in terms of both
cultural and sex role stereotyping.

See 0980. M. Pastine. "Articles on non-sexist, non-
racist children's literature."

See 0810. "Racism and sexism in children's books."

0737
    Salinas, Judy. "The Chicana image," paper
    presented at the Popular Culture Association
    Meeting, 1975. ERIC (ED 106 032).

    The literary conventions of "good woman" (kind, pas-
sive, motherly Virgin Mary) vs. "bad woman" (evil, passionate, manipulative Eve) are applied to Chicano literature. In traditional literature the "bad woman" was
punished for transgressions, hence the story where a
lesbian committed suicide. However in contemporary literature value judgments have been suspended. A prostitute
is portrayed compassionately as someone who is trying to

survive in a tough world.

See 0365. J. F. Seggar, "World of work on TV."

See 0367. D. W. Smythe, "Reality as presented by television."

0738
    "Summary of the script and program review of
    'Sesame Street' by the Chicano Study Center."
    Los Angeles: University of California, 1974.
    ERIC (ED 122 825).

    Criticism of heavy male representation among charac-
ters, voiceovers and sex stereotyped roles of men as
strong, aggressive, and smart while women were typed as
weak, passive, ignored or eliminated from scenes.
Heavy ethnic stereotyping and abuse of Spanish language
is also criticized.

0739
    Trevino, Diana. "The longest running put-down;
    Daisy Mae doesn't speak for Appalachian women,"
    Women's Agenda, February, 1977, 2(2):10+.

    Daisy Mae and Mammy Yokum of Lil Abner fame along
with their television counterparts Ellie Mae and Granny
Clampett of "The Beverly Hillbillies" are the media stereotypes of the young and sexy, and aged and wisecracking Appalachian women. Television is somewhat redeemed by the
positive image of mountain women in "The Waltons," but
even there emphasis is a stereotyped image of mountain activities: quilting and hymn humming. Trevino calls for
a more sensitive portrayal of mountain women with their
unique personalities and problems.

THE MEDIA IMAGE OF MEN

See 0001. K. Amundsen, "The American female, myth and reality."

See 0006. S. L. Bem and D. J. Bem, "Case study of a non-conscious ideology: training the woman to know her place."

0740
    Brenton, Myron. "The Dagwood Bumstead Syn-drome," *The American Male: A Penetrating Look at the Masculinity Crisis*, by M. Brenton. NY: Coward-McCann, 1966. pp. 141-144.

    The contemptuous attitude toward the American father is evident throughout the media. In comic strips the married man is a good natured buffoon while the bachelor is a swashbuckler. Television commercials portray domes-tically oriented men as "simpering mother-attached caricatures" and in television situation comedies his in-competence borders on imbecility.

See 0377. C. Christ, "Marcus Welby or Archie Bunker: will the real chauvinist pig please stand up?"

See 0259. M. R. Crask, et al., "The modern masculine life style."

0741
    Ewen, Stuart, "Father: the patriarch as wage slave," *Captains of Consciousness; Advertising and the Social Roots of the Consumer Culture*, by S. Ewen. NY: McGraw Hill, 1976. pp. 151-157.

    Advertising defines man as wage earner. He functions as wage earner in death as in life, hence the absolute necessity for large insurance premiums.

0742
    Farrell, Warren. "Image and aggression," *The Liberated Man, Beyond Masculinity: Freeing Men and Their Relationships with Women*, by W. Farrell. NY: Random House, 1974. pp. 156-157.

Television, radio and newspapers reinforce and encourage violence as a primary masculine value. The media equates masculinity with conflict power, and ultimately, war rather than with more positive traits such as human cooperation and care.

0743
    Farrell, Warren. "Masculine images in advertising," *The Liberated Man, Beyond Masculinity: Freeing Men and Their Relationships with Women*, by W. Farrell. NY: Random House, 1974. pp. 105-117.

A visible tattoo, leather, aloof cowboy, horses, wilderness and other symbols of masculinity help to create a masculine aura in cigarette ads. Automobile ads project an equally masculine, though slightly less independent image of men. The man who buys cars is more often seen with the burden of responsibility - a dependent woman leans on him. The image of masculinity strengthened by a parasitic wife operates even more blatantly in life insurance ads in which men are responsible for wives even after death. Two responsible people sharing a life rarely exist in advertising. In their fear of tampering with profits by eliminating sex role stereotypes, advertisers may be doing themselves a disservice. By marketing golf to surburban women, for example, golf courses would be populated all week. By shattering the masculine mystique surrounding golf, or the feminine mystique of children's dolls, potential markets could be doubled.

See 0665. C. W. Ferguson, "In the lighter vein."

0744
    Goodman, Andrew and Patricia Walby. *A Book About Men*. London: Quartet Books, 1975.

The media fantasies of masculinity, particularly in advertising and cinema, involve sexual slogans for after shave and nearly pornographic packaging of products. The advertising fantasy becomes personified in movies by John Wayne/James Bond types. The image of female sexuality is also explored especially in contrast to the other equally prevalent image of women - Motherhood.

See 0920. E. Goodman, "Mother Nature and sex roles."

0745
     Kaye, Harvey E. *Male Survival; Masculinity With-
     out Myth*. NY: Grosset and Dunlap, 1974.

     The "Superman Syndrome" operates in ads for cologne
and razor blades, in porn movies, *Playboy* and other aspects of the masculine mystique.

See 0757. Z. S. Klapper, "The impact of the women's
liberation movement on child development books."

0746
     Lohof, Bruce. "The higher meaning of Marlboro
     cigarettes," *Journalism Quarterly*, 1975, 52:
     309+; also in *Side-Saddle on the Golden Calf*,
     ed. by George H. Lewis. Pacific Palisades, CA:
     Goodyear publishing, 1972. pp. 25-37.

     Masculinity as defined by Marlboro cigarette ads
shows an image of the Marlboro Man whose clothes, habits
and face represent the sculptured, cragged, rugged environment in which he roams. The same masculine values
of mobility and independence operate in "trucker" songs
whereby the working class man feels a conflict between
sowing wild oats and putting down roots. These men are
competitive and flirt with and overcome danger.

0747
     McLuhan, Marshall. "Blondie," *The Mechanical
     Bride, Folklore of Industrial Man*, by H. M.
     McLuhan. NY: Vanguard Press, 1951. pp.
     68-70.

     McLuhan calls Dagwood "an apologetic intruder into a
hygienic dormitory." His wife, Blondie is twice-bathed,
deodorized and depilatorized, his children are confident
and successful, while Dagwood is a dope who sports a
cuckold's hairdo and spends his free time either napping
on the sofa with his face to the wall, or in front of the
icebox where his insecurity promotes "promiscuous gorman-
dizing." McLuhan predicted Dagwood's popularity remaining
intact in spite of a world becoming alienated to his image.

See 0933. "Male superiority and dominance being taught
to both children and adults."

See 0173. M. Mannes, "Television: the splitting image."

0748
    Mehlinger, Kermit T. "The image of black man
    and the media," *Journal of the National Medical
    Association*, 1970, 62:129-133.

    The image of black men in the media is that of pain-
ful exclusion. He is absent from photographic accounts
of World War I, as if he had been exempt from the draft,
and he has been essentially absent from the entertainment
field where black characters had been performed by white
people wearing blackface makeup. When a black male face
was seen in the media, it was the stereotypically happy
Uncle Ben or pickaninny. Since the civil rights movement
some changes have been made: advertising now shows black
people washing dishes and clothes, and eating food.

See 0936. T. P. Meyer, "Children's perceptions of favorite TV characters as behavioral models."

See 0760. E. Mitchell, "The learning of sex roles through
toys and books."

See 0324. S. Pingree, et al., "A scale for sexism."

See 0682. J. Russ, "Image of women in science fiction."

See 0700. M. Seligson, "Nude times...2."

0749
    Silverstein, Michael. "The history of a short
    unsuccessful academic career," *The Insurgent
    Sociologist*, 1972, 4:4-19; also in *Sex: Male/
    Gender: Masculine*, ed. by John W. Petras.
    Port Washington, NY: Alfred Publishing, 1975.

    Confessions of a man whose self-worth suffered because
he could not identify with the violent and competitive image of manliness he was exposed to in school, books and
movies.

See 0819. K. Skjonsberg, "Sex roles in boy's and girl's
books."

See 0285. J. R. Stuteville, "Sexually polarized products
and advertising strategy."

0750
    Ward, Francis. "Black male images in film,"
    Freedomways, 1974, 14:223-229.

    In art films as well as commercial films, stereotypes
of the black male image persist. Black men are portrayed
as strong, virile lovers of flashy cars, gaudy clothes and
beautiful women. They are usually violent super-heroes:
the black equivalent of John Wayne or Humphrey Bogart.
Occasionally they are molded by another white stereotype
and become the smooth, well educated black executive or
professional. Although the image of black superstud seems
to be pervasive, actors like Poitier, Davis and Cosby
manage to maintain their integrity. As more blacks gain
control of film production and distribution, roles for
blacks will acquire greater dignity.

See 0641. M. Wilkinson, "Romantic love: the great equalizer? Sexism in popular music."

CHILDREN'S MEDIA

General Media and Toys

0751
   American Association of University Women. California State Division. Status of Women Committee. *Jack and Jill; This is the World that
   Jack Built and Jill Came Tumbling After.* AAUW,
   1972.

   Discusses the influence of advertising and children's
nursery rhymes in exposing children to sex role stereotypes.

See 0003. K. Barrett, "Daughters."

See 0015. L. J. Busby, "Sex role research in the mass
media."

See 0102. *Booklegger Magazine.*

0752
   Grambs, Jean Dresden. "Books and sex bias,"
   *Sex, Does It Make a Difference?: Sex Roles
   in the Modern World,* ed. by J. D. Grambs and
   Walter B. Waetjen. N. Scituate, Mass: Dux-
   bury Press, 1975. pp. 133-138.

   Sex bias in children's literature begins with the
preaching of cultural values in the nineteenth century
McGuffey readers. The reinforcement of those values continue in the twentieth century picture books with female
teachers and male principals, bus drivers and school doctors; in elementary school history books which virtually
ignore women's contributions as they concentrate on male-
initiated wars and politics; and in comic books which
stereotype women as constantly love-struck and men as
aggressive, violent and death dealing.

0753
   Grambs, Jean Dresden. "Sex stereotypes in instructional materials, literature and language: a
   survey of research," *Women Studies Abstracts*,
   1972, 1(4):1-4+.

   Brave, resourceful Dorothy of the Oz series is a rare
exception to the sex stereotypes children encounter in
other works of fiction and comic books.

See 0032. B. G. Harrison, "June, 1971: a new beginning."

0754
   Howe, Florence. "The female majority: the
   education of willing slaves," *Conspiracy of
   the Young*, ed. by Paul Lauter and F. Howe. NY:
   World Publishers, 1970. pp. 306-315.

   Because of the mystiques surrounding boys' toys,
girls are reluctant to play with scientific toys that
girls "aren't supposed to know about." Boys are willing
to play with nurse kits only when they pretend they're
doctor kits. Children's books prepare girls for marriage
and teach them that they are lovable, meek, sensitive and
shy. Children's books prepare boys for a number of adult
occupations and teach them to acquire exciting, lively,
action-packed personalities. When offering models for
professional aspirations these books picture waitresses
working in diners while waiters work in fancy restaurants.
Female *volunteers* and *salaried* male legislators work together to solve governmental problems.

See 0608. "Joan Nicholson: on using employee publications
for affirmative action."

0755
   Juran, Carol Kline. *The Effects of Subject
   and Model Sex on Imitative Behavior with Sex
   Typed Toys*. Ph.D. dissertation, University
   of Maryland, 1971.

   When following a respected role model, traditional
sex "appropriateness" of toys was not a significant variable for 120 first and second grade children participating
in this experiment.

0756
   Kinsell-Rainey, Lynn. *Incidental Learning of
   Sex Role Characteristics*. M.A. thesis, Southern

Illinois University, 1972.

Analysis of toy advertisements in Sears, Roebuck and Co. catalogues for the years 1900-1970 revealed that the toys of 1900 encouraged boys to be rowdy, noisy and boisterous and girls to be non-competitive and quiet, while 1970's toys encouraged boys to be more quiet, passive and sedentary and encouraged girls to be more assertive. The results indicate a future trend toward decreased differentiation of sex roles.

0757
Klapper, Zelda S. "The impact of the women's liberation movement on child development books," *American Journal of Orthopsychiatry*, 1971, 41: 725-732.

Sex stereotypes in children's toys and child development books contribute to female lack of self-worth and prevalence of self-hatred and to the damaging effect on boys who are pressured to be "manly."

0758
Levy, Betty, and Judith Stacey. "Sexism in the elementary school: a backward and forward look," *Phi Delta Kappan*, 1973, 55:105-109+.

A review of the research involving sex role stereotypes in readers and math, science and social studies textbooks, toys and children's television. The authors suggest that reforming the symptom by adding token women does not guarantee a cure. Such reform does not challenge the elitist structure. There is a need to analyze the types of changes which will facilitate a genuinely liberating education for children.

0759
Lyon, Nancy. "A report on children's toys and socialization to sex roles," *Ms.*, December, 1972, 1(6):57.

An examination of the illustrations on children's toy packages reveals that pictures of boys appear more often on packages containing complex and expensive toys (e.g., erector sets) while girls appear more frequently on simple, less interesting toy packages (e.g., building blocks). The package illustrations also define the roles of parents with fathers joining the children as they play with the toys while mothers either act as spectator or perform cleaning duties in the background.

229

0760

Mitchell, Edna. "The learning of sex roles through toys and books: a woman's view," *Young Children*, 1973, 28:226-231.

Toy manufacturers refuse to change slogans to include appeals to girls, even if girls play with those toys. The rationale: "boys don't want toys that girls can also play with." Girls are sold toys that prepare them for a domestic future - baby dolls and cribs, kitchen appliances and battery operated sweepers, while boys play with trucks and artillery. Teen dolls train girls to become 18 year old Barbie clothes mannequins while boys who play with Big Jim and his flexing muscles learn the macho role. Children's books teach similar values. Tomboy girls must grow up to become ladies while adventurous boys aren't trained to outgrow creativity and action. Careless selection of toys and books by parents can "have an irreparable impact on the psychological growth" of children.

0761

Rachlin, Susan Kessler and Glenda L. Vogt. "Sex roles as presented to children by coloring books," *Journal of Popular Culture*, 1975, 8:549-556.

An examination of 30 coloring books by five publishers which were "prominently displayed and repeated from store to store" indicates that the coloring book medium maintains a definite sex role bias. The authors suggest alternatives to traditional stereotypes such as "Susie is the doctor for Ted's doll."

0762

Sanders, Marlene. *A Woman's Place.* 16mm, 52 mins., purchase, $600. Xerox Films, 245 Long Hill Road, Middletown, Conn. 06457.

Children's books, toys, motion pictures and advertising are among the media forces that influence children's acquisition of traditional sex roles in childhood and perpetuate them throughout life.

0763

"'Tear open the boxes' is new program on sexism in toy packaging and ads," *Media Report to Women*, April 1, 1977, 5(4):14.

A filmstrip, study guide and bibliography reveal toy packaging and advertising's "negative effect on children's growth, self-image and career motivation, particularly in girls."

0764
"Toys that care catalogue," available from Toys That Care, PO Box 81, Briarcliffe Manor, NY 10510. $2.00.

An educational guide and catalogue includes non-sexist, non-racist occupation puzzles, multi-media teaching aids, career dress-up, anatomically correct dolls, books and a plastic-coated career card game, "Robot", which is an alternative to the traditional "Old Maid."

Children's Literature

PICTURE BOOKS

0765
Conant, Margaret M. "Learning to be a boy, a girl, or a person, *PTA Magazine*, March, 1972, 66(7):18-21.

Children's books are among the most potent socializing forces in a child's life. Pre-schoolers find sex stereotyped occupations in living color in their picture books, and school children meet them again in math and reading books which introduce boys to the working world and prepare girls for marriage.

0766
Czaplinski, Suzanne M. *Sexism in Award Winning Picture Books*. Pittsburgh: KNOW, Inc., 1973.

A time study of the Caldecott and Lewis Carroll award winning picture books shows that sex bias in picture books decreased during the 1940's and 1950's, then greatly increased during the 1960's. Overall, female characters appeared in 20% of the texts and 30% of the illustrations. Male characters were portrayed as more physically active, emotionally controlled and intellectually superior than their passive, dependent, conforming sisters. The psychological implication of sex-typed behavior models indicates that children of both sexes prefer to identify with male roles than the less interesting female roles. Examples of sexist and non-sexist books are discussed in terms of Kate Millett's criteria for examining literature.

See 0955. K. B. DeFilippo, "Little girls and picture books; problems and solutions."

0767
    Fisher, Elizabeth, "Children's books: the
    second sex, junior division," *The New York Times
    Book Review*, May 24, 1970, p. 6+; also in *And
    Jill Came Tumbling After*, ed. by Judith Stacey,
    et al. NY: Dell, 1974. pp. 116-122.

Although the US population is 51% female, children's
picture books represent them as a 25% minority. Girls are
nearly invisible in the fantasy worlds of Maurice Sendak
and Dr. Seuss, as well as in most animal stories. Only in
several picture book versions of "Noah's Ark" are both
sexes equally represented. When female characters are
represented they still nearly border on invisibility. A
Richard Scarry book pictures boys engaged in 21 activities
and girls in two: watching and sitting.

See 0792. H. Fraad, *Sex role stereotyping and male-female
character distribution in popular, prestigious and sex
role defining children's literature.*

0768
    LaDow, Stephanie. "A content analysis of selected
    picture books examining the portrayal of sex roles
    and representation of males and females," 1976.
    ERIC (ED 123 165).

If literature helps shape the cognitive and emotional
development of the pre-school child, then children's textbooks should offer alternatives to the traditional sex
roles children find in picture books. A content analysis
of 125 picture books revealed underrepresentation of female
characters in illustrations, book titles and occupational
roles.

See 0972. E. Merriam, "A feminist alphabet."

0769
    Stewig, John and Margaret Higgs. "Girls grow
    up to be mommies: a study of sexism in chil-
    dren's literature," *School Library Journal*,
    January, 1973, 19:44-49; also in *Library Jour-
    nal*, 1973, 98:236-241.

Of 154 picture books analyzed, 83% showed women in
homemaking roles while 17% showed women in occupations.
The occupations included teacher, maid, nun, librarian,

gypsy, cafeteria worker and fat lady in a circus. While
most of the 17% female occupations require little or no
training, many of the male occupations require education
and/or talent: musician, sports player, principal, doctor, zookeeper, mayor. The authors call for a wider presentation of women's roles in picture books viewed by
children during the critical age of attitude formation.

0770
Stewig, John Warren and Mary Lynn Knipfel. "Sex-
ism in picture books: what progress?" *Elementary
School Journal*, 1975, 76:151-155.

In order to determine if recently published books
show mother in the lab as well as at the stove, 100 pre-
school picture books published from 1972 to 1974 were examined. Female invisibility still exists as evidenced in
the absence of female characters in nine books. Women are
shown in homemaking roles in 68% of the books examined and
in professional roles in 32%. This marks an improvement
over a 1971 study where the ratio was 84:17%. In the later
study women were rarely shown reading or playing musical
instruments. Although women enjoyed increased variety of
professional roles, they still had fewer types of occupations than men. Male recreational activities were action
oriented while female activities were sedentary. Men were
rarely shown performing household tasks that they commonly
do in reality. A more accurate portrayal of women's and
men's roles in picture books is still needed to present
children with positive attitudes of the sex roles.

0771
Sutherland, Zena. "Make no mystique about it,"
Saturday Review, March 20, 1971, 54:30-31.

Although the need exists for a changed image of girls
and women in picture books, the author hopes that not all
books will begin featuring aggressive female characters.

0772
Trumpeter, Margo and Linda D. Crowe. "Sexism
in picture books," *Illinois Library*, September,
1971, 53:499-503.

Of 33 Caldecott medal winners from 1950-1970 examined,
only seven (21%) feature female protagonists. Not only do
they see more male characters, but male readers are offered much more interesting role models than female readers: on an egg hunt boys are shown to find more eggs than
girls (connoting success) but girls find prettier eggs
(connoting beauty). Men give "wise" advice while mothers

scold.

0773
Vukelich, Carol, Charlotte McCarty and Claire
Nanis. "Sex bias in children's books," *Child-
hood Education*, 1976, 52:220-222; also in *Grow-
ing Free: Ways to Help Children Overcome Sex
Role Stereotypes*, by Monroe D. Cohen and Lucy
Prete Martin. Washington DC: International As-
sociation for Childhood Education, 1976.

Thirty-two picture books labeled "favorites" of young
children by 21 teachers were examined for sex stereotypes.
It was found that the main characters were 68% male, 22%
female. Those engaged in active play were 85% male, 15%
female. Those using initiative were 100% male, 0% female.
Although sex stereotyping in children's books has been
studied for five years, it was determined that teachers
are not evaluating picture books for sex bias when using
them with their students. Careful screening of these books
is needed.

0774
Weitzman, Lenore, Debora Eifler, Elizabeth Hokada,
and Catherine Ross. "Sex role socialization in
picture books for preschool children." *American
Journal of Sociology*, 1972, 77:1125-1150; also in
Sexism and Youth, ed. by Diane Gersoni-Stavn. NY:
Bowker, 1974. pp. 174-195; also in *Marriage and
the Family*, ed. by Carolyn C. Perrucci and Dena
B. Targ. NY: McKay, 1974. pp. 155-178.

An examination of the societal values presented to
preschool children who "read" picture books. Caldecott
award books, Golden Books, and preschool etiquette books
were examined. The most common stereotype shows an adventurous hero rescuing a passive princess who is restricted
by her long dress. The authors reveal the prevalence of
male camaraderie in many picture books, while female characters are rarely shown strictly with members of their own
sex. The impact of inadequate role models on girls' happiness is discussed, and suggestions are given for realistic
portrayals of both sexes.

0775
Yawkey, Thomas D. and Margaret L. Yawkey. "An
analysis of picture books," *Language Arts*, 1976,
53:545-548.

An examination of 26 picture books published prior
to 1965 and 26 published since 1965 revealed that the more

recent publications included a greater number of main
characters from all racial backgrounds. However no such
equality was found for female characters in the newer
books. Less than 10% of the 26 post-1965 imprints had
dominant female characters, in spite of the emergence of
the new feminism.

FAIRY TALES

0776
    Bettelheim, Bruno. "The sleeping beauty," *The
    Uses of Enchantment; The Meaning and Importance
    of Fairy Tales*, by B. Bettelheim. NY: Knopf,
    1976. pp. 225-236.

    Bettelheim defends the fairy tale genre against femi-
nist charges of sex role stereotypes by explaining that
the female character's passivity, coupled with the male
character's aggressiveness, together represent the two
sides of one self.

0777
    Donlan, Dan. "The negative image of women in
    children's literature," *Elementary English*, 1972,
    49:604-611; also in *Sexism and Youth*, ed. by
    Diane Gersoni-Stavn. NY: Bowker, 1974. pp.
    217-229.

    Quotations from popular nursery rhymes and fairy
tales expose recurring characterizations of women. Sympathetic females are usually sweet, little old ladies or
young beauties. "Good" women include the eccentric Mother
Goose who rides a gander, a befuddled Old Mother Hubbard
whose dog appeared to be dead and laughed at her when she
purchased its coffin, and Little Red Riding Hood's imper-
ceptive grandmother who was devoured by a wolf she had
confused with her granddaughter. Typical of the young
beauties are dull-witted Snow White, spiritless Cinderella,
passive Rapunzel and naive Sleeping Beauty, all of whom
are saved from death by an aggressive male of royal lin-
eage. Although they have never expressed love for their
princes, each beauty marries her savior. Through the
course of the tales the women all live in moral vacuums
and passively submit to their situations.

    Independent women who do control their own destinies
are unsympathetic characters. Cannibalistic, sadistic
and revengeful witches in "Hansel and Gretel," "Rapunzel"
and "Sleeping Beauty," who destroy innocence and beauty are
common, as are the greedy housewives who nag their husbands
or daughters in "Hansel and Gretel", "Snow White" and

"Toads and Diamonds."

0778

Dworkin, Andrea. "The fairy tales," *Womanhating*, by A. Dworkin. NY: Dutton, 1974. pp. 29-49.

Fairy tales clearly define good and evil people who function as childhood role models. Cinderella and Snow White both have good, pious, passive and ultimately dead biological mothers. They have greedy, ambitious, ruthless, powerhungry, evil stepmothers who victimize them. Like their good [dead] mothers, Snow White and Sleeping Beauty sleep. The prince is a good person. He is handsome, heroic, strong. He falls in love with the victim's corpse and inadvertently rescues her from catatonia. He is good. Her father is good. He may not intervene in her urgent situation or try to restore Cinderella's dignity, but because he does not initiate evil, he is good. Children reading fairy tales learn two definitions of women - the passive good victim and the actively plotting, evil woman. There is one definition of man: he is good, no matter what he does or does not do.

0779

Lieberman, Marcia R. "'Some day my prince will come': female acculturation through the fairy tale," *College English*, 1972, 34:383-395; also in *Sexism and Youth*, ed. by Diane Gersoni-Stavn. NY: Bowker, 1974. pp. 228-243.

Behavior patterns appearing in fairy tales seem to socialize children to accept certain cultural sex roles. In the "beauty contest" pattern beautiful women are good tempered, weak of character and are rewarded with a royal wedding while their physically ugly stepsisters are cruel, selfish people who are punished in the end. Not only is beauty rewarded by a lucrative marriage to the prince, but the beauty's meek passivity is rewarded often with gifts from a fairy godmother. The two positive female role models then are the suffering princess-to-be and the non-human fairy. Two types of women have power in fairy tales: witches who cast evil spells and wicked and jealous stepmothers with powers of extreme cruelty. Though few benevolent fairies do appear, the most powerful women are evil and physically repulsive. Most good characters are passive, sweet-tempered and beautiful. The author questions the psychological implications of fairy tales' inherent dichotomy of good vs. evil and beauty vs. ugliness.

0780
   Minard, Rosemary. *Womenfolk and Fairy Tales*.
   Boston: Houghton Mifflin, 1975.

   The most common female characters in popular fairy
tales are beautiful young women, magical fairy godmothers
and wicked stepmothers, while male characters in most
fairy tales are bold, courageous and clever young men.
This anthology presents 18 folk and fairy tales whose female protagonists are active, intelligent, capable and
courageous. The admirable human beings here offer girls
intelligent female role models to emulate and offer boys
exciting women to respect.

See 0973. V. Moberg, "A child's right to equal reading."

0781
   Northern California Association of Children's
   Librarians, Social Concerns Committee. "Active
   heroines in folktales for children," 1976.
   Available from Kendall Smith, P. O. Box 32485,
   San Jose, CA 95152. 25¢ and SASE.
   95132. 25¢ and SASE.

   An annotated list of 57 folktales, animal tales and
fairy tales with independent, clever heroines who each
have minds of their own.

0782
   Stone, Kay. "Things Walt Disney never told us,"
   Journal of American Folklore, 1975, 88:42-50.

   Although most heroines in the Grimm Brothers fairy
tales are docile, Gretel is momentarily violent as she
destroys the villain. Walt Disney's adaptations of fairy
tales, however, never allow for healthy female aggression.
His three passive female heroines are always victimized
by female villains. The article ends with quotes from interviews with 40 women of varying ages and backgrounds
concerning the impact of female stereotypes in fairy tales
on their personal development. Many claim to have been
bored as children by the "passive princess."

See 0066. S. Tobias and E. Kusnetz, "For college students:
a study of women, their roles and stereotypes."

FICTION

0783
Bernstein, Joanne. "The changing roles of females in books for young children," *Reading Teacher*, 1974, 27:545-549.

Children's books about boys outnumber those about girls by approximately 6:1. Girls are often found in auxiliary roles, but rarely in leading roles, therefore girls find few protagonists with whom they can truly identify. By developing adventurous female characters in books, not only will female readers find their imaginations more stimulated, but male readers will read the more exciting "girl's" books and grow into men who respect women's natural sense of adventure and capacity for good ideas. In this bibliographic essay 22 books are described in terms of their positive images of female protagonists.

0784
Bernstein, Joanne. "The image of female teachers as portrayed in fiction for young children," *School Library Journal*, January, 1973, 20:79-81; also in *Library Journal*, 1973, 98:271-273.

Examination of the image of teachers in 98 stories published 1935-1970 revealed that only six teachers were male and only eight female teachers were married. In 73% of the stories teachers were portrayed as compassionate and with highly developed sense of humor. A bibliography of books with positive images of female teachers follows the article.

0785
Blaubergs, Maija S. "On 'the nurse was a doctor'," paper presented at the Southeast Conference on Linguistics, 1975. ERIC (ED 115 115); also in *Views of Language*, ed. by R. Ordoubadian and W. V. R. Engle. Murfreesboro, Tn: Inter-University Publishing, 1975.

Linguistic sex role stereotypes in children's literature show female characters more often using supportive language, *gee, great* and qualifiers like *I guess, I think, what do you think we should do?* Accepted usage of the English language also suggest that females never grow up. A sample of job ads show 97 references to *girl* or *gal*, but only two references to *boy*.

0786
    Boston Area Women in Libraries. "Tea and mus-
    kets, a bicentennial booklist," available from
    author, Box 476, W. Somerville, MA 02144. $2.00
    plus self-addressed mailing label.

A group of Boston area children's librarians compiled
and annotated a bibliography of children's historical fiction with realistic portrayals of women and men suitable
for grades K-8. Predominate themes emerging in the books
are: "The Two Suitor Syndrome" in which the heroine is
forced to choose between two polarized romantic figures,
one homey, the other glamorous; "Destined from the Cra-
le," a theme in which the heroine grows up to meet her
destiny as a born teacher; and "The Converted Tomboy" who
discards her energetic, independent nature to become passive and subservient. Each book is rated as recommended,
not recommended, or recommended with reservations, according to its historical and character believability.

0787
    Cadogan, Mary and Patricia Craig. *You're a
    Brick, Angela! A New Look at Girls' Fiction
    from 1839 to 1975.* London: Gollancz, 1976.

Much girls' fiction of this century has been written
by men. The image of girls and women as passive, domesticated, brainless and decorative individuals are stereotypes based on nursery rhyme characterizations: Miss
Muffet is plagued by an irrational fear, Polly puts the
kettle on and takes it off again, and the female victims
whom Georgia-Porgie intimidates with a kiss, are stereotypes still apparent throughout children's literature.

0788
    Campbell, Patricia B. and Charlie Thompson.
    "Little girl's place, little boy's world."
    Atlanta: Project 70 Audio Services, 1974.
    Available from authors, Department of Educa-
    tional Foundations, Georgia State University,
    Atlanta, GA 30303. Rental, $3.00.

A 26 minute audio tape discussion of sex role stereotyping in children's readers and leisure books, designed
to facilitate group discussion.

0789
    Cheda, Sherrill. "See Dick run, see Jane sit,"
    Chatelaine, La Review Moderne, December, 1972,
    5:40+.

If children's books no longer depict blacks eating
watermelon and Mexicans sleeping under sombreros, then
the time has come to get mother out of her apron and into
realistic activities. She should be portrayed fixing
things around the house, driving cars, balancing checkbooks, fund raising for organizations, enjoying her children and working in responsible professions.

See 0733. "Children's books from the new China."

See 0717. M. W. Davis, "Black images in children's literature: revised editions needed."

See 0718. D. J. Dieterich, "Books that lie and lullaby."

0790
    Feminists on Children's Literature. "A femi-
    nist look at children's books," *Library Journal*,
    1971, 17:19-24; also in *Notes from the Third
    Year, Women's Liberation*. NY, 1971, pp. 30-
    36; also in *Edcentric*, December, 1971, 3:9-15;
    also in *Sexism and Youth*, ed. by Diane Gersoni-
    Stavn. NY: Bowker, 1974, pp. 249-259; also in
    Radical Feminism, ed. by Anne Koedt, Ellen
    Levine and Anita Rapone. NY: Quadrangle, 1973,
    pp. 94-106.

    Discussion of a number of Newbery award winners and
other notable children's books includes a list of titles
with positive images of the female sex. The authors call
for the elimination of the term "tomboy," and ask "Why
can't a girl who prefers baseball to ballet simply be a
girl who prefers baseball to ballet?"

0791
    Feminists on Children's Literature. *Little Miss
    Muffet Fights Back*, NY: Feminists on Children's
    Media, 1974; 1971 ed. available on ERIC (ED 957
    626).

    Ideas children are exposed to early in life have a
profound effect on their ideas and self-concepts, and may
determine the course of their later lives. Rigid sex
roles in children's books can deter healthy development
of the readers. This annotated bibliography lists picture
books, children's fiction, biographies and non-fiction
dealing with history and women's rights which portray
people as vital human beings. The criteria for each selection are well-written, provocative, interesting books,

free of sex role stereotypes.

0792
    Fraad, Harriet, "Sex role stereotyping and male-
    female character distribution in popular, pres-
    tigious, and sex role defining children's
    literature from 1959 to 1972. Ed.D. dissertation,
    Columbia University, 1975.

    Analysis of the sex role stereotypes of 170 picture
books classified as popular (*New York Times* bestsellers),
prestigious (Caldecott award winners) and sex role defining (written by feminists). The sample was limited to
books published from 1959 to 1972, in order to include the
seven years prior to and following the emergence of the
women's liberation movement. Results indicate a majority
of male characters in both periods and in all categories
except the feminist-written books. Female characters were
most frequently depicted negatively.

0793
    Gersoni-Stavn, Diane. "Feminist criticism: an
    overview, *Sexism and Youth*, ed. by D. Gersoni-
    Stavn. NY: Bowker, 1974. pp. 377-384; also
    in *School Library Journal*, January, 1974, 20:22+;
    also in *Library Journal*, 1974, 99:182+.

    Several feminist criticisms of children's fiction are
summarized. The Nancy Drew "Superwoman," positive character though she is, should be augmented with more realistic adventure stories in which the female protagonists are
less paragon-like. While female characters are given more
options, male characters should not suffer limited roles
in didactic use of role-reversals, but should be portrayed
in natural, nonstereotyped roles. Realistic reflections
of reality could include female foxes outwitting roosters,
intelligent housewives and mothers functioning adequately,
and little girls whose femininity does not preclude depth
of character. Because children are influenced by the
books they read, feminist critics hope that children's
books will be purged of the limiting sex role propaganda
in order to broaden the child reader's horizons and options.

0794
    Ginsburg, Jane. "And then there is good old
    Nancy Drew," *Ms.*, 1974, 2(7):93-94.

    Nancy Drew is a positive role model for young girls
who crave an active and brave female protagonist.

0795
Heilbrun, Carolyn G. "Human Women," *The New York Times Book Review*, July 15, 1973, p. 8+.

Heilbrun welcomes women into the world of children's literature where female representatives used to be strictly mommies, stewardesses, nurses and coeds. Even though children's books now show women in positive roles, the books are more often manufactured than they are created. She hopes for the feminist equivalent of *Charlotte's Web*, well-written and without contrived social assumptions.

See 0734. L. Herbst, "That's one good Indian: unacceptable images in children's novels."

0796
Hillman, Judith Zoe Stevinson. *An Analysis of Male and Female Roles in Two Periods of Children's Literature*. Ph.D. dissertation, University of Nebraska, 1973; summarized in *Journal of Educational Research*, 1974, 68:84-88.

Analysis of 60 children's books published in the 1930's and the mid 1960's to mid 1970's revealed the following: 1) less sex stereotyping appeared in the 1960's, 2) female behavior profiles exhibited significant change over three decades, 3) differences between the sexes were most apparent in occupational patterns.

0797
Hillman, Judith Stevinson. "Occupational roles in children's literature," *Elementary School Journal*, September, 1976, 77(1):1-4.

A comparison of occupational roles in 120 children's novels published in the 1930's and 1960's revealed little change in sex typed occupations taught to children though social changes had taken place during the 30 year span.

See 0735. "How children's books distort the Asian American image."

0798
Howe, Florence. "Liberated Chinese primers," *Women: A Journal of Liberation*, Fall, 1970, 1: 33-34; also in *Sexism and Youth*, ed. by Diane Gersoni-Stavn. NY: Bowker, 1974. pp. 214-216.

Four Chinese fiction books offer positive role
models for girls. Female characters are shown as a doctor,
as a sexually equal teacher's aid working alongside a male
in the same position, as a farm worker, and as a courageous
and quick-witted spy.

See 0706. J. P. Jones, "Nancy Drew, WASP super girl of
the 1930's."

0799
    Lanes, Selma. "On feminism and children's books,"
    School Library Journal, January, 1974, 20:23+;
    also in *Library Journal*, 1974, 99:183+.

Feminists who call for a predominance of non-sexist
books on library shelves are cautioned to remember the
difference between propanganda and literature. Although
portraying female children as potential baseball players
or US Presidents is healthy propaganda, such roles for the
sake of eliminating sexism should not be the main preoccupation of children's books.

0800
    Liljestrom, Rita. "The Swedish model: cultural
    lag in communication media," *Sex Roles in Chang-
    ing Society*, ed. by Georgene H. Seward and
    Robert C. Williamson. NY: Random House, 1970,
    pp. 209-212.

A content analysis of children's books reveals that
physiological changes such as blushing, cold shivers, nau-
sea and trembling voice more frequently occur in girls'
books (72 occasions) than in boys' books (26 occasions).
Another discrepancy in emphasis shows girls' books most
often concerned with main character's clothing while boys'
books emphasize main character's knowledge.

0801
    Lukenbill, W. Bernard. "Fathers in adolescent
    novels: some implications for sex role reinter-
    pretations," *School Library Journal*, February,
    1974, 20(6):26-30; also in *Library Journal*, 1974,
    99:536-540.

Analysis of the father image in 227 adolescent novels
set in the twentieth century United States revealed that
fathers were 84% middle class, and 45% in professional or
business oriented careers. They were the traditional breadwinners while mother figures assumed household and child
care roles. If literature does influence society, can the

isolated medium of adolescent fiction change conventional
sex role behavior by providing alternate sex role patterns?
If so, it should be done without overwhelming the story
with contrived, didactic sex role interpretations.

0802
    MacCann, Donnarae. "Children's books in a plura-
    listic society," *Wilson Library Bulletin*, 1976,
    51:154-162.

    Sexist and racist children's books harm the self
esteem of female and black children while encouraging a
false sense of superiority in white male children. "Slurs
and demeaning images...deny the child's freedom to exist
as an individual of equal worth with others." The article
includes testimony of harmful personal effects on children
who read "Little Black Sambo," Whitney Darrow's *I'm Glad
I'm a Boy! I'm Glad I'm a Girl!*, and concludes with a
discussion of stereotyped portrayals of Indians in Laura
Ingalls Wilder's *Little House* series.

See 0708. B. A. Mason, "The girl sleuth."

See 0051. G. Nelson, "The double standard in adolescent
novels."

0803
    Nightingale, Camilla. "Sex roles in children's
    literature," *Assistant Librarian*, October, 1972,
    74:154-158.

    Emphasizing a number of themes not examined in most
American analyses this British article discusses the
polarity of the sexes in children's books. While boys'
adventures take them all over three continents, girls'
books are set in schools. In a series of books about
dance school students, technical details of the art form
are avoided while boys' books of the same age level abound
with technicalities of motors, explosives and traps. Instead, girls' books emphasize the crucial importance of
romance and teach girls to think of little else. Boys are
also interested in dating, but their reading matter reveals other interests as well. Instead of dealing sympathetically with the puberty stage conflict between growing
awareness of self and the female role, rigid sex roles are
the literary form, denying the adolescent's feeling that
she is a person in her own right, independent of sex.

0804
　　Nilsen, Alleen Pace. "Books a la mode: a
　　reader's digest," *Elementary English*, 1973,
　　50:1029-1033.

Because most slow readers are boys, books for the
readers are "sugar coated" to appeal to boys. The brand
of sugar coating is detrimental because boys are enticed
by stories in which male egos are salved by inadequate
portrayals of girls. Books at the first through third
grade levels show boys participating in sports while girls
watch. In reality girls aged five through eight are every
bit as active as their male counterparts. When examining
a group of readers the author found 213 boys pictured and
80 girls, 618 masculine pronouns and 170 feminine. She
suggests introducing children to books that contrast the
usual stereotype by featuring a boy who cries, a girl who
likes snakes and a picture book that presents a variety of
female roles.

0805
　　Nilsen, Aleen P. "Women in Children's Litera-
　　ture," *College English*, 1971, 32:918-926; also
　　in *Women in English*, ed. by Susan McAllister.
　　Urbana, Illinois: National Council of Teachers
　　of English, 1971, pp. 72-80; also in *Sexism and
　　Youth*, ed. by Diane Gersoni-Stavn. NY: Bowker,
　　1974. pp. 163-173; also in *Undoing Sex Types*,
　　ed. by Marcia Guttentag and Helen Bray. NY:
　　McGraw-Hill, 1976. pp. 194-207.

Analysis of the plots and illustrations of 80 Caldecott award winners and runners-up determined that every
book had at least one male character while six books had
no female characters, and 25% of the books examined had
token females whose only value to the plot was to sew the
male hero's buttons in order to facilitate his action.
Action was repeatedly performed by male characters and observed by female characters. The author perceives the
need for four major changes in children's book approach:
1) If folk tales are a favorite of artists and publishers,
why not folktales with strong female heroes? Many exist.
2) Why the cult of the apron? Mothers should be portrayed
more realistically as driving cars, playing guitars and
going to work. 3) Low vocabulary, high interest level
books should have more female protagonists. Not only
Johnny, but Joanie, Janet and Jeannie must learn to read.
4) It's fallacious to believe that boys will not read
books about girls. *Harriet the Spy* is one of several
books with female protagonists that are extremely popular
with boys.

0806
"Old values surface in Blume Country," *Inter-racial Books for Children, Bulletin,* 1976, 7(5):8-10; also in *Language and Racism,* NY: Council on Interracial Books for Children, Inc., 1976. pp. 9-11; also in ERIC (ED 128 523), pp. 9-11.

Although her skillful writing catches the tempo of contemporary pre-teen behavior, the value of Judy Blume's fiction is considered questionable for racist and sexist reasons. Her attitudes toward racism are confusing and she tends to depict traditional sex roles as "cute."

0807
"Only you, Dick Daring!" *Publisher's Weekly,* March 22, 1971, 199(12):20-22.

The Feminist Collective on Children's Media spoke at a National Book Association meeting. Using slides, they showed how children's books project a negative image of girls and women while projecting a positive image of boys and men. They read sexist passages from some award-winning books, explained why some were considered "copouts" and others considered "positive" images.

See 0054. L. C. Pogrebin, "Down with sexist upbringing."

0808
Pogrebin, Letty Cottin. "Girls liberation," *The New York Times Book Review,* pt. 2, May 6, 1973, p. 4+.

After reviewing several recently published children's books the author asks why so many assertive female protagonists are given boyish names and why so many books with feminist consciousness are not particularly well written. Instead of a spate of new books about female astronauts and presidents, Pogrebin calls for books with strong, endearing female characters, and tender companionable males to establish a new standard of expanded sex roles in children's literature.

See 0736. D. Prida and S. Ribner, "Portrayal of women in children's books on Puerto Rican themes.

0809
Pyle, Wilma J. "Sexism in children's literature," *Theory into Practice,* 1976, 15:116-119.

Sexism in children's fiction includes the female image as passive, submissive, and incapable of physical or emotional strength. As adjuncts of their husbands women have traditionally been identified by the husband's name and occupation. This image denies girls the choice of making names for themselves in personal careers. Children's books have not adequately explored the interaction between fathers and daughters or mothers and sons, especially in divorce or single parent situations. Sexism in children's literature denies both sexes the opportunity to regard girls as interesting and exciting people. Although the importance of eliminating sexism is understood, the author stresses that quality writing should not be sacrificed for a didactic, ideological message.

0810
"Racism and sexism in children's books," *Crisis*, January, 1975, 82:21-23.

Publishers may be attempting to overthrow the more obvious racist and sexist stereotypes in children's readers, but in the process are creating other stereotypes. The barrio is overly-romanticized, minority mothers are too often depicted as cleaning ladies and factory workers, and female children are still not depicted as skilled, creative or dashing individuals. The new stereotypes could be dispelled if more minority women wrote realistic stories for children.

0811
Rinsky, Lee Ann. "Equality of the sexes and children's literature," *Elementary English*, 1973, 50:1075+.

A random selection of 600 children's literature titles from three respected book lists revealed that nearly as many men as women write children's books, therefore the prevalence of sexism in children's literature cannot be blamed solely on either sex.

0812
Roberts, Patricia Lee Brighton. *The Female Image in the Caldecott Medal Award Books*. Ed.D. dissertation, University of the Pacific, 1975.

An investigation of the stereotyping of the human, animal and inanimate female image in the texts and illustrations of 37 Caldecott winners revealed that some readers, under certain conditions, undergo attitudinal and behavioral changes as a result of reading a book.

0813
    Roberts, Patricia and Dewey Chambers. "Sugar
    and spice and almost always nice: a content
    analysis of the Caldecotts," 1976. ERIC (ED
    127 556).

    The Caldecott Awards for excellence in illustration
of children's books is compared to the coveted Academy
Awards for excellence in the visual medium. Caldecott
winners, which become "instant classics" upon announcement
of the award, are often sexist in nature. Theme analysis
of Caldecott winners reveals that the female image is most
often narrowly defined as subordinate to male characters,
she who fails, the female as nurturer, as caretaker and
the female in the home environment. Such restrictions
present a colorless picture of women and deny them the
"spice" from the "sugar and spice" cliche.

0814
    Rogers, Katherine. "Liberation for girls," *Satur-
    day Review*, June 17, 1972, 40(25):72+.

    Unlike fairy tales where girls passively accept mis-
fortune until rescued by the prince, the female characters
in the *Oz* series are all brave, resourceful, brilliant
and irrepressible. Role reversals operate in the later
Oz stories when boys are younger, beautiful and conspicuously stupid. The sex role stereotypes of older boy/
younger girl, active boy/passive girl do not operate here
at all.

0815
    Rose, Karel. "Sleeping Beauty awakes: chil-
    dren's literature and sex role myths," paper
    presented at the annual meeting of the National
    Council of Teachers of English, 1973. ERIC (ED
    089 322).

    Modern day renditions of "Sleeping Beauty" show an
apron clad mother/housekeeper living happily ever after
within the confines of her home. She is never shown driving, reading, weeding or voting. The "realistic" mother
in children's literature does not experience the activity
of the fairy godmother. Male lifestyles are equally myth-
ologized with boys like Rumplestilskin who have no responsibilities. Present day books damage individual
growth for girls by portraying them as passive and immo-
bile, and damage boys by burdening them with the expectation of perpetual achievement. Female caricature in
picture books repeatedly show girls wearing restrictive
clothing, sitting indoors, and participating in activity
as spectator. Picture book mothers do not work, though

six million preschool children have working mothers. Boys are taught leadership qualities, while girls, who learn dependence and passivity, are not taught how to function effectively in a democracy, and therefore must take inactive roles in society. Prevailing stereotypes must be dispelled in order to raise low aspirations taught female students.

0816

Rosen, Ruth. "Sexism in history or, writing women's history is a tricky business," *Journal of Marriage and the Family*, August, 1971, 33: 541-544.

History textbooks have traditionally been concerned with military, economic and political power. History of oppressed peoples has been ignored until recently when black history and women's history became acceptable. The problem with most women's history textbooks is the concern with defining women's nature. Most texts attempt to classify female and male activities and motives by mythical polarities. The author calls for a new textbook approach which records women's history seriously and without relying on myths and sex roles stereotypes.

0817

Boston Area Women in Libraries. *Sexism in Children's Books*. Available from author, 42 Cherry Street, Medford, Mass 02155, rental, $7, purchase, $475.

A slide/tape program produced by a group of feminist librarians to illustrate the narrowness of sexist roles as they are drawn in children's trade books. The slides are details from illustrations which exemplify the "typical" female and male roles - for children and adults. An audio tape describes these role models and their effect on the child. It has been used successfully for parent and teacher groups in libraries and schools in the US and Canada.   Author Abstract

0818

Siege, Selma R. "Heroines in recent children's fiction - an analysis," *Elementary English*, 1973, 50:1039-1043.

Children's fiction written for the age group ten and up now has a new type of heroine who is an "uneasy, independent, critical non-conformist." Twenty female protagonists from 14 books are examined in terms of their anger, insecurity and confusion typical (rather than stereotypical) of individuals in this age group whose personal crises involve divorced parents, retarded siblings or a hostile school environment. The author describes the psychological protest of the 20 girls as well as the ways they cope with their problems until their behavior improves.

0819
    Skjonsberg, Kari. "Sex roles in boy's and girl's books," *Hertha*, 1969, n5:44-47.

Anglo-American and Scandinavian children's books teach children adult roles which feed children's fantasies. Boys learn instrumentality in travel and work while girls learn expressiveness. Nancy Drew, Cherry Ames and other characters are instrumental as well as expressive, but boys rarely experience a personal scope in their reading. Boys rarely have the opportunity to admit fear or helplessness.

0820
    Smolover, Miriam. "Little women in literature," 1974. Available from KNOW, Inc., PO Box 86031, Pittsburgh, PA 15221. #251.

An analysis of three popular novels from the "Girls! Girls! Girls!" library shelves. Two of the three books examined cripple the minds and spirits of prepubescent girls by teaching them to value male attention and personal appearance above personal intelligence, creativity and female friendships. Only the third novel offers a young heroine who learns to fly a plane and develops close friendships with both female and male friends.

0821
    Stanek, Lou Willett. "Growing up female: the literary gaps," *Media and Methods*, September, 1976, 13(1):6-8.

General society has finally acknowledged that little girls are made of mind, muscle, bone and blood, and their literary roles now include realistically handicapped, dying, fat, bright girls who may be basketball players, beauty queens, lesbians or loners.

0822
    Stavn, Diane Gersoni. "Reducing the 'Miss Muffet Syndrome'" an annotated bibliography," *School Library Journal*, January, 1972, 18: 32-35; also in *Library Journal*, 1972, 97: 256-259; also in *Sexism and Youth*, ed. by D.

Gersoni-Stavn. NY: Bowker, 1974. pp. 289-298.

One hundred publishers of children's books were requested to send copies of their latest imprints which depicted female characters fairly and realistically. Stavn discusses the trends of plot and character types emerging in the study, and includes a bibliography of the 40 best books examined.

0823
Stavn, Diane Gersoni. "The skirts in fiction about boys: a maxi mess," *School Library Journal*, January, 1971, 17(5):66-70; also in *Library Journal*, 1971, 96:282-286; also in *Sexism and Youth*, ed. by Diane Gersoni-Stavn. NY: Bowker, 1974. pp. 260-271.

Books written for boys often portray mothers and girlfriends in negative, stereotypical light. The image of women as insipid, bitchy, witchy, security conscious, or overly freewheeling is found in 26 titles reviewed here. Any positive female character is usually introduced as "not like most girls." Gersoni-Stavn quotes some of the most sexist observations about women from each book, then counters the stereotype with a logical debate of the author's misogynistic point.

0824
Tate, Janice M. "Sexual bias in science fiction for children," *Elementary English*, 1973, 50: 1061-1064.

The once exclusively male genre of children's science fiction now satisfies a significant female audience. Examination of 49 children's science fiction novels revealed the following themes: 1) the trend in male dominated books showed active male characters with either total exclusion of female characters or else females who function as cooks or sex objects enshrined in glass. 2) the female dominated stories most often showed women propelled by magical forces rather than controlling their personal destiny, although two authors showed women with intelligence superior to men's. 3) books with equal sex domination showed both sexes interacting with respect for one another, as do the books with male heroes who interact with female characters of equal intelligence but less plot significance.

See 1015. M. L. Thetford, "Vocational roles for women in junior fiction."

0825
    Tibbetts, Sylvia-Lee. "Children's literature -
    a feminist viewpoint," *California Journal of Edu-
    cational Research*, 1975, 26:1-5.

Children learn that girls are inferior to boys from
books in which 1) boys outnumber girls as major characters,
2) female characters are shown in passive, subordinate,
incompetent roles, 3) girls do not excel, 4) girls are
intellectually confused, 5) girls have severely limited
social roles, 6) girls are trained to have low aspirations.
As instruments of acculturation books mold girls into restricted roles and train children of both sexes to regard
the female sex as inferior.

Educational Material

0826
    Bereaud, Susan R. "Sex role images in French
    children's books," *Journal of Marriage and
    the Family*, 1975, 37:194-207.

Although traditional notions of women's roles persist
in France, the female professional elite is much further
advanced than in the US. French women represent 42% of the
country's pharmacists, 29% of its dentists and 22% of its
medical doctors. An analysis of the two most popular series of French children's books revealed that the professional status of French women is ignored while rigid sex
role stereotypes are reflected. Stereotypical adult occupations include female salesclerk, ticket seller, teacher,
stewardess and nurse while male occupations include tech-
nician, pilot, race car driver, photographer. Women's
work is usually an extension of the maternal role while
men control large enterprises, own shops or have difficult,
strenuous jobs.

0827
    Berg, Karen Westman. "School books and roles of
    the sexes," *Hertha*, 1969, n5:48-53.

Sex stereotypes in Swedish schoolbooks show dainty
girls described as dutiful, tidy, passive and timorous
while boys are forgetful, untidy and disdainful toward
girls. Although French, German and English textbooks take
more patriarchal approaches than Swedish books, educational
radio most often features male voices as omniscient teachers while female voices represent the assistants who make

the mistakes corrected by male voices.

0828
    Bernard, Jesse S. "The achievement of dependency,"
Women, Wives, Mothers: Values and Options, by
J. S. Bernard. Chicago: Aldine, 1975. pp. 36-37.

Dependency is bred into girls who would otherwise be
independent and autonomous. School readers teach girls to
acquire helpless, passive behavior by portraying female
characters dependent on brothers and boys for help with
every seemingly difficult situation.

0829
    Bernstein, Jean. "The elementary school: train-
ing ground for sex role stereotypes," *Personnel
and Guidance Journal,* 1972, 51:97-101.

Basal readers stereotype nuclear family roles by
showing fictional fathers going off to work and mothers
cleaning house. Children's social studies texts carry the
sex roles a step further by stereotyping the contributions
of historic American women: Pocahontas and Sacajawea both
served men, Clara Barton was a nurse. Other important
post-Civil War figures, the independent Grimke sisters and
Sojourner Truth, however are not mentioned in children's
history texts.

0830
    Bissett, Donald J. "Books in the classroom,"
Elementary English, 1973, 50:1094-1100.

In searching for children's books with strong, independent heroines, a researcher found several examples
of positive female characters shrouded in poorly written
stories, while many other books of high literary quality
are marred by excessive portrayals of female incompetence.
In spite of this problem, 60 books were found which illustrated equality between the sexes, showed positive female
characters in traditionally female roles, and positive
female characters in nontraditional roles. Fifteen titles
and plot summaries end the article.

0831
    Britton, Gwyneth E. *Danger: state adopted
reading texts may be hazardous to our future.*
(Racism and Sexism Perpetuated in Reading series).
1974. Also ERIC (ED 096 611).

Of 5,242 stories examined, major characters were 59%

white male, 16% white female, 9% minority male and 3%
minority female. In reality Black, Mexican, Puerto Rican,
Chinese, Japanese and Filipino populations comprise approximately 16% of the US population. Females and minority group persons, then, are underrepresented in children's
readers. Stereotypes include portrayal of native American
men as medicine men or chiefs, career roles 200 years out
of date. The Native American female is excluded from most
stories. Asian Americans are also most frequently portrayed in career roles several centuries out of date.
Minority women were portrayed as mothers in 76% of the
stories, but rarely shown as scholars, decision makers,
problem solvers, or even competent house managers. In reality many women combine motherhood with careers just as
men combine fatherhood with careers. By promoting such
stereotypes it appears that the American tax dollar is actually being spent to teach racism and sexism to children.

0832
        Britton, Gwyneth E. "Why Jane can't win (sex
        stereotyping and career role assignment in read-
        ing materials)," paper presented at annual meeting
        of the International Reading Association, 1974.
        ERIC (ED 092 919).

        In an analysis of 4,144 stories, 14% of the stories
featured female characters. Of the stories involving
career roles, 86% were held by men, 14% by women, though
the 1972 US labor force was 42% female. In primary grade
reading stories, major characters were 59% male, 16% female; in grades four through six, 61% male, 13% female.
Role stereotypes show boys as builders, achievers and per-
severing individuals who were older than female siblings.
Girls were docile, self-effacing, incompetent, vacuous,
non-achieving, clean. From these books girls learn to
restrict themselves and sublimate their abilities in order to conform to a learned social norm. Some suggestions
for textbook change include showing children of both sexes
working together and respecting one another's abilities,
depicting female characters in leadership roles, and expanding career options available to female characters.

0833
        Burr, Elizabeth, Dunn, Susan and Norma Farquhar.
        "Guidelines for equal treatment of the sexes in
        social studies textbooks," *Sexism and Youth,* ed.
        by Diane Gersoni-Stavn. NY: Bowker, 1974. pp.
        326-338.

        Although writers and publishers of elementary school
social studies textbooks do not consciously ignore or
derogate women in their textbooks, the fact remains that

the content, language and literature of these books is male-oriented. Women are omitted from history or considered the "luggage" of their pioneer husbands. Men are glorified as bold, imaginative and foresighted even though many male immigrants were desperate, hesitant and unwilling. Women's struggle for equal rights is usually given no more than a paragraph though the suffrage movement lasted more than half a century. Occupational sex roles are assigned though women have labored in mines and cotton fields and men have worked as secretaries. Women are often excluded from illustrations and "girl watching" often appears in textbooks. Guidelines are offered for eliminating the language of inequality which transmits implicit values and sex role behavioral models.

0834
    Burr, Elizabeth, Susan Dunn and Norma Farquhar. "Women and the language of inequality," *Social Education*, 1972, 36:841-845.

    The sexist use of language in textbooks blurs men with people in general while separating women from people in general. Illustrations of male peasants, pioneers and farmers are captioned by the single word "peasants", etc., while illustrations of female peasants, pioneers and farmers are captioned "female peasants," etc. Women are not permitted to represent people in general.

0835
    Burstyn, Joan N. and Ruth R. Corrigan. "Images of women in textbooks, 1880-1920," *Teachers College Record*, 1975, 76:431-440.

    An examination of attitudes toward women in 38 children's textbooks written during the period of the women's suffrage movement indicates that geography, physiology and arithmetic texts written by men ignored women's roles, conveying an image of women as insignificant, while books on the same subjects written by women reflected women's increasing importance to US economic life and moral code. One physiology book written by a woman encouraged women to become doctors, architects and preachers, while those written by men implied that women were losers because their health was crippled by tight lacing.

0836
    Burton, Gabrielle. "Sex role stereotyping in elementary school primers," 1974. Available from KNOW, Inc., PO Box 86031, Pittsburgh, PA 15221. #253.

    Salient points from several of the most important

studies of sex role stereotyping in basal readers, elementary level biographies and social studies texts are applied to Montgomery County textbooks. Suggested action for concerned parents and teachers include influencing publishers to revise texts and to encourage teachers to pay careful attention to book selection.

0837
Campbell, Pat. "From tomboy to femme fatale," 1975. Available from author, Department of Educational Foundations, Georgia State University, Atlanta, GA 30303. Rental, $3.00.

A taped lecture designed to facilitate discussion concerning sex role stereotyping in children's textbooks and adolescent fiction.

0838
Chase, Dannis J. "Sexism in textbooks?," *Nation's School*, December, 1972, 90(6):31-35.

Since feminist groups have challenged publishers of textbooks, some of the sex bias has been eliminated. Some stories with adventurous heroes have been rewritten with adventurous heroines. Included with the article is a chart of nonsexist language and sentence structure.

0839
Chevat, Edith S. "Women and girls in readers and texts," paper presented at annual meeting of the International Reading Association, 1975. ERIC (ED 110 974).

After reviewing common sex role stereotypes found in basal readers, spellers, textbooks and literary classics, the author suggests student exercises, artwork, reading and discussions to raise student consciousness thereby offsetting the influence of stereotypes in educational material.

0840
Child, Irvin L., Elmer H. Potter and Estelle M. Levine. "Children's textbooks and personality development," *Psychological Monographs*, 1946, 60(3):1-7+.

Even in the earliest grammar school years educational opportunity for girls does not equal that of boys, because the two sexes receive different motivational training from their textbooks. "Females are shown as being definitely

256

inferior from a moral point of view [and are] portrayed as
lazy twice as often." The article includes a frequency
distribution table of 22 behavioral characteristics by sex.

0841
Council on Interracial Books for Children, Inc.
"Testing texts for racism and sexism," *Scholas-
tic Teacher*, February, 1973, 102(2):16-17.

Textbooks should be examined to determine if the overly white male orientation operates to the exclusion of
ethnic and female peoples. Teachers should test the index,
and illustrations for loaded words and inclusion of non-
white, non-male contributors to society.

0842
DeCrow, Karen. "Look Jane, look! See Dick
run and jump! Admire him!," *The Young Woman's
Guide to Liberation*, by K. DeCrow, NY: Bobbs-
Merrill, 1971. pp. 62-72; also in *Sex Differ-
ences and Discrimination in Education*, ed. by
Scarvia B. Anderson. (Series on Contemporary
Educational Issues, 2). Worthington, Ohio:
Charles A. Jones, 1972. pp. 44-49.

A content analysis of readers and social studies textbooks geared to grades K-3 revealed that mothers, girls
and boys cook, wash dishes and set tables, but fathers do
not help in the work of women and children. Whether or not
the reader shows Mother in the kitchen, her spirit is always present in the form of food cooking on the stove.
Social studies texts also show Mother cooking, this time
in the cave. Until feminists demand a change in the sex
role portrayals in children's books, mothers will continue
to function in no more authoritative position than chief
cook and bottle washer.

0843
"Do instructional materials reinforce sex stereotyping?," *Educational Leadership*, November, 1973,
31:119-122.

The feminine preoccupation for marriage and motherhood is not matched with a male concern for fatherhood in
adolescent readers. History textbooks almost totally omit
the female gender and accomplishments. The article ends
with suggestions for new role models.

0844
Doyle, Nancy. "Stereotyping in texts and toys,"

Woman's Changing Place: A Look at Sexism, by
N. Doyle. (Public Affairs Pamphlet, 509), 1974.
pp. 6-7. Available from Public Affairs Committee,
318 Park Avenue, South, NY, 10016. 35¢.

In order to counteract the psychic damage and distorted aspirations caused girls by sex role stereotypes
in textbooks, the American Federation of Teachers, AFL-CIO
threatened publishers with a boycott of sexist textbooks.
However textbook illustrations still picture girls watching male activity, but not participating. The toy situation is slowly changing. While boys are still the target
market for scientific toys, toy trains now use girl-
directed advertising which shows a mother gift wrapping a
train for her daughter.

0845

Dunnigan, Lise. *Analysis of Masculine and Feminine Stereotypes in Quebec Schoolbooks*. Quebec:
Quebec Council on the Status of Women, 1975.

Analysis of 154 elementary level textbooks revealed
that boys are portrayed as intelligent and brave while
girls are portrayed as non-autonomous domestic beings.
Books reflect only these rigid sex roles and do not reflect the reality of both sexes engaged in a variety of
occupations and activities while sharing domestic responsibilities.

0846

Eliasberg, Ann. "Are you hurting your daughter
without knowing it?," *Family Circle*, February,
1971. pp. 38+. Also available from KNOW, Inc.,
PO Box 86031, Pittsburgh, PA 15221. #169.

Elementary school readers introduce children to famous men in all fields, and to nurse Florence Nightingale
and singer Marian Anderson. Ignored women include pioneer
doctor Elizabeth Blackwell, poets Emily Dickinson and Anne
Bradstreet, archaeologist Iris Love and scientists Marie
Curie and Lise Meitner. While given few biographical
sketches of real women with whom a girl child may identify,
she does have the adventurous Nancy Drew as role model as
well as several other fictional heroines listed.

0847

Farquhar, Norma, Susan Dunn and Elizabeth Burr.
"Sex stereotypes in elementary and secondary education," 1972. Available from Westside Women's
Committee, PO Box 24D20, Los Angeles, CA 90024.
50¢ plus SASE.

To combat the white male orientation of reading texts, female characters must be portrayed more adequately. The argument that reading texts should appeal to boys with reading problems does not justify the portrayal of female characters strictly as props. Boys enjoy reading about adventurous children regardless of sex. By not portraying girls as adventurous all children are taught that girls are dull.

0848
Fasteau, Marc Feigen. "The roots of misogyny," *The Male Machine*, by M. F. Festeau. NY: McGraw Hill, 1974. pp. 36-50.

"Cutely" misogynistic features on the evening network news reinforce children's textbook image of females as lazy, weeping, traitorous and selfish people while males are natural leaders, strong and protective of their women. Both stereotypes dehumanize by limiting women and over-straining men.

0849
Federbush, Marsha. The sex problems of school math books," *And Jill Came Tumbling After*, ed. by Judith Stacey, et al. NY: Dell, 1974. pp. 178-184.

Female devaluation is common in the texts and illustrations of elementary level math books. Verbal stereotypes in New Math include sets of male doctors, chiefs, astronauts and female nurses, waitresses, stewardesses. The author suggests that an occasional female astronaut is in order, to give girls an option for a traditionally male career aspiration. A six step program of action is outlined to change the present sex stereotyped approach to math.

See 0850. A. S. Fishman, "A criticism of sexism in elementary readers."

See 1004. H. H. Franzwa, "Working women in fact and fiction."

0850
Frasher, Ramona and Annabelle Walker. "Sex roles in early reading textbooks," *The Reading Teacher*, 1972, 25:741-749.

A content analysis of first and second grade readers

from four basal reading series measured sex of main characters, adult occupations, adult family roles and children's activities.

0851

Frazier, Nancy and Myra Sadker. "Sex bias: the hidden curriculum in the elementary school," *Sexism in School and Society*, by N. Frazier and M. Sadker. (Critical issues in education). NY: Harper and Row, 1973. pp. 76-113.

With illustrations from the "overtly offensive" *I'm Glad I'm a Boy! I'm Glad I'm a Girl!*, the authors discuss the lack of female role models in children's history books and the image of girls and women cooking and sewing their way through arithmetic texts. Subservient roles, lower pay and lower status are still the norm for women in these books, even though publishers no longer accept these images as appropriate depictions of Blacks, Mexicans and Native Americans. Not only are female readers offered too few inspiring female role models, but are often humiliated and taught not to strive and not to achieve.

0852

Frisof, Jamie K. "Textbooks and channeling," *Women: A Journal of Liberation*, 1969, 1(1): 26-28; also in *Sexism and Youth*, ed. by Diane Gersoni-Stavn. NY: Bowker, 1974. pp. 303-308.

The text and illustrations of five elementary level social studies textbooks dealing with occupations in contemporary American society continually show women in traditionally female service-oriented roles while men are leaders or creative forces in government and business. In the same factory women are portrayed as seamstresses while men are clothes designers. Waitresses serve in small diners and waiters serve in expensive restaurants. Men speak in town meetings, women sell lemonade. Male characters are usually more interesting than female characters in the text: boys demonstrate curiosity in the number and quality of questions asked while questions asked by girls are few in number and silly at that! Boys find interesting shells at the beach, girls find none. Boys are pictured in the illustrations far more often than girls: in one book examined, the ratio was 117:15.

Use of the word "men" to refer to "humankind" is a poor choice of words when dealing with the very literal mind of the seven year old child. The text and illustrations of the five books examined seem to teach children that adult men are the only thinkers and achievers in contemporary American society, while adult women are "un-important, nonproductive, nonadventurous and unintelligent beings."

0853
    Gallagher, Kathleen and Alice Peery. "Bibliog-raphy of materials on sexism and sex role stereo-typing in children's books," 1976. Available from Lollipop Power, PO Box 1171, Chapel Hill, NC 27514.

A bibliography including some material not listed in this chapter. Not annotated.

0854
    Graebner, Dianne Bennett. "A decade of sexism in readers," *The Reading Teacher*, 1972, 26:52-58.

Children's readers underwent minimal sex role changes from 1962 to 1971. After nine years adult women wore aprons less often and carried fewer dishtowels, and their daughters dressed casually in slacks instead of prim dresses. Aside from dress few improvements were evident. Portrayal of female occupations increased from 5 to 56 while male occupations increased from 38 to 73. Unchanged sexist propensities found in the 1971 textbooks included passive female characters who say nothing contrasted with male characters who rarely had no dialogue. Textbook men outnumbered women 3:2 even though the real life ratio is 49:51% of the population.

See 0722. B. C. Graham, "Treatment of black American wom-en in children's encyclopedias."

0855
    Groseclose, Everett. "Sexism and schools," *What Do Women Really Want?*, ed. by Ellen Graham. Chicopee, Mass: Jones Books, 1974, pp. 164-169.

A news feature originally published in the *Wall Street Journal* quotes the head of Kalamazoo Michigan Committee who monitored elementary school textbooks in 1973, the elemen-tary education director of Kalamazoo, and a textbook edi-tor, all of whom were amenable to eliminating sex role stereotypes in children's textbooks.

0856
    Gunderson, Doris, "Reading and sex roles," paper

presented at annual meeting of the National Council of Teachers of English, 1975. ERIC (ED 116 180).

Typical stereotypes found in children's readers include a father who works, an apron clad mother who doesn't, two children (the brother is older than the sister) and two pets (the dog is older than the cat). Suggestions are given for more accurate portrayals of family members and for inclusion of women in social history textbooks.

0857
Gunderson, Doris V. "Sex roles in reading," paper presented at annual meeting of the American Educational Association, 1972. ERIC (ED 064 671).

Boys more commonly experience difficulty learning to read than girls. Although several factors may cause this difficulty, the reading matter itself is not the problem. Children's readers and textbooks present situations and characters with whom only boys may identify while disregarding the interests of girl readers.

See 0961. M. E. Hagar and S. Deffenbaugh, "Does Mama Bear always serve the porridge? Sex role stereotyping in school reading materials.

0858
Heyn, Leah. "Children's books," *Women: A Journal of Liberation*, Fall, 1969, 1(1):22-25.

Children's books repeatedly show men as principals, women as teachers; men as architects or engineers, women as secretaries; and men as veterinarians with no female counterpart. Even the book *Famous Men of Medicine*, written by a female MD, includes illustrations of male doctors only, although nurses of both sexes are pictured. Since many children's books are written by creative women it is curious that talented female characters are so scarce.

0859
Hurst, Gayle. "Sex bias in junior high school literature anthologies." National Organization for Women, St. Louis Chapter, 1973. ERIC (ED 085 763).

The image of women in textbooks has created a mythology that dehumanizes women and deprives them of a creative role in society. This hypothesis was proven in the examination of several textbooks. *Focus* is an attractive

text with liberal approach except when dealing with women.
Female characters are omitted in 18 stories. *Perception*
has five stories with female protagonists and 18 stories
with no female characters. *Adventures for Readers* has 53
stories; 25 have no mention of female characters. These
books not only do not reflect reality, many selections
totally ignore half the human race. An improved situation
would reflect women in the population, reflect their numbers in the workforce and give names and identities to female characters.

0860
     Hyde, Janet S. and B. G. Rosenberg. "Personality
     and stages of adjustment: childhood," *Half the*
     Human Experience: The Psychology of Women, by
     J. S. Hyde and B. G. Rosenberg. Lexington, MA:
     Heath, 1976. pp. 62-65.

Young girls regard children's readers and television
as important sources of information about the adult world,
and acquire sex stereotyped values projected in those
media.

0861
     Jay, Winifred Tom. *Sex Stereotyping in Selected*
     Mathematics Textbooks for Grades 2, 4, and 6.
     D.Ed. dissertation, University of Oregon, 1973.

Analysis of sex stereotyping in 12 textbooks according to the following categories: famous males and females,
male and female occupations, and examples of unusual, non-
stereotyped approaches to math problems.

0862
     Jederman, Jean E. *The Sexual Stereotype of*
     Women in Children's Literature. Ed.D. disser-
     tation, Northern Illinois University, 1974.

The marital, maternal and occupational status of
adult women in children's fiction are measured in relation
to the adult female population. Analysis of 889 female
characters from 301 books recommended in four children's
book lists and catalogs reveals 19 books with no female
characters, and 2% whose principal characters are women.
The research indicates a discrepancy between the actual
American scene and the trend observed in children's books
regarding the number of married, divorced, widowed and
separated mothers and non-mothers in the US workforce.
However the largest discrepancy involves working mothers:
18% of the book characters worked outside the home, while
in actuality mothers comprised 40% of the workforce in

1973. Another discrepancy is the book trend in which 38% of all characters were depicted as teachers, an exaggeration of the reality in which only 6% of all adult American women were employed as teacher.

0863
Jeffrey, Jan and Barb Craft. "Report of the Elementary School Textbook Task Force," Michigan; Kalamazoo Public Schools, 1973. ERIC (ED 127 234).

Evaluation of 172 textbooks and 89 other instructional media revealed that sexist portrayals of children and adults reinforce sexism and omit the career aspiration and self-esteem of the female audience.

0864
Jennings, Sally A. "Effects of sex typing in children's stories on preference and recall," *Child Development*, 1975, 46:220-223.

Children from day care centers and nursery schools were divided into small sexually segregated groups and each told two stories. The girls were told one story about a female ballerina and one about a female mail carrier. The boys were told one story about a male dancer and one about a male mail carrier. Both groups of girls and the day care boys had higher recall for the stories with reversed sex roles while the nursery school boys remembered the story with traditional sex roles. Even though the day care boys remembered the story with reversed roles, they disapproved of a male dancer and many refused to listen. The author mentions a "greater rigidity of the definition of the male role among lower income [day care] boys." A less rigid attitude toward sex roles in children's books could widen children's ideas of competence.

0865
Kalamazoo, Michigan. Board of Education. *Sex Discrimination in an Elementary Reading Program*. Kalamazoo: Board of Education, 1974.

The occupational stereotypes found in the readers for grades 1-6 give children the impression that sex is a bona fide occupational qualification for 95% of all jobs in the world. Other sex stereotypes treat women as dependent, fearful people who spend a great deal of time uncomplainingly cleaning house. In children's readers women's achievements are rarely mentioned, human female characters appear less frequently than male animals, and the pronoun "she" is taught in a late lesson vocabulary. Constant

exposure to sex discrimination in a mandatory reading program reinforces low self-esteem among female children,
influences their level of achievement throughout life and
discourages them from considering many occupational roles.
The Michigan Women's Commission also suggests that American woman's lack of political power is related to the indoctrination of a sex biased elementary reading program.

0866
    Key, Mary Ritchie. "The role of male and female
    in children's books - dispelling all doubt,"
    Wilson Library Bulletin, 1971, 46:167-176.

An assimilation of the findings from many simultaneously performed studies on sexism in children's fiction
and basal readers.

0867
    Kidd, Virginia. "'Now you see,' said Mark,"
    New York Review of Books, September 3, 1970, 15
    (4):35-36.

Children's readers expose them to the following sex
role stereotypes: Mothers cook, sew and iron but never
work outside the home or drive cars. Fathers come home
from work and play ball with Mark but never sympathize
with Janet or help clean Mark's room. Mark plays with
parachutes, rockets and spaceships and other astronaut
gear while Janet plays with dollhouse, buggy, dishes and
other domestic equipment. The stereotypes persist in animal stories where Mother Bear wears an apron, Little Bear
(male) actively seeks fun and adventure and Little Frog
(female) passively sits on a rock and asks how she should
spend her time.

See 1008. M. S. Kimmell, "Educational influences on career opportunities for women."

0868
    Kraft, Linda. "Lost herstory: the treatment of
    women in children's encyclopedias," *Library Jour-
    nal,* 1973, 98:218-227; also in *Sexism and Youth,*
    ed. by Diane Gersoni-Stave. NY: Bowker, 1974.
    pp. 339-357.

Five encyclopedias were examined to determine how the
role of women was presented in the following entries:
Women's-Rights-Suffrage, Colonial Life, the Revolution,
Civil War, Westward Ho, Labor Movement, Reform and Tem-
perence, the World Wars. The author found omissions of

significant women and events, stereotyped role assignments
with the glorification of men and denigration of women as
"luggage". Women were not portrayed as the gold seekers,
missionaries, homesteaders in the westward movement, or in
other roles that they historically held.

0869
Land, James L. *Sex Role Stereotyping in Elementary School Readers, Grades 1-6, adopted
by the State of Indiana for the Years 1973-1978.*
Ed.D. dissertation, Ball State University,
1974.

A sample of 280 stories in 56 readers were classified
by roles, relationships, activities, treatments, generalizations, future career directions and personal importance
of female and male characters. Results indicate females
were less frequently represented in central roles and as
intelligent people but were frequently represented as re-
cipients of derogatory comments and in situations which
reinforce culturally conditioned sexual characteristics.

0870
Levy, Betty and Judith Stacey. "Sexism in the
elementary school: a backward and forward look,"
Phi Delta Kappan, 1973, 55:105-109+."

Reviews the research involving sex role stereotypes
in readers and math, science and social studies textbooks,
toys and children's television. The authors suggest that
reforming the symptom by adding token women does not challenge the elitist structure and therefore does not guarantee cure. There is a need to analyze the types of changes
which will facilitate a genuinely liberating education for
children.

0871
Lewis, Jennifer. "What the publishers are doing
about sexism in textbooks," *Teacher, the Professional Magazine of the Elementary Grades,* October, 1972, 90(2):52-53.

Recounts the influence of *Dick and Jane as Victims*
(see 0899) on publisher's decisions to portray women more
realistically in textbook readers.

0872
Lobban, Glenys. "Sex roles in reading schemes,"
Educational Review, 1975, 27:202-210.

Previous content analyses of seven British primers revealed presentation of a world divided sharply by sex. Male characters predominated in this world while female characters were "naturally" inferior to males. This study analyzes two reading series, one with a non-traditional fantasy story base and the other with a linguistically impeccable scheme. Both had nearly twice as many male protagonists as female and five times as many male characters, even though British society is over 50% female. The two predominant female themes were nurturance and evilness. Women performed domestic nurturance while male characters expressed nurturance by caring for animals (but not the realistic care of children). Evil women outnumbered evil men 7:5.

0873
    McDonald, Gilda. "Look, Jane, look. See Tommy run. See Tommy jump. See Tommy play," *School and Community*, November, 1973, 60(3): 18+.

    Girls have few active role models in literature. While boys actively run, jump and play, girls sit, Miss Muffet-style, and watch.

See 0970. J. S. Macleod and S. T. Silverman, *"You Won't Do."*

0874
    McLure, John W. and Gail T. McLure. "Cinderella grows up: sex stereotyping in the schools," *Educational Leadership*, October, 1972, 30(1): 31-33.

    The schools are partially responsible for the waste of human talent in American society. Elementary primers subtly reinforce attitudes of female inferiority by illustrating girls as essentially passive creatures with hands clasped behind their backs and a limited range of facial expressions while boys actively use their facial and body muscles as they participate in adventurous activities.

0875
    Marten, Laurel A. and Margret W. Matlin. "Does sexism in elementary readers still exist?," *The Reading Teacher*, 1976, 28:764-767.

    Examination of 16 first and sixth grade textbooks by five publishers, half of which were published prior to

1971 and half since 1973, revealed a barely significant
increase in the percentage of female characters represented in illustrations and as story protagonists. In all
cases total female representation remained less than 40%.
Where female protagonists were represented they were often
portrayed as bumbling, forgetful or incompetent, while
male characters were independent, inventive and aggressive.
No significant change was noted in the image of women in
elementary textbooks published since 1973.

0876

Miles, Betty. "Harmful lessons little girls
learn in school," *Redbook*, March, 1971, 136(5):
86+.

In children's readers boys tell girls that they're
inferior - they're just girls, they're not thinkers. Adult
characters never contradict the boys' remarks, never tell
the girls that they are indeed valuable people. The research by Women on Words and Images and protest letters to
publishers concerning sexist bias in children's readers
are facilitating change in offering a positive image of
women and men in children's readers.

0877

National Education Association of the United
States. *Sex Role Stereotyping in the Schools*,
Washington, DC: NEA, 1973-1975.

"Sex role stereotyping: books" and "Cinderella is
dead" are two filmstrips included in the multi-media package which also includes books, cassettes and fact sheets
dealing with sex role stereotypes in the classroom, athletics and society.

0878

Northern Women's Groups Education Study Group.
"Sex role learning - a study of infant readers,"
*Body Politic: Writings from the Women's Liber-
ation Movement in Britain, 1969-1972*, ed. by
M. Wandor. London: Stage One, 1972. pp. 146-
149.

A short survey of British elementary primers whose
sex role stereotypes are considered an "ideological prison."
While Daddy reads Mummy works, and the two parents rarely
share activity. Brothers and sisters also share few activities: while he plays ball, she watches, he sails his
toy boat, she watches; he flies in an aeroplane with Father, she and Mother watch from the ground. These readers
pressure children to accept sexual roles as norms of

behavior without offering a choice of role-free behavior
which may better suit their natural inclinations.

0879
O'Donnell, Richard W. "Sex bias in primary social studies textbooks," *Educational Leadership*,
1973, 31:137-141.

A study of sex roles found in illustrations of first
and second grade level social studies textbooks revealed
that boys were shown in active roles three times as often
as girls, men were pictured in 83% of occupational roles
while women were in 17% and men were never engaged in
domestic duties.

0880
Oliver, Linda. "Women in aprons: the female
stereotype in children's readers," *Elementary
School Journal*, 1974, 74:253-259.

Common textbook stereotypes teach children that
mothers wash dishes, cook and scold children; fathers
work, read newspapers and take children camping; girls are
helpless and boys solve mysteries. The author offers six
ways to eliminate sexism in children's readers and
examines eight children's stories to uncover sexist subtleties in seemingly non-sexist stories.

See 0323. J. Papachristou, *Women Together, A History in
Documents of the Women's Movement in the United States.*

0881
Perreault, Gerri. "Q: Do the schools need women's
liberation? A: Yes, yes, yes, yes, yes...,"
Sexism in Education, by Emma Willard Task Force
on Education, 1972. Available from author, University Station Box 14229, Minneapolis, MN.

Lists the common sex role stereotyped activities,
adjectives and illustration captions found in children's
elementary readers.

See 1011. C. Rose, "Women's sex role attitudes: a historical perspective."

0882
Russo, Nancy Felipe. "Kids learn their lessons
early...and learn them well," *Confronting the*

Issues: Sex Roles, Marriage, and the Family,
ed. by Kenneth C. W. Kammeyer. Boston: Allyn
and Bacon, 1975. pp. 377-387.

Sex role stereotypes learned by pre-school age children are reinforced by the textbooks they are forced to
read in school. Pronatalism ranks among the most heavily
emphasized forms of socialization. While boys learn that
the US presidency is a realistic career goal, girls learn
to prepare for motherhood.

0883
Saario, Terry N., Carol Nagy Jacklin and Carol
Kehr Tittle. "Sex role stereotyping in the
public schools," *Harvard Educational Review,*
1973, 43:386-416.

By assimilating into one article the findings of
several important studies documenting sex role stereotypes in children's books the authors hope to prove that
such socialization "exerts a powerful and limiting influence on the development of sex roles" in children.

0884
Sadker, Myra and David Sadker. "Sexual discrimination in the elementary school," *National Elementary Principal,* October, 1972, 52(2):41-45.

When reading their elementary school history lessons
children see pictures and biographical accounts for all
the famous American founding fathers, and Betsy Ross.
Later they read about all the famous American explorers,
presidents and scientific geniuses, and Annie Oakley and
Amelia Earhart. Girls learn the reason for so few female
biographical subjects: their pleasure reading expounds
on female inferiority with "It's a man's world" and "It's
all right for girls to be scared silly." Children's
readers continue the image by showing boys doing magic
tricks or scientific experiments while girls do housework,
bake cookies or watch their brothers' activities. Teaching girls inferiority, docility and submissiveness robs
them of their self esteem and initiative. This loss of
human potential also has a devastating effect on society
as a whole.

0885
Salpukas, Agis. "Survey of textbooks detect less
bias against blacks but little to please feminists," *The New York Times,* March 28, 1973, p.
13.

Although the image of Blacks and Native Americans has been purged of the most blatant racism, the same cannot be said for the image of women.

0886
Schenck, John P. "Sexism in textbooks: a guide to detection," *American Vocational Journal*, October, 1976, 51(7):42-45.

Offers examples of sexist language in children's textbooks and reasons for eliminating these cues of gender-appropriate behavior. The late-1976 article is followed by a trade ad for a power tool attended by a mini-skirted model whose presence as sex object has no connection with the product.

0887
Schmidt, Dolores. "Sexism in education," *Female Studies*, 1972, 5:29-33.

A highly competent woman interested in the medical profession usually becomes a nurse instead of a doctor because, among other factors, the books she has read from nursery school to college insist on subordinate dependent roles for women. The findings of nine studies reveal sexism in textbooks: school books for grades 3-9 use the word "boy" 4,700 times, the word "girl" 2,200 times. Boys outnumber girls 3:1 in Newbery medal winning books. An American historical biography series of 165 books includes only six about individual American women. Eleanor Roosevelt is remembered as an asset to her husband rather than as a staunch advocate of civil rights. Woman's image in books is that of someone who accomplishes nothing in her own right but rather assists men: she is his muse and helpmate.

0888
Schulwitz, Bonnie Smith. "Coping with sexism in reading materials," *The Reading Teacher*, 1976, 29:768-770.

The five most prevalent sexist themes found in children's readers are: 1) women's limited role as wife/mother; 2) her negative characteristics as weak person lacking initiative, 3) omission of female characters, 4) limited occupational goals for women and 5) stereotyping of less than the full range of human interests for both sexes. Classroom teachers are given six suggestions for coping with sexism in readers, including changing the stories and omitting stories or books with blatantly sexist themes.

0889

Sexism and Racism in Popular Basal Readers. NY:
Council on Interracial Books for Children, 1976;
also in ERIC (ED 123 307).

Comparison of sexism and racism in four popular basal
reading series from 1964 to 1976 reveals limited improvement. In the most recent series female characters have
increased in number, express more active, resourceful and
courageous behavior, and wear aprons less often. Simi-
larly minority characters appear with more frequency and
fewer stereotyped characteristics in the more recent works.
However subtle sexism still exists in the form of language
bias, storylines based on anti-woman jokes and exclusion
of women from traditionally male-dominated occupations.

0890

Shirreffs, Janet H. "Sex role stereotyping in
elementary school health education textbooks,"
Journal of School Health, 1975, 45: 519-523.

An evaluation of the content and illustrations of
six health education textbooks published from 1969 to 1974
revealed that boys are encouraged to participate in many
active sports while girls are limited to modern dance and
volleyball. Hysterical mothers are common while fathers
are usually portrayed as calm and quick thinking during
crises. The danger of sex role stereotypes in health
textbooks lies in the threat to the female child's human
spirit. She should learn to have confidence in protect-
ing her personal health and be encouraged to expand her
nursing aspirations to MD level if she so desires.

0891

Stacey, Judith, Susan Bereaud, and Joan Daniels.
*And Jill Came Tumbling After: Sexism in American
Education.* NY: Dell, 1974.

Even though boys and girls share a classroom, boys
receive better education than girls. Learned sex roles
undermine female confidence and aspirations as "primer
after primer teaches children that men work and women
mother, boys climb and girls fall." Educational sexism
from kindergarten to academe is explored in this anthology.

0892

Stefflre, Buford. "Run Mama, run: women workers
in elementary readers," *Vocational Guidance Quarterly,* December, 1969, 18:99-102; also in *Sexism
and Youth,* ed. by Diane Gersoni-Stavn. NY:
Bowker, 1974, pp. 209-213.

Elementary school readers present a distorted image
of reality when they depict the marital and occupational
scenes as either/or situations for most adult women. Working women are usually shown to be teachers and rarely
shown in traditionally masculine fields such as engineering. Young girls need more realistic adult female models
with whom to identify and boys need realistic female literary figures to respect.

See 1013. M. Suelze, "Women in labor."

0893
Taylor, Marjorie E. "Sex role stereotypes in
children's readers," *Elementary English*, 1973,
50:1045-1047.

In the reading series examined girls are repeatedly
shown as uninteresting, emotionally flighty and ridiculous
while boys excel in physical tasks and creative activities.
Mothers are never shown engaged in activity common to reality: reading books, driving cars, balancing checkbooks.

See 1014. M. Thetford, "The case for the career book in
grades 5-8: a feminist view.

0894
Trecker, Janice Law. "Woman in US history
high school textbooks," *Social Education*, 1971,
36:249-261; also in *And Jill Came Tumbling
After*, ed. by Judith Stacey, et al. NY: Dell,
1974. pp. 249-268; also in *Sexism and Youth*,
ed. by Diane Gersoni-Stavn. NY: Bowker, 1974.
pp. 309-325.

Because school textbooks continue to transmit stereotypes of women and their capacities, the schools must share
responsibility for the diminished aspirations of female
students since the 1930's. History textbooks omit women
of importance and minimize the legal, social and cultural
disability women face. When important women are mentioned
it is still their male counterparts who are quoted. Recently published books now include black history but still
omit the historical accomplishments of black women.

0895
U'Ren, Marjorie B. "The image of woman in textbooks," *Woman in Sexist Society: Studies in
Power and Powerlessness*, ed. by Vivian Gornick
and Barbara K. Moran. NY: Basic Books, 1971.

pp. 218-225.

A discussion of plots, themes and characterization in children's readers. In a third grade book whose male protagonists outnumber female 7:1, the seven boys lead exciting lives and become civic heroes or paragons of virtue, while in 30 textbooks only two girls receive public acclaim. Textbooks stereotype girls as manipulative, lazy, incapable of independent thinking, selfish and often the butt of a joke. The author suggests that textbooks return to pre-1930 themes in which female characters handled physical danger, stood up against false opinion and were regarded with respect and a sense of "frontier equality."

See 1016. M. E. Verheyden-Hilliard, "Cinderella doesn't live here anymore."

0896
    Weitzman, Lenore J. and Diane Rizzo. "Biased textbooks: images of males and females in elementary school textbooks in five subject areas; what you can do about biased textbooks," 1974. Available from the National Foundation for the Improvement of Education, 1156 15th St. N. Suite 918, Washington, DC, 20005. $1.00. Also in ERIC (ED 119 114).

Analysis of the "latent" content of textbooks, i.e., images of appropriate sex role behavior implicitly conveyed with social studies, math, reading and spelling textbooks used by grade 1-6. Males appear in illustrations more often than females and are stereotyped as strong, silent people while girls are pictured as affectionate and emotionally expressive. Males are pictured in 150 different occupations while females are primarily mothers, and are thus cheated of other aspirations. Authors suggest action to be taken by teachers, administrators and parents to improve the image of women and men in textbooks.

0897
    Weitzman, Lenore and Diane Rizzo. *The Images of Males and Females in Elementary School Textbooks, A Slide Show*. Old Wesbury, NY: The Feminist Press.

Focuses on sex, race and age stereotypes in science, mathematics, reading, spelling and social studies textbooks.

274

0898
     Wiik, Susan L. "The sexual bias of textbook literature," *English Journal*, 1973, 62:224-229.

In an examination of 15 literature anthologies, 6% of the female characters had non-stereotyped personalities. Of this 6%, a disproportionate number of minorities demonstrated independence and resourcefulness, while very few white girls and women were depicted as emotionally independent or self sufficient. The author charges sex role stereotyping in literature with reinforcing low self concepts and low level career aspirations for female readers.

See 1017. T. J. Wirtenberg and C. Y. Nakamura, "Education: barrier or boon to changing occupational roles of women."

0899
     Women on Words and Images. "Dick and Jane as victims! Sex stereotypes in children's readers," 1972. Available from author, PO Box 2163, Princeton, NJ 08540. $2.00; also in ERIC (ED 065 832).

A NOW task force examination of children's readers revealed several stereotypes: while mothers are shown cooking and scolding, fathers and older brothers deal compassionately with frightened animals and arbitrate arguments, therefore "generativity and nurturing are removed from the mothering stereotype and assigned to men." Mothers often nag while fathers are fun people who help children build things. Old, mean people are repeatedly female while old, wise people are male. Since Mexicans are no longer stereotypically asleep under sombreros and blacks no longer eat watermelon on the stoop, the time has come to take off Mother's apron, let Jane climb a tree, Dick stroke a kitten and Father grill dinner inside the kitchen without charcoal.

0900
     Women on Words and Images. *Dick and Jane as Victims*. Available from author, PO Box 2163, Princeton, NJ 08540. Rental $40, purchase $300.

A slide program based on research by the same title. See 0899.

0901
     Women on Words and Images. "Look Jane look. See sex stereotypes," *And Jill Came Tumbling After*, ed. by Judith Stacey et al. NY: Dell, 1974. pp. 159-177.

An adaptation of "Dick and Jane as victims. See
0899.

See 0070. "Your daughter's education."

0902
Zimet, Sara Goodman. "Males and females in Ameri-
can primers from colonial days to the present,"
*What Children Read in School: Critical Analysis
of Primary Reading Textbooks*, by S. G. Zimet.
NY: Grune and Stratton, 1972. pp. 79-86.

Same as "Little boy lost." See 0903.

0903
Zimet, Sara Goodman. "Little boy lost,"
Teacher's College Record, 1970, 72:31-40.

An examination of children's primers from 1600 to
1966 revealed that the portrayal of sex roles has remained essentially the same since America was colonized.
The adult roles, illustrations and behavior messages in
children's textbooks have historically ignored socioeconomic, cultural and sexual differences in American
society.

0904
Zimet, Sara Goodman. "Reader content and sex
differences in achievement," *The Reading Teacher*,
1976, 29L758-763.

Research indicates that children enjoy reading about
characters with whom they identify. Multi-ethnic texts
featuring the non-stereotyped lifestyles, occupations,
recreation and fantasies of both sexes may solve the early
reading problems of young boys and the achievement reversals common to older girls.

0905
Zimet, Sara Goodman. *Sex Role Models in Primary
Reading Texts of the United States*, 1600-1966.
Ph.D. dissertation, University of Denver, 1968.

Examination of 18 primary reading texts from 1600-
1966 revealed that women have historically be portrayed
as dependent on men, however success and failure have
not been related significantly to one sex more than the
other.

0906
Zuersher, Dorothy J. "Bringing women into the curriculum," *Clearing House*, 1976, 50:111-115.

Stereotyped sex roles and the absence of inspiring female role models damage female self-esteem and aspirations by depriving women of a sense of pride and implying that women are incapable of assuming leadership roles. The stereotypic feminine role is culturally determined rather than innate. To offset the damaging stereotypes the author advises teachers to scrutinize new textbooks before purchase and suggest non-sexist films and activities to supplement curriculum units.

Children's Television and Film

See 0953. L. Artel and S. Wengraf, *Positive Images: A Guide to Non-sexist Film for Young People.*

0907
Baris, Jay R. "Study concludes that television promotes stereotypes that adversely affect children," *The New York Times*, March 23, 1975. p. 93.

A summary of the Donagher and Liebert findings (see 0380) is followed by quotes from Dr. Robert Liebert who cites the tragic effects of violent television programming when children faithfully recreate the masculine brutality/female victimization role stereotypes seen on television.

0908
Bendler, Deborah Dean. *The Female in Cartoonland: A Content Analysis of Sex Role Models in Saturday Morning Cartoon Programs*, Ph.D. dissertation, Ohio University, 1974.

Comparison of verbal and physical behavior of male and female characters on Saturday morning cartoons indicates that male characters outnumber female 3:1, female characters most often appear as teenagers or children and are portrayed as adults less often than men, male characters initiate more physical action and male characters are more often involved in occupations or professions.

277

0909

Bergman, Jane. "Are little girls being harmed
by 'Sesame Street'?," *The New York Times*, Janu-
ary 2, 1972, p. 13; also in *Sex Differences and
Discrimination in Education*, ed. by Scarvia B.
Anderson. (Series on Contemporary Educational
Issues, 2). Worthington, Ohio: Charles A.
Jones, 1972. pp. 50-53; also in *And Jill Came
Tumbling After*, ed. by Judith Stacey, et al.
NY: Dell, 1974. pp. 110-115.

For little girls, watching "Sesame Street" is a
lesson in invisibility. When a female character makes a
rare appearance her stereotyped role (strident mother,
simpering girl) furthers the damage to the female viewer.
The segments which teach reading and number skills are
all narrated by men and are about boys, with an occasional
female appearance. The films feature active boys and
girls functioning as spectators. Stories with minority
group themes typically show mothers cooking or mothers and
grandmothers making necklaces from corn, but do not show
women in active, vital roles. The ratio of adult male to
female performer is 7:3. The program averages one adult
female appearance per show. Parents who try to teach
their daughters to be "real" people rather than passive
puppets are given no support by "Sesame Street."

0910

Betancourt, Jeanne. *Women in Focus*. Dayton:
Pflaum, 1974.

The 16mm films listed are all non-sexist in theme.
Some comment on the sex role stereotyping in the American
culture, such as *Crash*, a film which Betancourt says
"symbolizes the icon quality of advertising." Each film
is described in terms of plot, outstanding image and
camera work. Suggestions for suitable age group and sup-
lementary reading follow each film description. An annotated bibliography of the supplementary reading titles
and an address list of film distributors are included.

See 1000. H. A. Britton, "Sex role stereotyping; a content analysis of 'Bread and Butterflies'."

0911

Busby, Linda Jean. "Defining the sex role standard in network children's programs," *Journalism
Quarterly*, 1974, 51:690-696.

Analysis of the physical attributes, behavior and
attitudes of characters in 20 Saturday morning children's

cartoons revealed that male heroic characters (usually unmarried) and most female characters (regardless of marital status) were usually slender in physique while married men were usually overweight. Application of 40 personality traits revealed that female cartoon characters were more often portrayed as dependent and weak while their male counterparts were usually ambitious and bold. On the cartoons sampled, no women worked outside the home even though the US labor force is almost 50% female.

0912
    Busby, Linda Jean. *Sex Roles as Presented in Commercial Network Television Programs Directed Toward Children: Rationale and Analysis.* Ph.D. dissertation, University of Michigan, 1974.

Twenty children's animated cartoon programs analyzed for plot themes and personality traits of major and minor characters, revealed that cartoon males more often exhibited personality traits applauded by society while cartoon females more often exhibited personality traits demeaned by society.

See 0333. "CPB study finds women underused and underserved."

0913
    Cathey-Calvert, Carolyn. "Sexism on 'Sesame Street'; outdated concepts in a 'progressive' program," 1971. Available from KNOW, Inc., PO Box 86031, Pittsburgh, PA 15331. #121.

Although the writers of "Sesame Street" have done an excellent job of including minority group characters in positive roles of leadership, creativity and independence, "Sesame Street's" female characters are half as visible as male characters, have 93% fewer speaking lines and are portrayed as subservient people who spend time cleaning and mothering.

0914
    Chafetz, Janet Saltzman. The bringing up of Dick and Jane: Media," *Masculine/Feminine or Human*, by J. S. Chafetz. Itasca, Ill: Peacock, 1974. pp. 81-85.

Sex role stereotypes were found in the examination of 100 commercials aired during children's programming and on the show, "Sesame Street" which has successfully avoided racial (but not sexual) stereotypes.

0915

Children's Television Commercials, A Content
Analysis, by Charles Winick, Lorne G. William-
son, Stuart F. Chusmir, and Mariann Pezella
Winick. (Praeger Special Studies in US Economic,
Social and Political Issues). NY: Praeger, 1973.

Female authority figures appear in 14.8% of the commercials examined, as compared to the 41.5% ads featuring
male authority figures. Women are portrayed exclusively
as mother or entertainment figure, while men have more
varied roles including professor, astronaut, king.

0916

Chulay, Cornell and Sara Francis. "The image of
the female child on Saturday morning television
commercials," 1974. ERIC (ED 095 603).

A statistical analysis of 294 television commercials
determined that female children are oriented by television to accept a lifetime role within the home. Women
are depicted as mothers and housewives in 53% of commercials studied while men are husbands and fathers in 2%;
girls are shown in a bedroom setting in 88% of commercials
studied, boys are in bedrooms in 6%; girls are depicted
outdoors in 4% of commercials studied, boys are outdoors
in 63%. The statistics include types of products advertised by each sex, sex of voice-over, and primary role
of the female. In no commercial studies were girls shown
as aspiring female athletes, businesswomen, scientists
or professors. If advertising reflects the "modern
world, it has failed to keep pace with the changing, growing and liberated female."

0917

Dohrmann, Rita Meade. Children's Television Programming: A Sex Socialization Agent, M.A. thesis,
Drake University, 1974.

Monitoring of 34 children's television programs revealed that male supremacy dominated the screen with 78%
visibility as compared to the 49% male population. Male
characters exhibited behavior patterns of active mastery,
while female characters exhibited passive, dependent behavior. The occupational and leadership roles on educational programs "Sesame Street" and "Electric Company"
were overwhelmingly male. Male authority and superiority
was evident even in male children who exhibited masterful
superiority over adult women. Children viewing television
are taught to accept the symbolic annihilation of girls
and the social superiority of boys. A recommendation is
made for vociferous lobbying to remove sexist content

from children's television programming.

0918
Dohrmann, Rita. "A gender profile of children's educational TV," *Journal of Communication*, 1975, 25:56-65.

Analysis of five educational programs for gender representation indicates that the adult male was visible 65% of the time while the female child (half the viewing audience) had only 8% visibility. The animals were male, animated non-human characters were male and even talking nuts and bolts had male voices. Dohrmann calls this significant lack of female participation "symbolic annihilation."

See 0141. J. Doolittle and R. Pepper, "Children's TV ad content: 1974."

0919
Gardner, Jo Ann, "'Sesame Street' and sex role stereotypes," *Women: A Journal of Liberation*, Spring, 1970, 1(3):42.

Besides enlivening the learning process the "Sesame Street" sketches seem to have another function: to stereotype the sex roles. Children are taught that men's work is heavy work, women's work is flower-arranging; fathers drive trucks, mothers do laundry; boys catch frogs, girls watch. Girls as well as boys should be taught assertiveness and independence.

See 0409. R. K. Goldsen, "Throwaway husbands, wives and lovers."

0920
Goodman, Ellen. "Mother Nature and sex roles," *Manhattanville College Magazine*, Fall, 1975. pp. 18-24.

Television advertising and toy packaging are two primary forces in socializing children to accept unnaturally rigid sex roles. Girls are pressured to limit their career aspirations and boys are pressured to inhibit their emotions.

0921
Hoffman, Heidi. "Report on monitoring of children's

television programming aired by WRC-TV: a comparison of male and female roles, *Women in the Wasteland Fight Back*, by National Organization for Women, National Capitol Area Chapter, Washington, DC: NOW, 1972. pp. 91-104.

Monitoring of children's programming included 10½ hours of cartoons, and comedy and dramatic educational shows. During this composite week 29% of the characters were female, 70% male. The only female lead character was a witch. Only one female instigated any action during the composite week while all remaining female characters either supported male characters or were acted upon by them. Male characters were passively acted upon in only 1/7 of the situations. In the chase scenes (featured in 80% of cartoon shows monitored) males usually chased males while females watched. There is a need for more active female participation in children's programming.

0922
> Houseman, Jerry Paul. *A Study of Selected Walt Disney Screenplays and Films and the Stereotyping of the Role of the Female*, Ph.D. dissertation, University of the Pacific, 1973.

Two Walt Disney films were shown to 234 elementary school children and 32 college students. Results indicate that some viewers undergo attitude changes as a result of film viewing, films may influence the social behavior of viewers, and some subjects disagreed with the stereotyping of the female role.

0923
> Howe, Florence. "Sexual stereotypes start early," *Saturday Review*, October 16, 1971, 54:76-77+.

According to the standard set by textbooks and television, fathers work and mothers stay home. Most children assume that their working mothers are "different" from the television norm.

0924
> Kaye, Evelyn. "Sexism," *The Family Guide to Children's Television: What to Watch, What to Miss, What to Change and How to Do It*, by E. Kaye. NY: Pantheon, 1975. pp. 53-54; also in ERIC (ED 096 941).

A quote from Letty Cottin Pogrebin warns parents to discourage children from watching specific television shows which stereotype women as brainless, deceptive and frivolous, and men as brave, courageous, without teaching children that women can also be intelligent and forthright and men can be nervous and express natural fears. If the average child watches 15,000 hours of television by age 18, it is important to counteract the influence of harmful sex role stereotypes.

0925
Leifer, Aimee Dorr, Neal J. Gordon and Sherryl Browne. "Children's television: more than mere entertainment," *Harvard Educational Review*, 1974, 44:213-245.

Children identify with television personalities with similar ascriptive characteristics. Black girls are most likely to follow role models of black women as teachers, lawyers, doctors or secretaries. As equal employment becomes a reality within the television industry, female characters will be cast in more prestigious and more numerous roles.

0926
Lesser, Gerald S. "Poorly represented constituencies," *Children and Television; Lessons from 'Sesame Street'*, by G. S. Lesser. NY: Random House, 1974.

Feminist criticisms of "Sesame Street" are answered here by a member of Children's Television Workshop, creators of the program. The early lack of female role models was due to "Sesame Street's" emphasis on strong male identification figures for inner-city children. Since the criticism began men are still shown in nurturing roles while women are also included in positive, distinctive roles.

0927
Levinson, Richard M. "From Olive Oyl to Sweet Polly Purebread: sex role stereotypes and televised cartoons," *Journal of Popular Culture*, 1975, 9:561-572.

Television socializes young children before they begin school. Later textbooks, pleasure reading, toys and toy packaging reinforce the initial sex role perception formed primarily by preschool attention to Saturday morning cartoons. In cartoons adult men outnumber adult women 4:1, while adolescent boys outnumber adolescent girls by only 2:1. Male roles outnumber female approximately 5:1. Most roles are sex stereotyped whether the

character is human, an animal or a robot. The author
cites research which questions the emotional damage of exposure to stereotyped role models.

See 0347. R. M. Liebert, "Modeling and the media."

0928
    Long, Michele and Rita J. Simon. "The roles and
    statuses of women on children and family TV pro-
    grams," *Journalism Quarterly*, 1974, 51:107-110.

A discussion of 22 children's and family shows in
terms of women's interaction with men, average women's
physical appearance compared with the average man's, and
the amount of time women and men appear on the screen.
Of the 34 married women, none worked outside the home.
The single and widowed women who work are rarely seen in
positions of authority or prestige. They are often portrayed as silly, emotional and dependent on men.

0929
    Lyle, Jack and Heidi R. Hoffman. "Children's
    use of television and other media," *Television
    and Social Behavior*, v. 4, ed. by E. I. Ruben-
    stein, G. A. Comstock and J. P. Murray. Wash-
    ington, DC: US Government Printing Office,
    1972. pp. 129-256.

Sex differences in television program preference among
first grade children show that boys tend to prefer action
programs which feature strong male leading characters
while girls tend to prefer family situation comedies in
which women predominate or are coequal with male leads.
Sixth and tenth grade sexual and racial preferences are
further examined in terms of movies, radio, records,
comics and other media.

0930
    McArthur, Leslie Zebrowitz and Susan V. Eisen.
    "Achievements of male and female storybook
    characters as determinants of achievement be-
    havior by boys and girls," *Journal of Personal-
    ity and Social Psychology*, 1976, 33:467-473.

One of three types of stories, (stereotyped role reversal, or control stories about animals) were read to 32
male and 36 female nursery school students. Although both
sexes exhibited chauvinistic preferences for stories about
same-sex characters, boys demonstrated more achievement
oriented behavior after hearing stories about male

achievement than female achievement while a nonsignificant trend in the opposite direction was observed for girls.

In order to expand women's role to greater representation in the "achieving" professions (doctor, lawyer, administrator) institutional changes must be supplemented with psychological changes. Sex role stereotypes are learned from live and symbolic models (films, television, books). This research attempts to prove that children model their achievement related behavior after that of like-sexed models presented in their storybooks.

0931
    Maccoby, Eleanor E. and William Cody Wilson. "Identification and observational learning from films," *Journal of Abnormal and Social Psychology*, 1957, 55L, 55:76-87.

Twenty-five seventh grade classes were shown a movie in which a teenage girl and boy were the two leading protagonists. It was found that the students identified themselves with the like-sexed characters. This 20 year old study significantly proves that women enjoy and remember characters with whom they can identify.

0932
    McGhee, Paul E. "Television as a source of learning sex role stereotypes." Paper presented at biennial meeting of the Society for Research in Child Development, 1975. ERIC (ED 111 528).

Excluding the influence of the nuclear family, children learn most of their sex role attitudes and behavior from television programming's role models. This hypothesis was suggested by giving the "It" test (a measure of sex typed activity using a stick figure) to a sample of 80 children in grades k, 2, 4, 6. Half of the children in each grade watched 25 hours of television per week, while the other half habitually watched 10 hours or less of television per week. The results of the "It" test, both from the initial testing and a second test 15 months later, indicate a marked difference in sex role attitudes between heavy and light television viewing habits of children.

0933
    "Male superiority and dominance being taught to both children and adults," *Media Report to Women*, September 1, 1974, 2(9):12.

Testimony by Mary Ellen Verheyden-Hilliard, NOW

Education Task Force leader, at Senate commerce committee hearings deals with television's influence on children's role acceptance and socialization. Television betrays its responsibility by teaching children "a grossly distorted and limited view" of the female role in society. Children see 27% female characters on television though the female population is far higher in American society. Girls learn to play supportive, subservient, submissive roles in society, learn to deemphasize intelligence and to be followers rather than leaders. Boys are taught that girls' ideas are unimportant, that girls will fail in a crisis, and that boys must be aggressive, unfeeling initiators of action. Sex role stereotyping must be eliminated on television in favor of a reasonable, balanced presentation of the varied roles held by both sexes.

0934

Maronde, Doreen Nelson. *What is She Like? A Study of Feminine Roles on Saturday Morning Children's Television.* M.S. thesis, Iowa State University, 1974.

A study of 32 cartoon segments confirmed that fewer female than male characters were presented, spent less time on screen and were presented more stereotypically especially in degree of adventurousness, emotionality and irrationality. Stereotypic behavior increased with age of female character. Women were overwhelmingly portrayed stereotypically, female teenagers assumed traditionally feminine roles in 3/5 of their appearances while female children almost never appeared in such roles.

0935

Meade, Marion. "Penelope Pitstop isn't enough!" *The New York Times,* September 13, 1970, p. D-25+.

Of the 50 televised children's cartoons only one stars a woman - Penelope Pitstop, a race car driver. The other female cartoon characters are all stereotypes: Witchipoo's independence is equated with evil, catatonic Nell Fenwick exists only to be saved by Dudley Doright (who loves his horse more than he loves Nell) and Wilma Flintstone whose sweet manipulation of Fred belies the castrating bitch she is underneath. "Sesame Street," "Captain Kangaroo," "Misterogers' Neighborhood" and "Romper Room" further demean women by disregarding them. Male supremacy operates in the read-aloud books with no female protagonists and in ads for vitamins featuring energetic boys while disregarding girls' health requirements.

0936
    Meyer, Timothy P. "Children's perceptions of
    favorite television characters as behavioral
    models," *Educational Broadcasting Review*, Feb-
    ruary, 1973, 7:25-33.

    Study indicates that many male children regard vio-
lent television characters as their role models.

0937
    Miller, Hannah, "Why children's films are not
    rated 'R'," *Wilson Library Bulletin*, 1971,
    46:183-184.

    Although sex does not exist in children's films, sex-
ism runs rampant. The most popular films, those recognized as among the best by Library Associations, and those
shown on children's television primarily feature male heroes engaged in activities that could realistically include
girls, such as in scenes where a child cleans a dog. Only
the "Many Americans" film series shows a fair number of
positive female role models - all minority group children
such as a Chicana girl who teaches English to her uncle and
a Chinese American girl who takes dancing lessons.

0938
    Mischel, Walter. "A social-learning view of sex
    differences in behavior," *The Development of Sex
    Differences*, by Eleanor E. Maccoby. Stanford:
    Stanford University Press, 1966. pp. 56-81.

    Acquisition and reinforcement of sex-typed behavior
in children is learned from live and symbolic models found
in films, television and books.

0939
    O'Kelly, Charlotte G. "Sexism in children's tele-
    vision," *Journalism Quarterly*, 1974, 51:722-723.

    A study of seven hours of children's television re-
vealed that of 242 program characters, 85% were male and
15% female. Commercial messages were 67% male, 33% female.
Other measurements include adult occupations and play activities. The author concludes that television remains a
stronghold for sex role images.

See 0181. S. Pingree, *A Developmental Study of the Attitudinal Effects of Nonsexist Television Commercials under
Varied Conditions of Perceived Reality*.

0940
    Sheikh, Anees A., Kanti V. Prasad and Tanniru R.
    Rao. "Children's TV commercials: a review of
    research," *Journal of Communication*, 1974, 24
    (4):126-136.

Saturday morning advertisements aimed at children had
49% male central characters, 16% female and 35% mixed
groups. Beauty and popularity were selling points for
girls' products while size, power, noise and speed sold
boys' products.

0941
    Stein, Aletha Huston. "Mass Media and young
    children's development," *Early Childhood Educa-*
    tion (National Society for the Study of Education.
    Yearbook. v. 71, pt. 2). Chicago: NSSE, 1974.
    pp. 191-202.

Children are typically more attentive to characters
similar to themselves in sex, age and ethnic background.
Television and films show more male than female central
characters, therefore male viewers see more characters
with whom to identify. When the media does feature women,
they are overly represented in passive and domestic roles.

0942
    Sternburg, Janet. "Kids' flicks: move over,
    Donald Duck," *Ms.*, December, 1974, 3:101-104.

Condensed version of "Non-sexist films for children."
See 0943.

0943
    Sternburg, Janet. "Non-sexist films for chil-
    dren," *Sightlines*, Fall, 1974, 8(1):7-8+.

An annotated catalogue of short films all of which
depict children of both sexes and many racial and social
backgrounds enjoying unusual adventures. The films appeal
to children ages 4-13.

0944
    Sternglanz, Sarah H. and Lisa A. Serbin. "Sex
    role stereotyping in children's TV programs,"
    Developmental Psychology, 1974, 10:710-715.

A study of 12 sex role appropriate behavior patterns
taught on children's television. One behavior pattern
outstandingly attributed to female characters was magic

ability. Four of the five female title-role stars were witches of one kind or another.

0945
    Streicher, Helen W. "The girls in the cartoons," *Journal of Communication,* 1974, 24(2):125-129.

A discussion of sex role differences in Saturday morning cartoons and advertisements.

See 0738. "Summary of the script and program review of 'Sesame Street' by the Chicano Study Center."

0946
    TV: The Anonymous Teacher, produced by United Methodist Communications, 1976, 16mm, 15 mins., rental, $20, purchase, $225. Available from Mass Media Ministeries, 2116 N. Charles St., Baltimore, MD 21218.

A child's psyche is subtly shaped by the influence of violence and sexual and racial stereotyping on television and in advertising.

0947
    Varlejs, Jana. "Cine-opsis," *Wilson Library Bulletin,* 1976, 51:80-81.

Films that demonstrate sex role socialization of children are juxtaposed with films showing non-stereotypic roles. "Cine-opsis," a monthly column in *Wilson Library Bulletin,* regularly reviews 16mm films with feminist themes.

See 0207. M. E. Verna. "The female image in children's TV commercials."

0948
    Vogel, Susan, Inge Broverman and Jo-Ann Evans Gardner. "'Sesame Street' and sex role stereotyping - updated with suggestions for eliminating objectionable features," 1971. Available from KNOW, Inc., PO Box 86031, Pittsburgh, PA 15221. #042.

Recommendations for eliminating sex role stereotyping on "Sesame Street" and other programs produced by Children's Television Workshop include: increased

frequency of female model presentation, elimination of
stereotypes in projected "Sesame Street" episodes, sub-
stitution of female models for male in episodes involving
action and use of implements, introduction of counter-
stereotypic models as new and continued characterizations
(such as female architect or city planner).

0949
    Waters, Harry F. "What TV does to kids: the
view from the victims," *Newsweek*, February 21,
1977. 89(8):65+.

A survey of television programming and advertising
revealed that men outnumber women 3:1, and women display
incompetence twice as often as men. Men are portrayed
as dominate, authoritative and sole economic source of
the family. These distorted sex roles do not reflect a
woman's thoughts or emotions.

See 0399. Women on Words and Images, *Channeling Children*.

Counterbalances

0950
    Adell, Judith and Hilary Dole Klein. *A Guide
to Non-Sexist Children's Books*. Chicago:
Academy Press, 1976.

An annotated list of fiction and nonfiction titles
written for a preschool to twelfth grade audience, which
show people of both sexes in nontraditional roles and
situations. Girls make decisions, boys fantasize and both
sexes function together in healthy, respecting relationships.

0951
    Ahlum, Carol and Jacqueline Frally. *Feminist
Resources for Schools and Colleges, A Guide to
Curricular Materials*. Old Westbury, NY: The
Feminist Press Clearing House on Women's Stud-
ies, 1974.

A resource list of materials suitable for elementary
school through college level classes. Photographs, records and films are among the resources rated as sexist,
non-sexist or questionable.

0952
Artel, Linda. "Free our children, free ourselves; selected resources for non-sexist education," *Booklegger*, 1976, 3(15):16-19.

An annotated bibliography of non-sexist children's books, films and curricular material.

0953
Artel, Linda and Susan Wengraf. *Positive Images: A Guide to Non-Sexist Films for Young People.* San Francisco: Booklegger Press, 1976.

In this electronic age the mass media is one primary source from which children develop a self-image and value system. Glamorous yet limiting sex roles reinforced by the media restrict the emotional, intellectual and physical development of both sexes. Womanhood is defined as passive, dependent and incompetent, while manhood is limited by a competitive, violent, unfeeling nature. This annotated list of films, filmstrips and photographs may be used by teachers, librarians and educators as an attempt to counterbalance the distorted stereotypes reinforced by television and film.

See 0783. J. Bernstein. "The changing roles of females in books for young children."

See 0733. "Children's books from the new China."

0954
Council on Interracial Books for Children. *Human (and Anti-Human) Values in Children's Books.* NY: CIBC, 1976.

Full page book reviews and a values rating checklist for 235 children's books published in 1975 rate the illustrations and language of each book according to sexist, racist, ageist, elitist and individualistic values. A subject index of the 235 books is especially useful for librarians, educators and parents.

0955
DeFilippo, Kathy Byrne. "Little girls and picture books: problems and solution," *The Reading Teacher*, 1976, 29:671-674.

In order to present preschool children with a fair and balanced picture of the female sex, the author offers

an annotated list of picture books with non-stereotyped
sex roles.

See 0718. D. J. Dieterich, "Books that lie and lullaby."

0956
    Edwards, Richard and Bruce E. Gronbeck. "A
    partial list of educational, instructional and
    documentary films treating women's roles, prob-
    lems and communications strategies," 1975.
    ERIC (ED 113 763).

    See title for description.

0957
    "Eliminating sexism in schools and educational
    materials, a roundup of national developments,"
    Library Journal, 1974, 99:1171-1172.

    Report of the various national and state level legis-
lative bills eliminating sexism in schools, with particu-
lar emphasis on purging textbooks. (See 0993-0997)

0958
    Fishman, Anne Stevens. "A criticism of sexism
    in elementary readers," *The Reading Teacher*,
    1976, 29:443-446.

    Most of the basal readers criticized by feminists are
now out of print. Feminists should begin to examine more
recently published books especially those of publishers
who have issued guidelines for elimination of sexism in
textbooks.

0959
    Free to be...You and Me, ed. by Marlo Thomas.
    NY: McGraw-Hill, 1974.

    Marlo Thomas calls this book a "celebration" of who
children are and who they can be, regardless of sex. The
stories, poems and songs celebrate boys who cry and cross
the street for the first time, girls who make wishes and
pitch on the softball team, and families who share the
housework and breadwinning responsibilities. The only
princess is not only awake but races alongside her fastest
suitor. Another subtle stereotype is broken in a tale of
sibling rivalry involving an eldest girl (The Great One)
and her younger brother (The Pain). A number of well known
authors, composers and illustrators contributed to the

collection.

0960
Free to Be...You and Me. Available from Free to
be Foundation, Inc., 370 Lexington Ave., Dept
4FTB, NY, 10017.

A recording and a 16mm film are both based on the
print version (see 0959).

0961
Hagar, Margaret E. and Sue Deffenbaugh. "Does
Mama Bear always serve the porridge? Sex role
stereotyping in school reading materials,"
paper presented at annual meeting of the College
Reading Association, 1974. ERIC (ED 099 806).

By portraying the sexes in "typical" behavior and
denying children the totality of their humanity, both
sexes suffer. Recommendations for eliminating sex role
stereotypes in readers include complaints to publishers
and school boards, use of outside curricular materials
role reversal games and consciousness-raising activities
in class.

0962
Haller, Elizabeth S. "Images of women: a bibliography of feminist resources for Pennsylvania
schools." Harrisburg: Pennsylvania State Department of Education, Bureau of Curriculum
Services, 1973. ERIC (ED 090 470).

A bibliography of books, films and tapes with favorable portrayals of women in non-traditional roles in
biographies, careers, fiction, history, literature and
the arts, psychology and sociology material which all offer
options for women.

0963
Harrison, Barbara. "Feminist experiment in education," *New Republic*, March 11, 1972, 166:13-
17; also in *And Jill Came Tumbling After*, ed.
by Judith Stacey, et al. NY: Dell, 1974. pp.
377-389.

A group of feminist mothers convinced the administrators of a liberal private school to eliminate sexist curricula just as they had eliminated racism. The revised
curricula offer students viable female models: The Grimke
sisters, Anne Bradstreet, Sojourner Truth as well as

lesser known women whose taped interviews provide the oral history of daughters of pioneers, slaves, immigrants.

0964
Hoffs, Tamar. *Ms. Goose: A Lib-retta.* Los Angeles: Avondale Press, 1973.

Liberated rhymes replace the traditional Mother Goose.

0965
Hooray for Captain Jane. (Women in Literature Series). NY: Caedmon Records, Inc.

Ten non-sexist stories for children on record and cassette.

0966
Humphreys, Di. "Kid's books," *Catonsville Runner*, December, 1973, n50:9+.

The British Ladybird reading series indoctrinates children to accept sexist values and behavior. To counter this sexism a group has sent out a plea of help, via this article, to meet with education authorities concerning purchase of non-sexist books and to persuade publishers to produce the group's material which offers alternatives to traditional sex roles in children's books.

0967
Kram, Judith. "Sex role stereotyping in textbooks: where to go from here," 1974. ERIC (ED 104 980).

In order to eliminate sex roles in instructional material, feminists must adopt specific action: publicize problems by writing letters to editors, radio and television stations, Congress, State board of education; lobby for strong legislation and work closely with textbook publishing companies and school librarians.

0968
Lacy, Dan. "Man's words; women's roles," *Saturday Review*, June 14, 1975, 1:25+.

McGraw-Hill's senior vice-president discussed the publishing company's goals for eliminating sex role stereotypes from its publications. Sex role stereotypes limit female aspirations and block male emotional development, therefore the publisher plans to treat the sexes equally

within its publications. In keeping with their guidelines
(see 0994) the editors also plan to eliminate sexist bias
from the language without artificially distorting acceptable English style.

0969
    Lollipop Power. "Children and books." Avail-
    able from author, PO Box 1171, Chapel Hill,
    NC 27514. 25¢.

The sex role stereotypes of many children's picture
books present a narrow view of adult life and ignore the
existence of working mothers, nurturant fathers, one-
parent families, child care centers and poverty level
minority group families. In contrast, paperback picture
books published by Lollipop Power, Inc. offer the images
of independent, emotional, expressive girls and boys in a
variety of social settings and family lifestyles.

0970
    Macleod, Jennifer S. and Sandra T. Silverman.
    *"You Won't Do." What Textbooks on US Govern-
    ment Teach High School Girls.* Pittsburgh,
    KNOW, Inc, 1973. Also in ERIC (ED 091 255).

Social studies and government textbooks tend to
either omit considerations of women and their political
movements in the texts or demean and belittle them in the
cartoons. Recommendations for improving the role of
women in textbooks include: quotations from knowledgeable
women as well as men should be included in the text, and
class discussions hypothesizing why so few women have en-
tered the fields of politics and law. A comprehensive,
annotated source list is included.

0971
    "Man! Memo from a publisher," *The New York
    Times Magazine,* October 20, 1974, p. 38+.

Excerpts from McGraw-Hill publisher's guidelines.
See 0994.

0972
    Merriam, Eve. "A feminist alphabet," *News-
    week,* August 2, 1976, 88:11.

A clever counter to the "M is for Mother" image of
women in children's alphabet books, this alphabet says
"K is for king: most powerful court person, sometimes
known familiarly as a billiejean."

See 0780. R. Minard, *Womenfolk and Fairy Fales.*

0973

Moberg, Verne. *A Child's Right to Equal Reading.*
Old Westbury, NY: The Feminist Press, 1972; also
published by Washington, DC: National Education
Association, 1974.

Ideas for consciousness raising workshops geared toward parents, teachers and school administrators include
many alternatives to sex role stereotyping in children's
books, including a non-stereotyped retelling of "Cinderella."

0974

Motomatsu, Nancy R. *A Selected Bibliography of
Bias-free Materials: Grades K-12.* Olympia:
Washington Office of the State Superintendent of
Public Instruction, 1976. ERIC (ED 127 408).

A bibliography of fiction, nonfiction and biographies
which present positive images of both sexes.

0975

Ms. Liberty: You Can Be What You Want To Be!,
available from Golden West Publishers, 4113 N.
Longview, Phoenix, AZ 85014. $1.00.

In this coloring book girls are encouraged to aspire
to traditionally male dominated occupations such as architect and clown.

0976

"A new list of books for free children," *Ms.,*
September, 1976, 5(3):95-97.

To counteract the stereotypes of children's television,
this annotated list of books for ages preschool to 12+ includes themes of strong female heroes, poor families, divorce, parent/child conflict, puberty, street life, love,
and other themes.

See 0804. A. P. Nilsen, "Book a la mode: a reader's
digest."

0977

Nilsen, Aleen P. "New kinds of books for new kinds
of girls," *Elementary English,* 1973, 50:1035-1038.

An annotated bibliography of elementary level books with interesting and individualistic female protagonists. One major character is a "girl with grit" and another delights in the rain. In none of the stories are the female characters confined to unrealistic, stereotyped roles.

0978
"Notes on people: Francoise Giroud," *The New York Times*, October 5, 1974. p. 19.

Giroud proposes the rewriting of French schoolbooks to get Mama out of the kitchen, let Papa try his hand at cooking, and let them buy the car together.

0979
180 Plus: A Framework for Non-Stereotyped Human Roles in Elementary Media Center Materials. Kalamazoo: Kalamazoo Public Schools, 1976.

An annotated bibliography of 183 non-sexist picture books, fiction, biographies, science and social science textbooks.

0980
Pastine, Maureen. "Articles on non-sexist, non-racist children's literature," 1975. ERIC (ED 117 654).

A bibliography of articles on non-sexist and non-racist children's books, alternative publishers of children's books and sources of children's book reviews.

0981
Pogrebin, Letty Cottin. "Toys for free children," *Ms.*, December, 1973, 2,(6):48-53+; also in *Sexism and Youth*, ed. by Diane Gersoni-Stavn. NY: Bowker, 1974. pp. 407-428.

Toys are one children's medium that can influence a child's future occupational choice by providing the inspiration for the child's fantasy development. In order to give children toys designed to facilitate growth, parents are instructed to discard the sexist packaging and rewrap the toys in plastic. Children of both sexes can develop positive values from sports equipment, lightweight tools, plant kits and creative art equipment without being brainwashed by sex-limiting pictures on boxes. The article ends with a shopping list of sexually neutral toys for children.

0982
>Rennie, Susan and Kirstin Grimstad. "Children's books and toys," *New Woman's Survival Sourcebook*. NY: Knopf, 1975. pp. 77-81.

>Lists non-sexist books and toys.

0983
>Rosenberg, Max. "Evaluate your textbooks for racism, sexism!," *Educational Leadership*, 1973, 31:107-109.

A checklist for evaluating textbooks and learning materials for sexist and racist bias.

0984
>Schmid, Anne McEvoy. "Let brother bake the cake," *American Teacher*, November, 1972, 57(3):CE4-CE5; also in *Sexism and Youth*, ed. by Diane Gersoni-Stavn. NY: Bowker, 1974, pp. 107-112.

Teachers searching for non-sexist teaching methods are advised to change pronouns and employ role reversals when reading stories to the class.

See 0888. B. S. Schulwitz, "Coping with sexism in reading materials."

0985
>Schumacher, Dorin. "Changing the school environment," *Women: A Journal of Liberation*, 1972, 2(4): 33-36; also in *Sexism and Youth*, ed. by Diane Gersoni-Stavn. NY: Bowker, 1974. pp. 113-119.

A woman and her nine year old daughter discussed the one-sided approach to women on television and in school textbooks. After raising her daughter's consciousness the woman took on the schoolteachers and PTA. Among other recommendations was the counterbalancing of women's negative image in literature by effective use of class discussion.

See 0110. S. Seed, "Saturday's child."

0986
>"Sex equality in educational materials." (American Association of School Administrators Executive Handbook Series, 4). Available from AASA,

1801 N. Moore St., Arlington, VA 22209. $2.50.
Also on ERIC (ED 111 096).

Television, periodicals and popular fiction all reveal a stereotyped image of women that reinforces present
attitudes. The educational system is equally guilty by
teaching books that ignore, exclude or distort the historical and present situations faced by women. School administrators and concerned members of the community can
change the situation by analyzing textbooks and contacting
publishers. Included are guidelines for analyzing textbook images of female and male characters, attitudes towards women's work, and language bias.

0987
     "Sex stereotyping in instructional materials,"
     Educational Product Record, December, 1973, 7:2-
     8; also in ERIC (ED 090 550).

Publishers guidelines for improving the image of wom-
en in textbooks is only a first step. Books have consistently underrepresented women, have shown them in limited,
stereotyped roles; reinforced cultural conditioning toward
passive, dependent personalities; and have failed to in-
still an appreciation of women's contribution to history,
literature, science and other areas of American life.
Sexism in education may be challenged under Title IX, Office of HEW and a number of State commissions.

0988
     Shargel, Susan and Irene Kane. *We Can Change It!*
     San Francisco: Change for Children, 1974.

An annotated bibliography of children's books which
offer role models of both sexes and many ethnic groups as
independent, adventurous, curious, confident, sharing,
considerate, sensitive human beings. Well-rounded girls
and boys coexist as friends and playmates.

0989
     Sprung, Barbara. "Annotated bibliography of non-
     sexist picture books," *Non-Sexist Education for
     Young Children, A Practical Guide*, by B. Sprung.
     NY: Citation Press, 1975. pp. 103-107.

An annotated bibliography of non-sexist picture
books.

0990
     Sprung, Barbara. "Non-Sexist materials,"

Non-Sexist Education for Young Children, a Prac-
tical Guide, by B. Sprung. NY: Citation Press,
10 1975. pp. 91-102.

Block accessories, photography, puzzles, records,
dolls and filmstrips distributed by Women's Action Al-
liance reflect role-free multi-racial and multi-ethnic
reality in both format and package design.

See 0943. J. Sternburg, "Non-sexist films for children."

See 0674. G. Trudeau, "Joanie: cartoons for free children."

0991
"Women beginning the sex-stereotype rollback,"
Media Report to Women, April 1, 1974, 2(4):7.

The editors of *Humpty Dumpty Magazine* for children
and *Baby Talk* for expectant parents tell of their concern in eliminating sexism from the publications. *Humpty
Dumpty* quotes apron-clad fathers as well as mothers,
and often edits the names of active major characters from
Billy to Betty so that children of both sexes will have
active role models. *Baby Talk* avoids stereotypes with
articles about the feelings of new fathers, the needs of
working mothers, and baby furniture ads picturing both
parents feeding, bathing and carrying infants.

See 0399. Women on Words and Images, *Channeling Children.*

0992
"Women's Rights Policy, AFT," *New Woman's Survival
Catalog*, ed. by S. Rennie and K. Grimstad. NY:
Coward, McCann and Geoghegan, 1975.

The women's rights policy resolution of the American
Federation of Teachers, AFL-CIO resolves to use teaching
material with non-sexist language, positive image of wom-
en in a variety of roles and physical sizes, among other
recommendations.

PUBLISHER'S GUIDELINES

0993
Guidelines for Creating Positive Sexual and

Racial Images in Educational Materials, 1975.
Available from The Macmillan Company, 866 Third
Avenue, NY 10022; also in ERIC (ED 117 687).

0994
*Guidelines for Equal Treatment of the Sexes in
McGraw-Hill Book Company Publications*, 1974.
Available from McGraw-Hill Book Company, 1221
Avenue of the Americas, NY 10020; also in ERIC
(ED 098 574).

0995
*Guidelines for Improving the Image of Women in
Textbooks*, 1972. Available from Scott Foresman
and Company, 1900 E. Lake Avenue, Glenview, IL
60025.

0996
*Guidelines for the Development of Elementary
and Secondary Instructional Materials*, 1975.
Available from Holt, Rinehart, Winston, 383
Madison Avenue, NY 10017.

0997
*Guidelines for the Fair and Adequate Representa-
tion of Women and Minorities*, 1976. Available
from Silver Burdett, 250 James Street, Morristown,
NJ   07960.

The publishers guidelines all seek to eliminate sex
role bias in language and content in children's textbook
publications.

THE IMPACT OF MEDIA STEREOTYPES ON
OCCUPATIONAL CHOICES

See also Classified Advertising, 0295 - 0302

See 0372. H. L. Arenstein. "The effect of television on children's stereotyping of occupational roles."

0998
Beuf, Ann. "Doctor, lawyer, household drudge,"
Journal of Communication, 1974, 24(2):142-145.

Interviews with 63 children reveal the influence of television programming on children's sex-typed career aspirations.

0999
Bird, Caroline. "The invisible bar," *Born Female, the High Cost of Keeping Women Down,* by C. Bird with Sara Welles Briller. NY: David McKay, 1974. pp. 47-71.

From preschool books children learn that girls must be clean, polite and tender while boys may be active and noisy. When they grow up girls become mommies and nurses while boys become men or doctors. Girls who deviate from the early message crash into the invisible bar of sex discrimination in employment when they reach adulthood.

1000
Britton, Helen Ann. "Sex role stereotyping: a content analysis of 'Bread and Butterflies'," 1975. ERIC (ED 116 699).

If children identify with the situation and characters found on television then their future adult roles may be influenced by the media definition. This major premise was applied to an examination of "Bread and Butterflies," a career development instructional television series. The portrayal of the sex roles in this series falls into five categories: 1) female job ghetto (14 women as secretary, store clerk, nurse), 2) male career domain (35 men as doctor, lawyer, architect), 3) women in men's job

(four occasions), 4) men in women's job (twice), and 5)
non-sexist career presentation (23 brief appearances
rather than role of major characters). "Bread and Butterflies" stresses female fears and insecurities while male
fears are overlooked, and women are expected to accomplish
the "near impossible" in order to prove themselves as competent.

1001

Brown, Jane Delano. *Role of Communication in
the Development of Sex Role Orientations*. M.A.
thesis, University of Wisconsin - Madison, 1974.

Examines the influence of mass and interpersonal communications on socialization and career choice. Results
indicate that family values most strongly direct female
sex role orientation.

See 0016. L. J. Busby, "Women and society: the mass
media."

1002

Chafe, William Henry. "Women in professions,"
*The American Woman, Her Changing Social, Economic
and Political Roles, 1920-1970*, by W. H. Chafe.
NY: Oxford University Press, 1972. pp. 89-111.

Following the passage of women's suffrage, women's
magazines of the 1920's decade published articles dis-
couraging women from acquiring jobs outside the home.
"Home Engineering" was declared a woman's profession.
Potential career women who were not discouraged by this
attitude in magazines had no successful female role models
to emulate. Novels and magazine fiction portray working women unflatteringly.

1003

Clarke, Peter and Virginia Esposito. "A study
of occupational advice for women in magazines,"
Journalism Quarterly, 1966, 43:477-485; also in
The Professional Woman, ed. by Athena Theodore.
Cambridge: Schenkman, 1971. pp. 142-155.

Three popular magazines aimed at the 20-30 year old
woman were examined for vocational information. The study
indicates that the career motivated college women sampled
did not seriously consider entering the field of African
missionary work or other highly unusual though romantic
and exciting careers commonly featured in magazine articles.

See 0134. J. D. Culley and R. Bennett, "Selling women, selling blacks."

See 0022. A. K. Daniels, "The mass media as 'educational supplements'."

See 0336. H. H. Franzwa, "The image of women in television: an annotated bibliography."

1004
    Franzwa, Helen H. "Working women in fact and fiction," *Journal of Communication*, 1974, 24(2): 104-109; also in *Mass Media and Society*, ed. by Alan Wells. Palo Alto, CA: Mayfield, 1975. pp. 398-402.

The image of women in advertising, toy catalogs, children's books and children's songs discourages career aspirations in female children and discourages non-traditional career choices in career-oriented women. The article focuses on the portrayal of women in magazine fiction, 1940-1970. Most plots revolve around a woman's acquiring or keeping a man, with career or work as a secondary theme, if present at all. The stories sampled had no working women, 1955-1970. Prior to 1955 work was often dropped upon the advent of marriage.

See 0852. J. K. Frisof, "Textbooks and channeling."

1005
    Garbarino, James and Susan Turner. "Television and vocational socialization." Cambridge, MA: Marketing Science Institute, Harvard University, 1975.

An examination of a number of content analyses dealing with vocational sex role socialization is followed by a research strategy proposal, one of whose purposes is the measure of vocational sex role content on television and how this content influences the vocational aspirations of female children and female adolescents. Commercial and Public television programming and television advertising will be included in the study.

1006
    Goldberg, Ruth E. "Sex role stereotypes and the career versus homemaking orientations of women," *The Emerging Woman: Career Analysis and Outlooks,*

ed. by Samuel H. Osipow. Columbus, Ohio: Merrill, 1975. pp. 99-115.

Sex role stereotyping in advertising and the media (as well as the influence of church, laws, customs) prescribes sex role behavior. Early socialization partially explains why most women's jobs are an extension of work performed in the home.

See 0920. E. Goodman, "Mother Nature and sex roles."

See 0797. J. S. Hillman, "Occupational roles in children's literature."

See 0754. F. Howe, "The female majority: the education of willing slaves."

See 0865. Kalamazoo, Michigan Board of Education, "Sex discrimination in an elementary reading program."

1007
Kaniuga, Kancy, Thomas Scott and Eldon Gade. "Working women portrayed on evening television programs," *Vocational Guidance Quarterly*, 1974, 23:134-137.

The occupations of the principal adult characters of 44 prime time television shows were surveyed. Of the 43 women, 30 were employed outside the home, 13 were full time housewives. Of the 30 employed women, only 3 were married, when in reality 60% of American working women are married. Eighty three percent of the female workers were in sex stereotyped occupations: nurse, secretary or teacher, while only four were in pioneer type or male dominated professions. The typical television woman worker is single and young. This rigid adherence to female work stereotypes can limit women's work expectations and aspirations. Because television has great socializing power, viewers exposed to unrealistic occupational roles begin to believe these role stereotypes. This rigid adherence to female work stereotypes can limit women's work expectations and aspirations.

1008
Kimmel, Marcia S. "Educational influences on career opportunities for women." (Teacher Education Forum Series, v. 2, no. 13). Bloomington: Indiana University School of Education, 1974; also

in ERIC (ED 099 323).

Stereotypic images of women in basal readers are among the school related factors teaching girls and young women to avoid success in high school, college and later in careers. From elementary school throughout life women should be encouraged to achieve their full potential.

See 0930. L. Z. McArthur and S. V. Eisen, "Achievements of male and female storybook characters as determinants of achievement behavior by boys and girls."

See 0970. J. S. MacLeod, *You Won't Do*.

1009
    Manes, Audrey L. and Paula Melnyk. "Televised models of female achievement," *Journal of Applied Social Psychology*, 1974, 4:365-374.

Using as basic premise the evidence proving that filmed models influence behavior, this study measures the influence of female televised role models on female viewers' achievement attitudes. A correlation is found between successful careers and unsuccessful marriages among female television characters. Only women at low levels of professional achievement and housewives are shown to have successful marriages. Therefore female television viewers learn to inhibit achievement oriented behavior in order to have a successful marriage, a correlation that in real life is not necessarily true.

See 0106. B. Medsgar, *Women at Work, A Photographic Documentary*.

See 0352. M. M. Miller and B. Reeves, "Dramatic television content and children's sex role stereotypes."

1010
    Plost, Myrna. *Sex of Career Models Affect Girls' Occupational Choices*. M.A. thesis, California State University - Fullerton, 1973.

A study of eighth grade students revealed that 1) students prefer like-sex career models in media exposure, 2) girls express preference for careers depicted by like-sex models more often than boys, and 3) students of both sexes rate male depicted occupations higher than female depicted occupations. The author suggests that instructional and vocational materials depicting women in traditionally female roles may profoundly limit girls' career goals and aspirations.

See 0981. L. C. Pogrebin, "Toys for free children."

See 0108. L. C. Pogrebin, "Women on the tube."

1011
　　Rose, Clare. "Women's sex role attitudes: a historical perspective," *Meeting Women's New Educational Needs*, ed. by C. Rose. (New Directions for Higher Education, 11). San Francisco: Jossey-Bass, 1975. pp. 1-30.

Though learned elsewhere, sex role standards are heavily reinforced by children's books and the mass media. Textbooks neglect female achievement while the media, especially television, portray women in traditional roles of wife and mother with personalities that are usually stupid, helpless and docile. This acculturation is so strong that if a woman does not enter college her aspirations are limited by the types of careers the media has projected as acceptable for women.

1012
　　Sandler, Bernice. "Women: the last minority," *Journal of College Placement*, December, 1971-January, 1972, 32:49-52.

Even though women comprise 43% of the workforce, advertising, television and other media rarely portray women workers, and when they do, the women are almost always secretaries, nurses and teachers.

See 0110. S. Seed, *Saturday's Child*.

See 0365. J. F. Seggar, "World of work on TV."

See 0892. B. Stefflre, "Run Mama Run: women workers in elementary readers."

1013
　　Suelze, Marijean. "Women in labor," *Trans-Action*, November/December, 1970, 8:50-58; also in *Sexism: Scientific Debates*, ed. by Clarice

Stall. Reading, Mass: Addison-Wesley, 1973. pp. 92+.

Among the seven myths concerning the female involvement in the labor force is myth I: "Women naturally don't want careers, they just want jobs." This myth is perpetuated in textbooks which place a ceiling on the aspirations of female children, in toy catalogs which picture household appliances but omit chemistry sets or astronaut costumes as preparation for female adulthood, and television advertising which presents women rendered helpless by a basket of soiled laundry while the male voice of authority directs her to a detergent. With no inspiring female role models girl children are trained to aspire to less prestigious occupations.

1014
Thetford, Mary. "The case for the career book in grades five to eight: A feminist view," *Elementary English*, 1973, 50:1059-1060.

In order to choose careers free of sex bias, children need role models in a greater variety of fields. However career fiction, a popular genre with this age group, shows a prevalence of traditional vocational stereotyping with boys as doctors and girls as nurses. The author suggests weeding libraries of stereotyped career fiction while building a collection with more alternatives so that children will have realistic vocational role models.

1015
Thetford, Mary Louise. "Vocational roles for women in junior fiction," 1974. ERIC (ED 102 553).

Analysis of female sex roles in junior high school level career fiction reveals that women were most commonly portrayed as passive people employed in service occupations. Junior high women, considering potential careers, are given more encouragement and reinforcement to enter stereotyped female occupations than non-stereotyped.

See 0825. S. L. Tibbetts, "Children's literature - a feminist viewpoint."

1016
Verheyden-Hilliard, Mary Ellen. "Cinderella doesn't live here anymore," *Womenpower*, 1975, 11:34-37; also available from KNOW, Inc., PO

Box 86031, Pittsburgh, PA 15221. #299.

It seems that vocational education students are being better prepared for Cinderella style roles than they
are for jobs. Cinderella's lifestyle consisted of cooking, cleaning and looking beautiful for the prince. That
glass slipper no longer fits. Proposed state and federal
legislation, workshops and programs are hoped to rid vocational education of sex role stereotypes in textbooks
and career aspirations.

See 0896. L. J. Weitzman and D. Rizzo, "Biased textbooks."

1017
    Wirtenberg, T. Jeana and Charles Y. Nakamura.
    "Education: barrier or boon to changing occu-
    pational roles of women." *Journal of Social
    Issues*, 1976, 32:165-180.

Sex biases in textbooks contribute to the stereotypic role models whom school children have been taught
to follow. However the trend presently developing provides for centers with curriculum packages and guidebooks
for non-sexist career guidance to overcome bias taught in
textbooks.

1018
    Women on Words and Images. *Help Wanted*. Avail-
    able from WOWI, PO Box 2163, Princeton, NJ
    08540. Book: $2.00, slide program, $40,
    rental, $300 purchase.

A content analysis of sex role stereotypes in career
education materials that track students in traditional sex
biased occupations.

Dooley, Janet L. 0261
Doolittle, John 0141
Dopp, Bonnie Jo 0617
Douvan, Elizabeth 0002
Downing, Mildred 0404
Doyle, Nancy 0459, 0844
Drew, Dan G. 0592
Dunn, Susan 0833, 0834, 0847
Dunnigan, Lise 0845
Durdeen-Smith, Jo 0405
Dworkin, Andrea 0778
Edgar, Joanne 0664
Edgar, Patricia 0381
Edwards, Richard 0956
Efron, Edith 0382, 0406
Eifler, Debora 0774
Eisen, Susan V. 0930
Eliasberg, Ann 0846
Elliot, Linda Anne 0719
Ellis, Katherine 0126
Embree, Alice, 0142
Ephron, Nora 0231, 0476
Epple, Ron 0537
Epstein, Cynthia Fuchs 0225
Esposito, Virgina 1003
Ewen, Stuart 0144, 0145, 0741
Farber, Stephen 0477, 0478
Farrell, Warren 0742, 0743
Farquhar, Norma 0833, 0834, 0847
Fasteau, Marc Feigen 0848
Faust, Jean 0026
Faxon, Pookie 0538
Fearing, Franklin 0672
Federbush, Marsha 0849
Feminists on Children's
    Literature 0790, 0791
Ferguson, Charles W. 0665
Ferris, Abbott Lamayne 0146
Fidell, Linda 0232, 0246
Firestone, Shulameth 0148
Fine, Gary Alan 0147
Fischer, Lucy 0479
Fisher, Elizabeth 0767
Fishman, Anne Stevens 0958
Flora, Cornelia Butler 0563
Fontes, Brian L. 0724
Foster, Anne Tolstoi 0149, 0262, 0263
Fraad, Harriet 0792
Frally, Jacqueline 0951
Francis, Sara 0916

Frankfort, Ellen 0233, 0234
Franzwa, Helen H. 0564, 0565, 1004
Frasher, Ramona 0850
Frazier, Nancy 0851
Freeman, Lucinda 0720
Freese, Arthur S. 0703
Freyer, Ellen 0539
Friedan, Betty 0150, 0337, 0566
Friedman, Leslie J. 0151, 0361
Friend, Beverly 0677
Frisbie, John M. 0215
Frisof, Jamie K. 0852
Frueh, Terry 0338
Frum, Barbara 0339
Fry, William F. 0647
Frye, Jerry K. 0264
Gabor, Mark 0687
Gade, Eldon M. 0408, 1007
Gadfield, Nicholas J. 0645
Gadlin, Howard 0152
Gallagher, Kathleen 0853
Gans, Herbert J. 0480
Gant, Liz 0481
Garbarino, James 1005
Gardner, Jo-Ann 0919, 0948
Gelber, Alexis 0153
Gelfman, Judith S. 0430
Gerard, Lillian 0482
Gerbner, George 0027, 0340
Gersoni-Stavn, Diane 0793, 0822, 0823
Gess, Sandra 0379
Gilburt, Naome 0483
Ginsburg, Jane 0794
Glicksohn, Susan Wood 0666
Goldberg, Ruth E. 1006
Golden, Bernette 0721
Goldfield, Evelyn 0028
Goldsen, Rose K. 0409
Goleman, Daniel 0704
Good, Mashinka 0082
Goodman, Andrew 0744
Goodman, Ellen 0920
Gordon, Neal J. 0925
Gorney, Sondra 0154
Graebner, Dianne Bennett 0854
Graham, Beryl Caroline 0722
Grambs, Jean Dresden 0752, 0753
Grant, Don 0265

Macleod, Jennifer S. 0970
McLuhan, H. Marshall 0171,
 0747
McLure, Gail T. 0874
McLure, John W. 0874
McNeely, Patricia G. 0088
McNeil, Jean C. 0349,
 0350, 0450
McRee, Christine 0239
Manes, Audrey L. 1009
Mannes, Marya 0089, 0172,
 0173, 0417
Mant, Andrea 0240, 0299
Margulies, Leah 0175
Mariani, John 0390
Maronde, Doreen Nelson
 0934
Marshe, Surrey 0692
Marston, William Moulton
 0669
Marten, Laurel A. 0875
Martin, Joanna Foley 0043
Martin, Judith 0276
Martineau, Barbara 0509
Marx, Janet 0126
Mason, Bobbie Ann 0708
Mather, Anne D. 0576
Matkov, Rebecca Roper
 0577
Matlin, Margaret W. 0875
Matre, Marc 0711
Maynard, Richard A. 0510
Mead, Marion 0300, 0622,
 0623, 0935
Meadow, Wendy 0660
Media Women's Association
 0059
Medsgar, Betty 0106
Meehan, Eileen Rose 0174
Mehlinger, Kermit T. 0748
Mellen, Joan 0511, 0512
Melnyk, Paula 1009
Merriam, Eve 0972
Meyer, Karl E. 0351
Meyer, Timothy P. 0936
Michener, Charles 0513
Miles, Betty 0399, 0876
Miles, Virginia 0277
Miller, Hannah 0937
Miller, Judith 0175
Miller, Susan H. 0592,
 0598
Mills, Kay 0451
Millum, Trevor 0176

Minard, Rosemary 0780
Minton, Lynn 0514
Mischel, Walter 0938
Mitchell, Edna 0760
Moberg, Verne 0973
Moore, Allan J. 0693
Morris, Monica B. 0599
Moskowitz, Samuel 0680
Motomatsu, Nancy R. 0974
Munaker, Sue 0028
Murphey, Mary 0048
Murray, James P. 0727
Mussell, Kay J. 0709
Naegel, Lana 0440
Nagel, Glennis L. 0610
Nakamura, Charles Y. 1017
Nanis, Claire 0773
Nash, Abigail Jones 0441,
 0442, 0446
National Advertising Review
 Board 0278
National Education Associa-
 tion 0877
National Organization for
 Women, Kalamazoo Area Chap-
 ter 0353, National Capitol
 Area Chapter 0354, New
 York Chapter 0050, San
 Francisco Chapter 0093,
 San Jose Chapter 0463
Neale, John M. 0348
Nelson, Gayle 0051
Nelson, Gunvor 0177
Nicholson, Joan 0157, 0694
Nietzke, Ann 0651
Nightingale, Camilla 0803
Nilsen, Alleen Pace 0804,
 0805, 0977
Northcott, Herbert C. 0356,
 0724
Northern Women's Groups Edu-
 cation Study Group 0878
Nunes, Maxine 0052
Nye, Russel Blaine 0579
O'Brien, Sally Ann 0279
O'Connor, John J. 0357
O'Donnell, Richard W. 0879
O'Kelly, Charlotte G. 0178,
 0939
Oliver, Linda 0880
Ontario Status of Women
 Council 0116
Orloff, Katherine 0626
Orth, Maureen 0515

Paisley, William 0017, 0324
Palmore, Erdman 0652
Papachristou, Judith 0323
Park, Lynn 0244
Partridge, Robert 0628
Passovoy, Janice Sue 0180
Pastine, Maureen 0980
Patrick, Robert 0516
Paulsen, Virginia M. 0245
Peck, Ellen, 0053, 0325, 0358
Peery, Alice 0853
Pepper, Robert 0141
Perebinossoff, Philippe 0670
Perreault, Gerri 0881
Peters, Margot 0707
Pincus, Ann 0393
Pingree, Suzanne 0181, 0324
Plost, Myrna 1010
Poe, Alison 0182
Pogrebin, Letty Cottin 0054, 0095, 0108, 0326, 0808, 0981
Porter, Sylvia 0183
Posner, Judith 0653
Potter, Elmer H. 0840
Poulos, Rita Wicks 0380
Poverman, Marian F. 0419
Prasad, V. Kanti 0940
Prather, Jane 0246
Press, Tina 0359
Preston, Marilynn 0611
Prida, Delores 0736
Pyle, Wilma J. 0809
Rachlin, Susan Kessler 0761
Rao, Tanniru 0940
Rauch, Gail E. 0140
Ray, Louelle 0580
Rea, James Michael 0186
A Redstocking Sister 0187
Reed, Rex 0517
Reich, Michael 0057
Reichert, Julia 0058
Rennie, Susan 0109, 0630, 0671, 0681, 0982
Resko, Beth Gabrielle 0168
Reynolds, Fred D. 0259
Reynolds, Lessie M. 0518
Ribner, Susan 0736
Richardson, John Adkins 0696
Ris, Hania W. 0247
Richards, Carol R. 0600
Richler, Mordecai 0697

Rinsky, Lee Ann 0811
Rivers, Caryl 0188
Rizzo, Diane 0896, 0897
Roberts, Patricia Lee Brighton 0812, 0813
Robinson, Florett 0646
Robinson, Lillian 0126
Rock, Gail 0394, 0519
Rodnitzky, Jerome L. 0631, 0632
Rogers, Katherine 0814
Rogowski, Phyllis L. 0423
Rosbrow, Susan R. 0582
Rose, Clare 1011
Rose, Karel 0815
Rosen, Diane 0360
Rosen, Marjorie 0520-0522
Rosen, Ruth 0816
Rosenberg, B. G. 0860
Rosenberg, Max 0983
Rosenstone, Robert A. 0633
Ross, Catherine 0774
Ross, Susan Deller 0452
Rossi, Alice S. 0361
Rossi, Lee 0698
Rupp, Carla Marie 0601, 0612
Russ, Joanna 0682
Russo, Nancy Felipe 0882
Saario, Terry N. 0883
Sadker, David 0884
Sadker, Myra 0851, 0884
Salinas, Judy 0737
Salpukas, Agis 0885
Sampson, Glenda 0611
Sanders, Marlene 0762
Sandler, Bernice 1012
Santi, Tina 0282
Saperstein, David 0060
Sargent, Pamela 0679, 0683, 0684
Sarris, Andrew 0523
Schenck, John P. 0886
Schien, Muriel 0126
Schmid, Anne McEvoy 0984
Schmidt, Dolores 0887
Schrib, June 0583
Schultz, Dodi 0225
Schulwitz, Bonnie Smith 0888
Schumacher, Dorin 0985
Schumann, Suzanne I. 0120
Scott, Rosemary 0284
Scott, Thomas 1007
Screen Actor's Guild 0189

319

321

toys (continued) 0920,
    0927, 0981, 0982, 0990,
    1012
Truffaut, Francois   0501
Turner, Tina   0622
Tyson, Cicely   0731
U.P.I.   0098
U.S. News & World Report
    0076
underground newspapers
    0018, 0028
United Nations 0010, 0044,
    0065, 0012, 0203
vaginal spray *See* personal
    products
Vanity Fair   0587
Varda, Agnes   0543
Verheyden-Hilliard, Mary
    Ellen   0933
villain, woman as   0406,
    0777-0779
violence   0056, 0201, 0336,
    0340, 0341, 0347, 0348,
    0379, 0390, 0396, 0470,
    0472, 0476, 0478, 0633,
    0664, 0669, 0671, 0672,
    0688, 0742, 0749, 0907,
    0936, 0946
*Virgo Rising: The Once and
    Future Woman*   0631
voice of authority   0011,
    0026, 0089, 0096, 0127,
    0133, 0156, 0157, 0163,
    0189, 0190, 0204, 0270,
    0916, 1013
Volner, Jill   0085
volunteerism   0754
von Hoffman, Nicholas   0605
Walters, Barbara   0075
"Waltons, The"   0739
Warner Brothers   0629
Washington Post, The   0597,
    0607
Wayne, John   0744
"Marcus Welby"   0377
West, Mae   0473
Weston, Edward   0696
Wichita Beacon, The   0602
Wisk   0373
"Woman Alive"   0552
Woman Under the Influence
    0504
Womansongs   0617

Women Against Violence
    Against Women 0056, 0625,
    0629
Women's movement, coverage
    of   0035, 0043, 0064,
    0076, 0091, 0093, 0094,
    0382, 0430, 0560, 0577,
    0583, 0584, 0590, 0591,
    0599, 0604, 0662
Wonder Woman   0664, 0665,
    0669
Mai Zetterling   0529, 0543